Playesque
Volume 1

Playesque
Volume 1

Plays for Amateur and Scholastic Venues

Written and Illustrated by
Joan Garner

Teacher Ideas Press, an imprint of Libraries Unlimited
Westport, Connecticut • London

Library of Congress Cataloging-in-Publication Data

Garner, Joan.
 Playesque : plays for amateur and scholastic venues / written and
Illustrated by Joan Garner.
 p. cm.
 ISBN 1-59158-344-6 (pbk. : v. 1 : alk. paper)
 I. Title.
 PS3557.A716673P55   2006
 812'.54--dc22   2006004495

British Library of Congress Cataloguing in Publication Data is available.

Copyright © 2006 by Joan Garner

All rights reserved. No part of this book may be reproduced in any form or by any electronic or mechanical means, including information storage and retrieval systems, without permission in writing from the publisher, except by a reviewer, who may quote brief passages in a review. An exception is made for individual librarians and educators who may make copies of portions of the scripts for classroom use. Reproducible pages may be copied for classroom and educational programs only. Performances may be videotaped for school or library purposes.

Library of Congress Catalog Card Number: 2006004495
ISBN: 1-59158-344-6

First Published in 2006

Libraries Unlimited/Teacher Ideas Press, 88 Post Road West, Westport, CT 06881
A Member of the Greenwood Publishing Group, Inc.
www.lu.com

10 9 8 7 6 5 4 3 2 1

Table of Contents

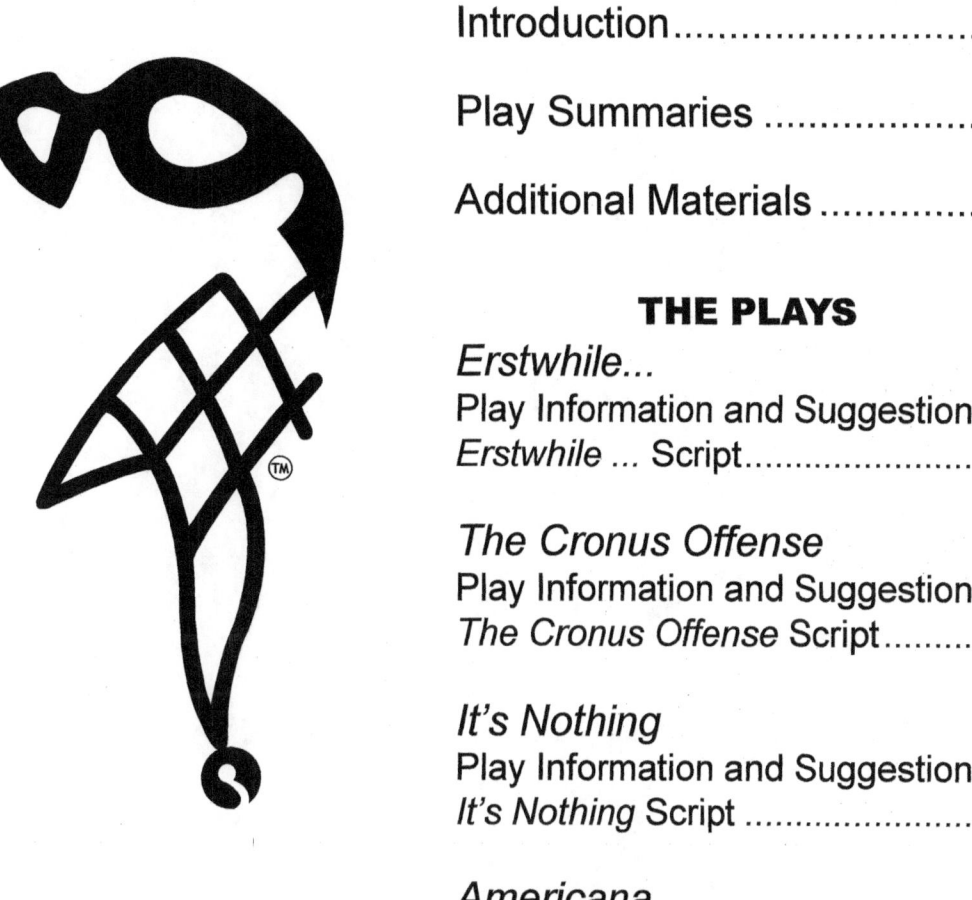

FRONT MATTER
Table of Contents v

Preface vii

Introduction..................................... ix

Play Summaries x

Additional Materials xv

THE PLAYS
Erstwhile...
Play Information and Suggestions............ 3
Erstwhile ... Script................................... 19

The Cronus Offense
Play Information and Suggestions........... 61
The Cronus Offense Script...................... 69

It's Nothing
Play Information and Suggestions........... 93
It's Nothing Script 103

Americana
Play Information and Suggestions......... 133
Americana Script 147
Author Profile.. 224

Page numbering for each script provided directly above book page number.

Preface

By Definition What is **Playesque**?

1. In defining the word: PLAY—a literary work written for performance on stage. And ESQUE—a suffix meaning in the manner of. Simply, **Playesque** is a manner of play.

2. In defining the concept: **Playesque** exists somewhere in the vast bastion of terms such as, "serious profession," "legitimate theatre can only be found on Broadway," and "dramaturgy." In other words, **Playesque** is for the real world.

Playesque plays are entertaining, short and feature length works with equal consideration given to production requirements as well as drama. Sound cues, costume changes, dialogue, and movement—all are carefully crafted into an overall, appealing piece of theatre.

In addition, **Playesque** plays are especially designed to accommodate frugal budgets, limited stage area, and inexperienced participants by incorporating (in general):

- One costume per PLAYER. If more than one costume is called for, it will usually be an easily found garment, or consist of pieces added to the original ensemble. (More than one costume may be needed for characters in feature-length plays.)
- One stationary set, or quickly made/inexpensive set change options. Lighting and sound effects that can be done even with the most limited equipment.
- Easily executed special effects.
- More detailed stage directions (narrative) than found in typical actor's scripts to be used verbatim or at the director's discretion.

Copyright The playwright, Joan Garner, holds copyright for each play in this volume. All rights are reserved on story and content.

Poster illustrations for each play are owned exclusively by the playwright and may not be copied and used for promotional purposes.

Script Reproduction Instructions

Individual scripts for each cast member of a **Playesque** play are not available through Teacher Ideas Press or the author. Each script in this volume is specially formatted for reproduction on most copy machines. Text is placed on the page to prevent lost or warped type during the copying process due to spine interference. After copying, this area may be used in writing down notes and blocking directions.

Although the copying of **Playesque** scripts is permitted for rehearsal use, the plays themselves cannot be reproduced and given to other instructors or theatre groups. Nor can they be copied and distributed throughout the school district or other drama organizations for general use.

Students and theatre group members finding this book in the library may copy sections of **Playesque** scripts for personal study, class performance, or try-out purposes.

Videotaping Performances

- Amateur performances of a **Playesque** play may be videotaped for private viewing.
- Reproduction of your videotape and selling for profit is not permitted and against the law.
- Showing your private videotape and charging admission is not permitted and against the law.

(The term videotaping *includes any form of taping and/or recording via DVD, audiocassette, digital, or any other form of recording yet to come.)*

Royalties

Schools and Amateur Theatre Groups
Playesque plays performed by schools and amateur theatre groups do not require royalty payments.

Professional Companies
Permissions and privileges permitted within this book are for school and amateur venues specifically. Professional and for profit theatre companies need to query the author concerning royalty payments. Please address these queries to:

JOAN GARNER
c/o Teacher Ideas Press
88 Post Road West
P.O. Box 5007
West Port, CT 06881-5007

Allow four to six weeks for response.

Introduction

Dramatic Classification

The following categories apply to **Playesque** plays:

Type

FANTASY—dragons; wizards; time travel; the unexplained; the miraculous.
SCIENCE FICTION—space ships; future worlds; aliens; futuristic themes.
PERIOD PIECE—of a specific time in the past; also known as Costume Drama.
AVANT GARDE—presentation outside the realm of conventional theatre.
CONTEMPORARY—current time and story.

Genre

COMEDY—situation providing humorous action and reaction.
FARCE—pratfalls; broad physical humor; outlandish situations.
BLACK COMEDY—macabre presented as the norm; an absurdity.
DRAMADY—dramatic overtones interwoven in the comedy.
DRAMA—high drama and angst; exploring morals and behavior.
TRAGEDY—extreme situation ending in catastrophe and death.
THRILLER—involving mystery and suspense.
HORROR—ghosts; monsters; things that go bump in the night.

Skill Level

BEGINNER—simple enough for the novice to perform and produce.
INTERMEDIATE—for the more theatre knowledgeable and experienced performer and designer.
ADVANCED—a good challenge for the actor and artist.

Considerations

CONTENT—identification of possible objectionable or controversial subject matter.
PRODUCTION—identification of possible difficult to construct set elements; special effects; expensive pieces; or hard to find prop items.

*(The **Playesque** plays in this volume include: period piece, science fiction, and contemporary TYPES; comedy, farce, and drama GENRES.)*

Play Summaries

ERSTWHILE...

TYPE: Period Piece.
GENRE: Comedy.
SKILL LEVEL: Beginner +.
CONSIDERATIONS: None.

STORY: As the kingdom of Interlocken prepares to welcome their new princess, two wayward Vikings storm the castle—well, quasi-plunder the castle. Princess Angeleen arrives unannounced and immediately falls in love with Prince Steven. Unfortunately, Princess Angeleen is in Interlocken to marry Prince Crispen. To avoid marrying Prince Crispen, Princess Angeleen pretends to be Lady Vivien, who in turn pretends to be the princess. In the meantime, Her Majesty Tallulah concentrates on making the evening's festivities the height of the social season and His Majesty Walter appears preoccupied with the Sacred Stone of Loch Bowie.

TIME PERIOD: Near the end of the 9th Century, A.D.
LOCALE: The island of Interlocken above Scotland.
SET: Single, stationary set. The great room in the royal castle of Interlocken.
COSTUMING: Gowns, robes, crowns, helmets, tunics, shifts, tights, boots, cloth shoes.
LIGHTING AND SOUND: Basic lighting. One sound effect.
PROPS: Nothing of special note.
SPECIAL EFFECTS: None.
LENGTH OF PLAY: Approximately 50 to 55 minutes.
ROLES: 9 + Males. 6 + Females.

DEGREE OF DIFFICULTY TO STAGE

Easy ▲ ———————————————————— Difficult

Play Summaries

THE CRONUS OFFENSE

TYPE: Science Fiction.

GENRE: Drama.

SKILL LEVEL: Intermediate.

CONSIDERATIONS: Production. *(Special props to be made.)*

STORY: In the future the exchange of commerce, technology, and political power will be decided through an elaborate system of games. Called the Ultra Olympics, countries and governments participate to win/gain land, water rights, manufactured goods, commodities and so forth. Into this intriguing event comes a small team in desperate need, but with little talent to win anything—especially the final set of games known as the Cronus Offense. As in Greek Mythology, the God Cronus eliminates his enemies by gobbling them up. The inferior team works to gobble-up it's more powerful opponents.

TIME PERIOD: The future.

LOCALE: Ultra Olympics.

SET: Single stationary set. A preparatory level below the Olympic Stadium.

COSTUMING: Futuristic.

LIGHTING AND SOUND: Normal lighting. No sound effects.

PROPS: Some special requirements.

SPECIAL EFFECTS: None.

LENGTH OF PLAY: Approximately 35 to 40 minutes.

ROLES: 11. Optional Casting.

DEGREE OF DIFFICULTY TO STAGE

Easy ▲ Difficult

Play Summaries

IT'S NOTHING

TYPE: Contemporary.
GENRE: Farce.
SKILL LEVEL: Beginner +.
CONSIDERATIONS: Production.

STORY: Cindy and Greg are getting married today. This is the plan. However, if they do get married today, it will be nothing short of a miracle. You name it, it happens. From the wedding being called off to too many flower sprays being delivered, from a rather exuberant wedding coordinator, to a crazy ex-girlfriend, the family does its best to get the ceremony going.

TIME PERIOD: Present.
LOCALE: The upper-middle class home of the Caulfield's.
SET: Single, stationary set. The hallway leading to two bedrooms.
COSTUMING: Wedding fare. Gowns and tuxedos.
LIGHTING AND SOUND: Basic lighting. Easily found sound effects.
PROPS: Some special requirements. (Flower and wedding cake.)
SPECIAL EFFECTS: None.
LENGTH OF PLAY: Approximately 40 to 45 minutes.
ROLES: 4 Males. 7 Females.

DEGREE OF DIFFICULTY TO STAGE
Easy ─────────────────────── Difficult

Play Summaries

AMERICANA

TYPE: Costume.
GENRE: Drama.
SKILL LEVEL: Intermediate.
CONSIDERATIONS: Production.

STORY: LaVonne Dunn is preparing a sweet sixteen birthday party for her daughter Penny. Neighbors and Ted, Penny's boyfriend, are expected at this special supper. LaVonne also invites an army sergeant who has wandered in from an adjoining apricot orchard. Preparations are going well until Ted proposes to Penny and then promptly announces his plans to enter the service before age eligibility. After placing this upsetting development on the back burner, the supper is once again interrupted by a most unexpected visitor—an escaped prisoner of war who has followed LaVonne's sister-in-law home from Hill Air Force Base.

TIME PERIOD: 1944.
LOCALE: Hardin, Utah (fictional town).
SET: Single, stationary set. Exterior Dunn house and front yard.
COSTUMING: Period costuming of World War II.
LIGHTING AND SOUND: Basic lighting.
PROPS: Bicycle, wagon, and other items of the period.
SPECIAL EFFECTS: None.
LENGTH OF PLAY: Approximately 120 minutes.
ROLES: 5 Males. 5 Females.

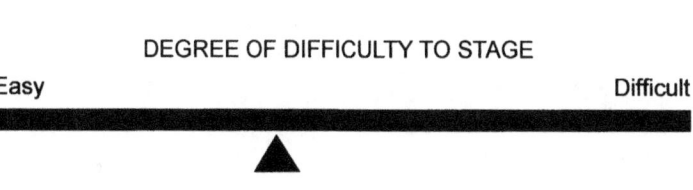

Additional Materials

Production notes and suggestions are provided with each play. These notes may include, but are not limited to:

Director's Notes

Overall Tone
Identifying the play as an entertaining and light-hearted fair or dramatic work with specific intent.

Essence of Play
Explaining what should be realized to help assist in projecting the theme and issues of the play. Mood.

Moral of Play
Recognizing the moral hoped to be learned and taken away by the performers and audience and/or the moral of the play as it relates to the specific story.

Symbolism
Revealing elements and dialogue representing ideals other than the obvious/literal representation in the play.

Attention Required for Specific Characters
Notations of a character trait or personality quirk that could be implemented for better clarification of that character. An extended description of a major character not provided in the **Character Analysis** section.

Scenes and Moments Requiring Special Attention
Describing a particular scene or moment critical in enhancing the story line that may not be realized while reviewing or rehearsing the play.

Dialogue and Accents
Dialogue to be considered due to its importance to the story or difficulty in delivery and accents that should be applied or regarded necessary to the character.

Character Traits to Enhance Performances
Suggestions of personality quirks or physical habits the PLAYER(S) might use to help define the role.

Movement of Players/Staging
Recommendation of PLAYER placement, especially in setting up large casts on stage. Additional suggestions of movement for PLAYERS not otherwise indicated in the narrative.

Character Analysis

A one or two line description of character personality and foibles the PLAYER may wish to incorporate into their performance.

Production Notes

Design Concepts
A brief overview of design style appropriate for the play.

Costume Narrative
Costume ensemble description and suggestions for each character that includes possibilities for:

(FULL PRODUCTION) Ultimate costume suggestion that would be used should the play be produced as written and intended by the playwright.

(GOOD REPRESENTATION) Costume description with modifications to the full production costume that reduces time and expense in construction, yet maintains a good visual representation of intent.

(MINIMAL REPRESENTATION) What can be put together with the least amount of effort and cost, yet still give a satisfactory visual representation of intent.

Costume Illustrations
Black and white illustrations of costumes per character for a FULL PRODUCTION staging.

Set Design Narrative
Description of set utilizing the same three possibilities used above (FULL PRODUCTION, GOOD REPRESENTATION and MINIMAL REPRESENTATION). This section also includes furniture and set accessory suggestions.

Set Design Illustration
A blueprint/floor plan illustration of the set using the FULL PRODUCTION intent.

Lighting and Sound Requirements
Notation of lighting and sound needs and alternative equipment implementation to achieve similar effects.

Prop Lists
List(s) of props not included in the **Set Elements**, **Set Furniture** or **Set Accessories** Sections.

Erstwhile...
a Comedy
by Joan Garner

Play Information and Suggestions

Director's Notes

Overall Tone — **Erstwhile...** is a gentle comedy. It's a Much Ado About Nothing. There's much fuss and mild desperation, but the audience should always believe that bouts of peril and mayhem are only temporary. **Erstwhile...** isn't an *uproariously funny* comedy. It's more of a *grinning through the whole thing* play.

Essence of Play — Modern ideas, issues, and buzzwords generously pepper the script. Although placed in the Dark Ages, **Erstwhile...** is anything but dark. It's a light, nonsensical affair.

Moral of Play — Simply good over evil.

Symbolism — As this is a little comedy, symbolism isn't a concern.

Attention Required for Special Characters — If any one actor is not fully grasping their character, the following comparisons may help:

THOR—A big and strong, but not especially brainy football player.

SWAINE—In this day and age, **SWAINE** would be a super model with nothing in her refrigerator—not that she would know how to cook it.

CYRIL—A glasses wearing accountant or computer geek.

TALLULAH—A wannabe perfect hostess of the world.

WALTER—Suspiciously and quite possibly one of Santa's elves.

STEVEN—All American homespun young man next door.

AUGUSTY—Thinks he's clever to always be on the winning side, but not clever enough to know which side is winning.

CRISPEN—A pampered Hollywood star in the making.

SIR DUKE LORD—A heroic cowboy or foreman on a ranch.

ANGELEEN—Cheerleader, class president, homecoming queen, future CEO and soccer mom.

VIVIEN—Sidekick, best pal, comic relief, pleasing and amiable

Scenes and Moments Needing Special Attention — This is a direct play; the scenes progress to move the plot forward. But perhaps there are three relationships that need watching to make sure they remain on track because of their importance for a good deal of the play's humor and purpose.

Director's Notes

Scenes and Moments Needing Special Attention

1. As implied, **TALLULAH'S** attitude towards **WALTER** has been one of dismay for some time. There's a feeling he was a good king, but has turned into a comical buffoon. Of course there's a good reason for this strange behavior, but **TALLULAH** doesn't know this. The pained expression on her face when **WALTER** enters, or look of hopelessness when he leaves will help convey this difference to the audience.
2. **STEVEN** and **ANGELEEN** are just precious together. If they continue to be sweet and endearing, the love at first sight plot device won't seem so unbelievable.
3. **THOR** and **SWAINE** are also a great couple in a different way. Although fond of each other, they are partners in all they do—equally responsible for their successes and failures. They may argue between themselves, but will always fiercely defend the other when necessary.

Dialogue and Accents

Apply Scottish accents when convincing. A rolling Scottish brogue for **SIR DUKE LORD** would be ideal. **THOR**, **SWAINE**, **ANGELEEN**, and **VIVIEN** wouldn't have Scottish accents.

Character Traits to Enhance Performances

Besides his strutting about, an arrogant hand on hip would show **CRISPEN'S** vanity. **VIVIEN** might be like a joyful teenage young woman, she could jump up and down and squealing with delight when excited. **TALLULAH** might sometimes straighten up and look outward soulfully searching the Heavens for some decorum. **SIR DUKE LORD** could scratch his head or place hand to chin when pondering. This will show his worldliness and good sense which would be opposite **WALTER'S** childlike reasoning. **AUGUSTY** beams an evil grin here and there. But be careful, too much sneering or leering would detract from his cowardliness. **THOR** would probably adjust his neck and flex a muscle or two like athletes preparing for their sport.

Movement of Players/Staging

Because of the large number of PLAYERS on stage—especially at the end—placement will be a bit challenging. Fortunately, the larger group consists of minor characters that can stand in a semi-circle around center stage where the main action takes place. And, because there is little seating or need for sitting, most of the actions can be down, center stage. This will also be best for audience viewing.

Character Analysis

THOR—Large, muscular, and ferocious looking, but is a sensitive, Twenty-first Century kind of guy. Although they live in a time long ago, **THOR** and **SWAINE** are contemporaries. Their modern approach to their predicament lends a humorous touch to the story.

SWAINE—Xena Warrior Princess type pressed with stereotypical and personal growth issues.

CYRIL—Probably tall and skinny, he's the smartest yet saddest character in Interlocken. Casting against type gives him a comic advantage.

3 WANDERING MINSTRELS—The three must show their personalities through expression and gesture of body and face only. Their movement should be graceful and though funny, never distracting to the primary action of the play.

HER MAJESTY TALLULAH—Upper mobile society speaking. **TALLULAH** strives to bring Interlocken class, good taste, and sophistication. So far she has had little success. She carries herself well as nobility would, but there's a slight weariness.

LADIES-IN-WAITING—Are like wind-up Barbie dolls doing everything the same.

HIS MAJESTY WALTER—Though Scottish, **WALTER** is an Irish Leprechaun in manner and spirit. He must keep a scatterbrain aura to help make the ending a surprise. But through it all, **WALTER** is likable.

PRINCE STEVEN—The good guy who's always overlooked. **STEVEN** has built up an armor of good humor and an easygoing attitude to combat the slights he receives all the time. More like his father, **STEVEN** is a gentle and kind soul.

CHAMBERLAIN AUGUSTY—Thinks he's smart, but is dumb. Thinks he's brave, but is cowardly. Thinks he knows what's going on, but hasn't a clue.

PRINCE CRISPEN—Handsome yet vain. **CRISPEN** may look good, but he's smarmy. He's spoiled and deceitful, but there needs to be a spark of decency shining through, otherwise **VIVIEN** wouldn't be smitten with him.

SIR DUKE LORD—Competent with an itty-bitty sense of "what am I doing here?" attitude that comes through from time to time. But he's loyal and trustworthy.

PRINCESS ANGELEEN—Usually a practical and common-sense young woman, she turns into a giddy, love-struck young woman on seeing **STEVEN**. But she remains determined to have a "happily-ever-after" life and will use her vast talents to get it.

LADY VIVIEN—She's not as beautiful as **ANGELEEN**, but just as smart. She's also not as privileged. At times she appears clever and other times a little ditsy. But one is never sure if either is just an act.

PEOPLE OF THE COURT—Look good standing off to the side; able to mumble idle background platter.

Production Notes

Design Concepts

This being a "wink of the eye" comedy, realism isn't necessary. Broad, bold colors would work well. Accuracy isn't important. A middling effort to create the proper look should do.

Costume Narrative

THOR

(FULL PRODUCTION) Gray and white fur vest showing chest and arms. Chainmail, half thigh-length kilt. Gold metal belt with medallion buckle. Gray and white, calf-high fur boots bound with black leather strips. Red, small cone shaped helmet* with a gold metal band around the crown. Jewels on band. Two small cow-like horns sticking out on either side of the helmet. Short metal broadsword with leather wrapped hilt. Blonde, long Algernon mustache. Blonde, long hair with one braid braided down one side of the head (natural wig).

(GOOD REPRESENTATION) Gray leather vest showing chest and arms. Gray leather, half thigh-length kilt. Gray leather belt with silver metal medallion buckle. Gray, calf-high leather laced sandals. Silver metal headband. Short wooden broadsword with cloth wrapped hilt. Blonde, long Algernon mustache (yarn). Blonde, long hair with one braid down one side of the head (yarn wig).

(MINIMAL REPRESENTATION) Gray cloth vest showing chest and arms. Gray cloth, half thigh-length kilt with ragged hem. Gray cloth sash. Gray, calf-high cloth boots bound with shredded cloth strips. Gray cloth shredded headband and wrist "wraps." Painted, short wooden or plastic broadsword. Long or semi-long, tousled hair.

SWAINE

(FULL PRODUCTION) Green leather, formfitting halter top. Green molded armor breastplate. Green leather, knee-length skirt. Gold metal belt with gold medallion buckle. Gold, calf-high laced sandals. Green, tall coned helmet with gold "wing" adornments on either side. Gold metal upper arm bracelets. Short metal broadsword with leather wrapped hilt. Flaming red, free-flowing, long curly hair (natural wig).

(GOOD REPRESENTATION) Green cloth, formfitting halter top. Black leather breastplate. Green cloth, knee-length skirt. Black leather belt with gold medallion buckle. Black, calf-high leather laced sandals. Silver metal headband. Black leather upper arm bracelets. Short wooden broadsword with cloth wrapped hilt. Red, long hair braided with two braids on either side of the head (yarn wig).

(MINIMAL REPRESENTATION) Green cloth, formfitting halter top laced up the front with tan laces. Green cloth, knee-length skirt with ragged hem. Green cloth sash. Tan, calf-high cloth boots bound with shredded cloth strips. Tan cloth shredded headband and upper arm "wraps." Painted, short wooden or plastic broadsword. Long, tousled hair.

It is acknowledged that Vikings didn't really wear helmets with horns and such, but this play design isn't especially concerned with realism.

Production Notes

Costume Narrative

CYRIL

(FULL PRODUCTION) "Cap and bells" jester costume: Red, formfitting long sleeved blouse with no collar. One arm of blouse is light blue. Light blue stars and yellow decorative stripes applied to blouse. One leg light blue and one leg red, formfitting hose or tights. Yellow felt cloth, long toed shoes. Light blue, floppy fool's cap with yellow stars applied and large jingle bell attached to the extended point on cap. Short brown (buzz cut) hair.

(GOOD REPRESENTATION) Red, long sleeved spandex "cyclist top" with colorful diamond pattern applied. Black, full leg spandex "cyclist pants" with colorful diamond pattern applied. Black socks pulled over bottom legs of pants. Red stocking cap with a large jingle bell attached to the extended point on cap. Short brown (spiked) hair.

(MINIMAL REPRESENTATION) Red, long sleeved sweatshirt with light blue and yellow stripes or diamond pattern applied. Red, full leg sweatpants with light blue and yellow stripes or diamond pattern applied. Light blue or yellow socks pulled up over the bottom of the sweatpants. Yellow or light blue stocking cap that comes to a point. Short hair.

3 WANDERING MINSTRELS
Alter outfits according to casting of males or females in parts.

(FULL PRODUCTION)
WANDERER 1: (as a male) Lime green, long sleeved tunic, thigh-length with a yellow cord or rope tie around the waist. Red hose or tights. Orange felt cloth, long toed shoes. Blonde, straight hair shaved straight across in the back from the top of the left ear to the right (natural wig).
WANDERER 2: (as a male) Light blue, short puffy sleeved tunic at mid high-length with a purple, long sleeved blouse underneath with a yellow cord or rope tie around the waist. Purple hose or tights. Light blue felt cloth, long toed shoes. Dark blue cap with extended point. Red semi-long, hair (natural wig).
WANDERER 3: (as a female) Blue, sleeveless, surcoat. Red, long sleeved blouse/chemise underneath. Blue, floor-length bliaut (skirt). Red cloth sash at the waist. Red hose or tights. Red felt cloth shoes. Red, short pointed cap. Brown hair braided with one long braid down the back (natural wig).

(GOOD REPRESENTATION)
WANDERER 1: Lime green rectangle piece of cloth with hole for head to go through cut in the middle (poncho) tied at the waist with a rope. Lime green, long sleeved sweatshirt underneath. Tan sweat pants. Tan socks pulled up over the bottom of the sweatpants for shoes. Tan stocking cap. Yellow tousled hair (yarn wig).
WANDERER 2. Light blue rectangle piece of cloth with hole for head to go through cut in the middle (poncho) tied at the waist with a rope. Gray, long sleeved sweatshirt underneath. Gray sweatpants. Gray socks pulled up

Production Notes

Costume Narrative

over the bottom of the sweatpants for shoes. Gray stocking cap. Brown, semi-long hair (yarn wig).

WANDERER 3: Blue jumper dress, floor-length with red blouse underneath. Red hose or tights. Red socks with tops rolled down to ankles for shoes. Brown hair braided with one long braid down the back (yarn wig).

(MINIMAL REPRESENTATION)
WANDERER 1: Green rectangle piece of cloth with hole for head to go through cut in the middle (poncho) tied at the waist with a rope. Tan shirt and pants underneath. Tan socks pulled up over the bottom of the sweatpants for shoes. Short hair.

WANDERER 2: Light blue rectangle piece of cloth with hole for head to go through cut in the middle (poncho) tied at the waist with a rope. Gray shirt and pants underneath. Gray socks pulled up over the bottom of the sweatpants for shoes. Semi-long, tousled hair.

WANDERER 3: Red, long sleeved blouse tucked into a floor-length blue skirt. Blue triangle piece of cloth over the shoulders like a shawl with ragged hem. Red hose or tights. Red socks with tops rolled down to ankles for shoes. Little triangle piece of cloth (any color) tied to the back of the head (around the hair). Straight hair.

HER MAJESTY TALLULAH

(FULL PRODUCTION) Purple velvet, sleeveless short surcoat. Blue satin, floor-length chemise. Silver lamé cape flowing to the floor with light blue satin lining. Light blue hose or stockings. Silver lamé slippers. Silver, bejeweled brooches. Silver, bejeweled crown with short, light blue veil falling down the back of the head from underneath. Brown hair braided with one braid down the back (natural wig).

(GOOD REPRESENTATION) Altered blue nightgown with added silver cloth pieces to adorn and disguise the nightgown. Light blue velvet rectangle piece of cloth for cape. Blue hose and stockings and white ballet slippers. Silver band for crown with jewels attached and a short blue veil falling down the back of the head underneath the silver band. Hair pulled back into a bun under the crown and veil.

(MINIMAL REPRESENTATION) Altered blue nightgown with added silver cloth pieces to adorn and disguise the nightgown. Light blue velvet rectangle piece of cloth for cape. Blue knee-high stockings. Silver plastic headband for crown with short blue veil falling down the back of the head underneath the silver band. Hair pulled back into a bun under the crown and veil.

LADIES-IN-WAITING

(FULL PRODUCTION) Pink, floor-length bliaut with gold embroidery decoration around neckline. Pink, long surcoat. White hose or stockings and pink slippers. Long pink veil draped over the head and flowing down to below waist. Brown, long free-flowing hair (natural wig).

Production Notes

Costume Narrative

(GOOD REPRESENTATION) Altered pink nightgown with added gold cloth pieces to adorn and disguise the nightgown. Pink hose or stockings and white ballet slippers. Long pink veil draped over the head and flowing down to below waist. Brown, long free-flowing hair (yarn wig).

(MINIMAL REPRESENTATION) Altered pink nightgown with added gold cloth pieces to adorn and disguise the nightgown. Pink square of cloth folded into triangle and used as a shawl. Cardboard band covered with pink cloth. Pink piece of cloth attached to the back of the band and covering the pulled back hair.

HIS MAJESTY WALTER

(FULL PRODUCTION) Purple, long sleeved tunic, knee-length. Trimmed with gold braiding. Purple hose or tights. Knee-length, dark red velvet cape attached in the front with a gold amulet. Gold lamé, half-calf high boots bound with gold buckles. Gold belt. Gold and bejeweled crown. Black and gray, semi-long, tousled hair (natural wig). Black and gray bushy mustache.

(GOOD REPRESENTATION) Dark red rectangle piece of cloth with hole for head to go through cut in the middle (poncho) tied at the waist with a rope. Purple, long sleeved sweatshirt underneath. Purple sweatpants. Purple socks pulled up over the bottom of the sweatpants for shoes. Gold band for crown with jewels attached. Black, semi-long hair (yarn wig). Mustache painted on.

(MINIMAL REPRESENTATION) Dark red rectangle piece of cloth with hole for head to go through cut in the middle (poncho) tied at the waist with a rope. Black shirt and pants underneath. Black socks pulled up over the bottom of the sweatpants for shoes. Gold plastic headband for crown. Semi-long hair.

PRINCE STEVEN

(FULL PRODUCTION) Light blue, long sleeved tunic, upper thigh-length. Trimmed with gold braiding. Yellow hose or tights. Short, dark blue velvet cape attached in the front with a gold amulet. Gold lamé tall boots (above the knees) bound with gold straps. Gold belt. Gold and bejeweled crown. Black, short curly hair (natural wig).

(GOOD REPRESENTATION) Light blue rectangle piece of cloth with hole for head to go through cut in the middle (poncho) tied at the waist with a rope. Dark blue, long sleeved sweatshirt underneath. Dark blue sweatpants. Dark blue socks pulled up over the bottom of the sweatpants for shoes. Gold band for crown with jewels attached. Black, short hair (yarn wig).

(MINIMAL REPRESENTATION) Blue rectangle piece of cloth with hole for head to go through cut in the middle (poncho) tied at the waist with a rope. Dark blue shirt and pants underneath. Dark blue socks pulled up over the bottom of the sweat pants for shoes. Gold plastic headband for crown. Short hair.

Production Notes

Costume Narrative

CHAMBERLAIN AUGUSTY

(FULL PRODUCTION) Red, high-collar, super long-sleeved "officials" robe flowing down to the ankles. Trimmed with gold and blue braiding. Red hose or tights. Gold and blue broad collar (Egyptian collar). Red velvet, small, square corner cap. Brown hair, shaved straight across in the back from the top of the left ear to the right (natural wig). Brown goatee.

(GOOD REPRESENTATION) Dark red rectangle piece of cloth with hole for head to go through cut in the middle (poncho) tied at the waist with a rope. Purple, long sleeved sweatshirt underneath. Purple sweatpants. Purple socks pulled up over the bottom of the sweatpants for shoes. Brown, short hair (yarn wig). Goatee painted on.

(MINIMAL REPRESENTATION) Dark red rectangle piece of cloth with hole for head to go through cut in the middle (poncho) tied at the waist with a rope. Black shirt and pants underneath. Black socks pulled up over the bottom of the pants for shoes. Short hair.

PRINCE CRISPEN

(FULL PRODUCTION) Red, high still collar, long sleeved tunic, upper thigh-length. Trimmed with gold embroidery and jewels. Laced with gold cording across the chest. Yellow hose or tights. Gold lamé, ankle-high boots. Gold belt. Gold and bejeweled crown. Black, semi-long hair (natural wig).

(GOOD REPRESENTATION) Orange rectangle piece of cloth with hole for head to go through cut in the middle (poncho) tied at the waist with a rope. Red, long sleeved sweatshirt underneath. Red sweatpants. Red socks pulled up over the bottom of the sweatpants for shoes. Gold band for crown with jewels attached. Black, semi-long hair (yarn wig).

(MINIMAL REPRESENTATION) Orange rectangle piece of cloth with hole for head to go through cut in the middle (poncho) tied at the waist with a rope. Dark brown shirt and pants underneath. Dark brown socks pulled up over the bottom of the pants for shoes. Gold plastic headband for crown. Semi-long hair.

SIR DUKE LORD

(FULL PRODUCTION) Chain-mail collar. Green, short, no sleeved tunic, waist-length. Green, floor-length pants. Yellow, mid calf-high boots. Yellow belt. Short metal broadsword with leather wrapped hilt. Brown hair, shaved straight across in the back from the top of the left ear to the right (natural wig). Brown mustache.

(GOOD REPRESENTATION) Gray loosely knitted and fitting turtle neck collar to look like chain-mail. Green rectangle piece of cloth with hole for head to go through cut in the middle (poncho) tied at the waist with a rope. Brown, long sleeved sweatshirt underneath. Brown sweatpants. Brown socks pulled up over the bottom of the sweatpants for shoes. Short wooden broadsword with cloth wrapped hilt. Brown, short hair. Mustache painted on.

Production Notes

Costume Narrative   (MINIMAL REPRESENTATION) Green rectangle piece of cloth with hole for head to go through cut in the middle (poncho) tied at the waist with a rope. Dark brown shirt and pants underneath. Dark brown socks pulled up over the bottom of the pants for shoes. Painted short wooden or plastic broadsword. Short hair.

PRINCESS ANGELEEN
(FULL PRODUCTION) Mint green, floor-length bliaut. Velvet green, long surcoat with gold embroidery trim. (No cape.) Flesh colored hose or stockings with mint green slippers. Gold, small crown with jewels. Blonde, long free-flowing hair (natural wig).

(GOOD REPRESENTATION) Altered green nightgown with added gold cloth pieces to adorn and disguise the nightgown. Green velvet rectangle piece of cloth for cape. Green hose or stockings and white ballet slippers. Gold band for crown with jewels attached. Blonde, long free-flowing hair (yarn wig).

(MINIMAL REPRESENTATION) Altered green nightgown with added gold cloth pieces to adorn and disguise the nightgown. Green velvet rectangle piece of cloth for cape. Green knee-high stockings. Gold plastic headband for crown. Long, free-flowing hair.

LADY VIVIEN
(FULL PRODUCTION) Purple, floor-length bliaut with long sleeves. Trimmed with gold and green braiding. (No cape.) Purple colored hose or stockings with gold slippers. Green, shot hennin (hat) with green, waist-long veil flowing underneath. Red, long free-flowing hair (natural wig).

(GOOD REPRESENTATION) Altered purple nightgown with added purple cloth pieces to adorn and disguise the nightgown. Purple velvet rectangle piece of cloth for cape. Purple hose or stockings and black ballet slippers. Green piece of cloth covering top of head and flowing down the back. Red, long free-flowing hair (yarn wig).

(MINIMAL REPRESENTATION) Altered purple nightgown with added purple cloth pieces to adorn and disguise the nightgown. Purple velvet rectangle piece of cloth for cape. Purple knee-high stockings. Long, free-flowing hair.

PEOPLE OF THE COURT
Suggestions from (FULL PRODUCTION, GOOD REPRESENTATION, and MINIMAL REPRESENTATION) may draw from the primary characters to construct costumes for the **PEOPLE OF THE COURT**.

Production Notes

Costume Illustrations

THOR & SWAINE

SIR DUKE LORD

CYRIL

3 WANDERING MINSTRELS

LADIES-IN-WAITING

Production Notes

Costume Illustrations

PRINCESS ANGELEEN & PRINCE STEVEN

PRINCE CRISPEN & LADY VIVIEN

CHAMBERLAIN AUGUSTY

HER MAJESTY TALLULAH

HIS MAJESTY WALTER

Production Notes

Set Design Narrative

(FULL PRODUCTION)

SET ELEMENTS:
- SKY: Backdrop with painted blue sky and clouds.
- Back WALL: Faux stone paneling with stone molding around open arches/windows.
- Left and Right WALLS: Same faux stone paneling. TAPESTRY on Right WALL. TORCHES on Left WALL. (See *SET ACCESSORIES* below for more on the TAPESTRY and TORCHES.)
- PLATFORM: Wooden frame raised roughly 9" from the ground. Semi-circle "stage" slatted on top.
- FIRE PIT: 9" high semi-circle border with mortared top (for sitting). Should be the same dimensions as the stage. Long branches stacked upright and tied at the top in PIT.

SET FURNITURE:
- THRONES: Wooden chair with tall back and arms. Decorative molding facade applied to exposed wooden areas. Red velvet cushioned seat and back.
- BANQUET TABLES: Long, folding tables. (See *SET ACCESSORIES* below explaining TABLECLOTHS needed for the TABLES.)
- STOOLS: STOOLS are hidden behind the TABLECLOTHS and can be of any material and style.

SET ACCESSORIES:
- TAPESTRY: (On Right WALL.) TAPESTRY should be big enough for **THOR** and **SWAINE** to hide behind. A good 4' x 6' tapestry with a medieval scene depicted on it would work nicely.
- FIRE PIT: Several long branches stacked up tepee style. Fire is cold.
- TORCHES: (On Left WALL.) Wooden torches hollowed out in center. Electric cording threaded through center with bulb socket fixture at end. Light bulb shaped like a flame. Bulbs that flicker light like a flame would work best.
- TABLECLOTHS: Cloth that fully covers the TABLE and falls to the floor. Multicolored cloth of large checkered pattern.
- BANNERS: BANNERS with Scottish heraldic images may hang on the Back WALL. These are optional.

(GOOD REPRESENTATION)

SET ELEMENTS:
- SKY: Blue scrim or backdrop painted blue or blue cloth or curtain.
- Back WALL: Flats painted to look like stone. Archways/windows with fortified ledges.
- Left and Right WALLS: Flats painted to look like stone. (See *SET ACCESSORIES* below for more on the TAPESTRY and TORCHES.)
- PLATFORM: Wooden frame riser or wagon in front of flats.
- FIRE PIT: Two-by-four(s) aligned to make a pit. Branches stacked up inside.

Production Notes

Set Design Narrative

SET FURNITURE:
- THRONES: Chairs with cloth draped over.
- BANQUET TABLES: Sheets of plywood sitting on cinder blocks or plastic mike crates. (See *SET ACCESSORIES* below explaining TABLECLOTHS needed for the TABLES.)
- STOOLS: STOOLS are hidden behind the TABLECLOTHS and can be of any material and style.

SET ACCESSORIES:
- TAPESTRY: (On Right WALL.) TAPESTRY with a medieval scene painted on WALL. (**THOR** and **SWAINE** can hide behind the WALL.)
- FIRE PIT: Several long branches stacked up tepee style. Fire is cold.
- TORCHES: (On Left Wall.) Wooden TORCHES not lit.
- TABLECLOTHS: Cloth that fully covers the table and falls to the floor.
- BANNERS: BANNERS with Scottish heraldic images may hang on the Back WALL. These are optional.

(MINIMAL REPRESENTATION)

SET ELEMENTS:
- SKY: Blue scrim or black curtain, or anything that covers or blocks stage or classroom.
- Back WALL: Long folding tables turned on side and propped up. Possible cardboard or cloth covering painted to appear like stone. Center table strongly supported and padded for PLAYERS to climb and fall over.
- Left and Right WALLS: If on a standard stage, use teasers for entering and exiting. If performed in an open space, PLAYERS need only to leave the area of action.
- PLATFORM: Not required. The **THREE WANDERING MINSTRELS** need only perform their antics off to the side.
- FIRE PIT: Not required.

SET FURNITURE:
- THRONES: THRONES can be hidden from view like the STOOLS.
- BANQUET TABLES: Several folding tables butted up against each other to create a table long enough to accommodate the number of PLAYERS sitting there. (See *SET ACCESSORIES* below explaining TABLECLOTHS needed for the TABLES.)
- STOOLS: STOOLS are hidden behind the TABLECLOTHS and can be of any material and style like stacked plastic crates.

Production Notes

Set Design Narrative

SET ACCESSORIES:
- TAPESTRY: (On Right WALL.) Not required.
- FIRE PIT: Not required.
- TORCHES: (On Left WALL.) Not required.
- TABLECLOTHS: Bedsheets.
- BANNERS: Not required.

Lighting and Sound Requirements

LIGHTING:
- Standard Lighting: Perhaps a bit dime as it's approaching evening. Room lighting should be satisfactory.

SOUND:
- The sound of a splash can either be a recording or a heavy object plopped in a tub of water (offstage).

Prop List

- A Court Jester's CLOWN STICK for **CYRIL**.
- 3 large SACKS stuffed with wigs, costumes, masks, and anything and everything cast and crew can think of to put in sacks specifically including lots of hats.
- Large, GOLDEN AMULET.
- HANDHELD MIRROR.
- A slice of GOOSEBERRY PIE.
- WIMPLE.
- Big, gaudy JEWELRY and gold chains.
- Medium-sized, GOLD FRAMED MIRROR.
- PLACE SETTINGS/COMPOTES (one for each **LADY-IN-WAITING**).
- SACRED STONE OF LOCH BOWIE (which is a big rock). This can be a rock or a papier-mâché rock stone.
- ROAST BOAR on a large TRAY. This may be of papier-mâché as well.
- STRETCHER device for carrying ROAST BOAR.

Production Notes

Set Design Floor Plan

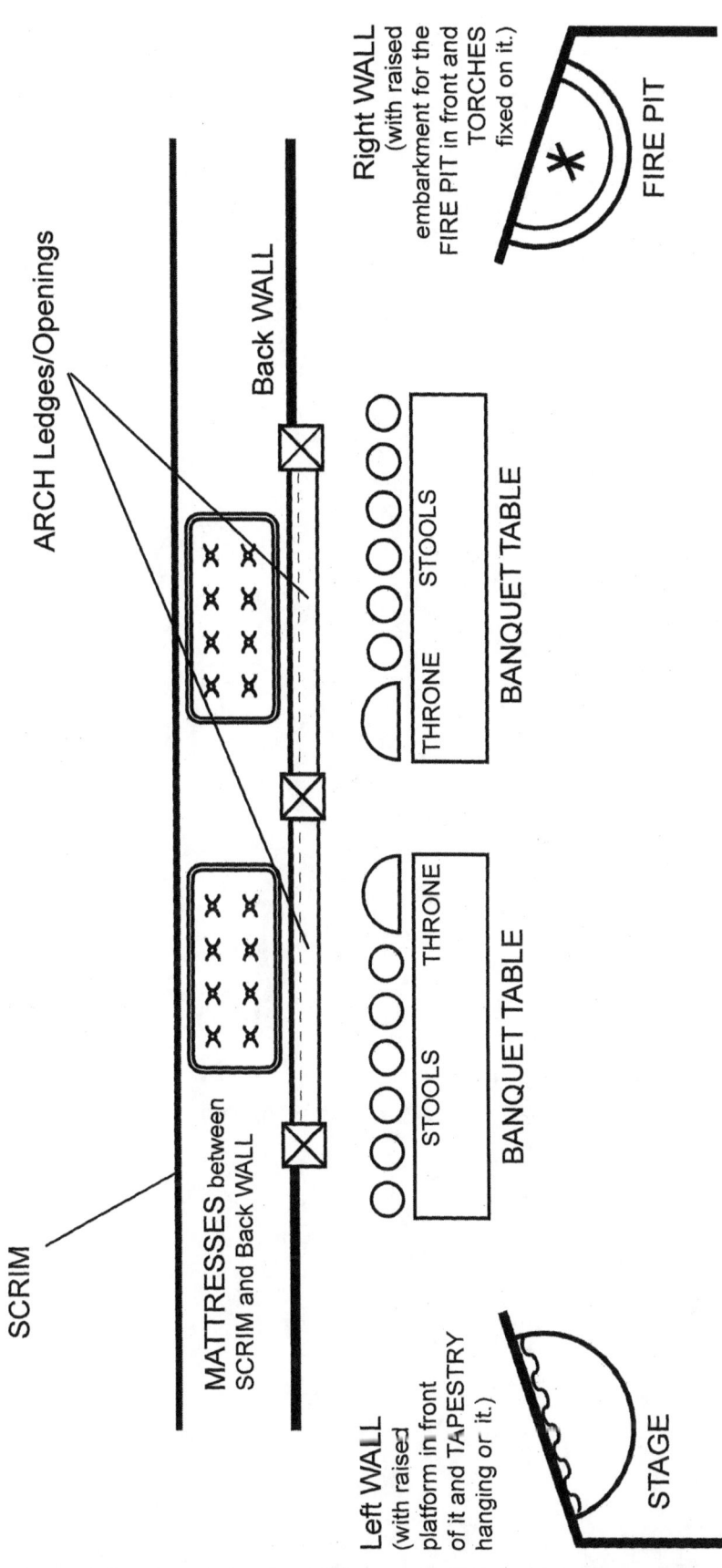

Erstwhile ...

a Comedy
by Joan Garner

CAST OF CHARACTERS *(in order of appearance)*

THOR—A Viking Warrior
SWAINE—A Viking Warrioress
CYRIL—The Court Jester
3 WANDERING MINSTRELS
HER MAJESTY TALLULAH—The Queen
HER MAJESTY'S LADIES-IN-WAITING
HIS MAJESTY WALTER—The King
PRINCE STEVEN—The Second Son
AUGUSTY—Lord Chamberlain
PRINCE CRISPEN—The First Son
SIR DUKE LORD—Captain of the Guard
PRINCESS ANGELEEN—The Betrothed
LADY VIVIEN—Angeleen's Companion
PEOPLE OF THE COURT

SET

The great hall of the royal castle of Interlocken. Two long BANQUET TABLES extend out along the back WALL upstage. There should be an opening between the TABLES at center. Behind each TABLE, on either side of the opening, is a THRONE. **HIS MAJESTY WALTER'S** THRONE is behind the right TABLE, and **HER MAJESTY'S TALLULAH'S** THRONE is behind the left TABLE. Stools also sit behind the TABLE. TABLECLOTHS reaching down to the floor drape the TABLES. The back WALL of the room has two open ARCHES (windows) that look out onto a blue SKY. The window ledges should be high enough to be seen by the audience and not hidden from the tables in front of them. There needs to be space between the back WALL containing the windows and the far back WALL or SKY SCRIM. The right WALL holds a large TAPESTRY. Upstage from the right WALL is an opening that exits out right. In front of the TAPESTRY is a small, semicircular, raised platform (like a little STAGE). The left WALL is similar to the right with an exit upstage that leads out stage left. It also has a semicircular structure in front of it which is a FIRE PIT. A two-or three stone high half circle embankment defines the PIT. (Normally, the FIRE PIT is in the center of a great hall, but for practical purposes here, it's off to the left—away from the action.) Logs are stacked inside the FIRE PIT teepee style. The fire is cold during the play.

AT RISE

- INTERLOCKEN, an itty-bitty kingdom on a teeny-weeny island north of Scotland.
- Near the turn of the 9th Century, A.D.
- Late afternoon.

*(All is quiet and calm. The room is empty of **PLAYERS**. Momentarily a pair of hands come up and clutch onto the ledge of the right ARCH opening on the back WALL. Then **THOR** [a Viking warrior] hoists himself up bracing the upper part of his body with his arms on the ledge. Pleased with himself, **THOR** lets out a victorious "humph." However, he loses his grip and slowly slips back down behind the*

WALL. BEAT. Another set of hands come up to clutch the ledge of the left ARCH opening of the back WALL. Next, a sandaled foot sticks up in the opening. Now **THOR'S** hand comes back onto the ledge of the right ARCH opening. There's grunting and sounds of much effort until **THOR** is up bracing himself again with his arms. And now, **SWAINE** [a Viking warrioress] hoists herself up in the left ARCH opening to take the same position as **THOR**. They both lean inward and "hush" each other. With great difficulty and noise, the two climb over the ledge and drop/fall to the floor. They fumble and clang about with their shields and swords until both are standing. Again they "hush" each other. Once inspected and adjusted of armor, cloaks, helmets, and so on, they step center stage—ready to attack. Then **THOR** motions for **SWAINE** to follow him, and the two tiptoe out to the right—continuing to make a racket. BEAT. Entering from the left is **CYRIL** [the court jester] with the **3 WANDERING MINSTRELS** following. The **3 MINSTRELS** carry large cloth SACKS stuffed full of items.)

CYRIL: —And this is where you will be entertaining the royal court later this evening. This is the great hall.

(The **3 MINSTRELS** look incredulously at one another.)

CYRIL: *(Continued.)* Yes, I know. "Great" doesn't properly describe this room, but you see the royal coinage in the royal counting house dwindled down dramatically before the royal builders got to this room. Presently—and we are all counting on very soon here—the royal counting house will once again be brimming with gold and jewels and other treasures society uses to set up the caste system. When this comes to pass, the royal builders will expand the room out this way over the cesspool, naturally relocating the current cesspool... Any questions?

(The **3 MINSTRELS** look at one another again, then back to **CYRIL** with blank expressions.)

CYRIL: *(Continued.)* All right, then. You may set up over there.

(**CYRIL** points to the right. The **3 MINSTRELS** obediently step to the side of the room. They place their large cloth SACKS down on the little STAGE and take out wigs, props, clothing, and so on.

During the duration of the play—up and until the time of their performance—the **3 MINSTRELS** will fuss with makeup, masks, footwear, hats, musical instruments, banners, flags, and whatever else they have stuffed in the SACKS. From time to time—between the coming and going of others—something completely unrelated and absurd will be pulled out of the SACKS for the audience to see.

CYRIL begins to exit stage left, notices the audience out of the corner of his eye, and steps back to center stage to address the audience.)

CYRIL: *(Continued.)* Oh, you're here. We weren't expecting you for a bit. But since you're here, best of the day to you and yourn. Welcome to the kingdom of Interlocken. Never heard of it, you say? Well, here in Interlocken, we like to keep a low profile. I am Cyril, jester to the royal court. Granted, I'm not what one would expect a jester to look like, but when I ventured into this community, it was the only opening available. I'm doing my best to fit into my new vocation, but I fear praise and accolades will never come my way. The royal physicians have diagnosed it to be a right brain/left brain malady. I have no idea what they're talking about. They're always talking in terms the layperson doesn't understand. But, as I'm not medically inclined myself, I must trust the knowledge of the good doctors.

Anon, the kingdom is much a buzz this day. Today we await the arrival of our queen to be, Princess Angeleen, the lovely and fair. Or so this is what we are told, fore no one here in Interlocken has seen the lovely and fair Angeleen. The marriage has been prearranged for some time now. Angeleen is to marry our Crispen, first son to His Majesty Walter and Her Majesty Tallulah. When Prince Crispen marries Princess Angeleen in the 'morrow, he'll then be crowned as our new king. All neat and tidy... Well, that should be all you need to know for now... *(CYRIL looks over to the 3 MINSTRELS, then readdresses the audience.)* Oh. Tonight there is to be a wonderful banquet in honor of Princess Angeleen. You're all invited to stay and partake of the festivities if you like. There will be food and drink and entertainment.

(CYRIL gestures in presenting the 3 MINSTRELS who stop and look over to CYRIL deadpanned.)

CYRIL: *(Continued.)* Yes, well, we can only hope. Please stay and make yourselves to home. I'll return soon.

(CYRIL exits out stage right. Entering from stage left is HER MAJESTY TALLULAH [the queen] and her LADIES-IN-WAITING. The number of LADIES-IN-WAITING can range from 2 to infinity. Whatever the count, they should all walk and speak in unison, dress alike, and keep the same facial expression.)

HER MAJESTY TALLULAH: —And be certain the cook removes the eyes from the roast boar this time. There's nothing quiet as unappetizing as having your dinner stare back at you....

LADIES-IN-WAITING: Yes, Your Majesty.

TALLULAH: Good, because everything must be perfect tonight.

LADIES-IN-WAITING: Oh, it will be, Your Majesty.

TALLULAH: I wish I could be as optimistic, but I have this unsettling feeling the night will end in disaster.

LADIES-IN-WAITING: But why, Your Majesty?

*(Enter **HIS MAJESTY WALTER** [the king] from stage right. He stops and bows grandly towards the women.)*

TALLULAH: Well, there's one reason right there.

*(Enter **CYRIL** with **PRINCE STEVEN** [the second son] from stage right.)*

TALLULAH: *(Continued.)* And there's the other.

PRINCE STEVEN: Slow down, Cyril. I fear we've come onto the path of a tempest.

TALLULAH: Steven, have you seen your brother?

STEVEN: Brother Crispen? The first son? The heir apparent? The blessed one? I suggest you search out a mirror. Undoubtedly Crispen will be standing in front of it.

TALLULAH: Steven, will you ever come to the realization that the only one who finds you amusing is you?

STEVEN: Oh, probably not, Mother.

TALLULAH: Mm... Come along, ladies. I want to double check all the preparations for this evening. Absolutely nothing can go wrong tonight. Nothing!

*(**TALLULAH** begins to exit stage left with her **LADIES-IN-WAITING**, and then turns back.)*

TALLULAH: *(Continued.)* Walter, are you planning to wear that outfit this evening?

HIS MAJESTY WALTER: *(Looking over his clothes.)* What's wrong with this?

TALLULAH: *(Not thrilled.)* Mm....

*(**TALLULAH** exits stage left with the **LADIES-IN-WAITING**.)*

WALTER: It seems we both manage to irritate Her Majesty, my son. When you tease her about Crispen, it plays especially bad.

STEVEN: Annoying the queen is my self-appointed mission in life, Father. As it's obvious I'll receive nothing else from this monarchy, I must satisfy myself with lighthearted moments from time to time.

WALTER: But you *will* receive something, Steven. You are to be deeded Loch Bowie the day of Crispen and Angeleen's marriage.

STEVEN: Yes, Father. And I'm sincerely grateful. It's just that Crispen gets the crown, the kingdom, and the beautiful princess. All I get is a parcel of swampland on the south end of the island.

WALTER: Ah, but there is a mountain behind the swamp, my son. Look to the mountain.

STEVEN: Yes, Father. It's a very pretty if not tiny mountain. Thank you.

WALTER: There can be much more to a mountain besides the landscape.

STEVEN: What are you trying to tell me, Father?

WALTER: In good time, Steven. All will reveal itself in good time.

   (WALTER exits out stage left.)

STEVEN: His Majesty is most mysterious today.

CYRIL: Your father is a good man, Your Highness. Trust him.

STEVEN: Oh, I do, Cyril. I do.

   *(Enter **AUGUSTY** [Lord Chamberlain] and **PRINCE CRISPEN** [the first son] from stage left.)*

STEVEN: *(Continued.)* Crispen, Mother is looking for you.

PRINCE CRISPEN: What of it?

STEVEN: Nothing of it. I merely relay the message.

CRISPEN: It won't be long now until I'm the ruling sovereign. Then Her Majesty will have to answer to *my* beck and call.

STEVEN: But of course. I see how reverently you hold the responsibilities of being king. Does the phrase "usurping one's power" have any meaning for you, Crispen?

CRISPEN: Does the phrase "no one remembers the one who comes in second" have any meaning for you, Steven?

STEVEN: *(Sarcastically.)* Oh, ouch. How you bruise my frail ego, Brother. Not to worry. Come the day you're crowned, I'll be far, far away—on some small mountaintop, I suspect.

CRISPEN: Why wait until that day?

STEVEN: Good point. Adieu to you.

   (STEVEN bows slightly and exits stage left.)

CRISPEN: *(To CYRIL.)* And adieu to you, too.

   (CYRIL bows and exits stage left while saying:)

CYRIL: "Adieu to you, too." Gosh, I wish I was that clever.

AUGUSTY: Please, Your Highness, allow me to fry that one in his own unfunny fat.

CRISPEN: *(Ignoring AUGUSTY.)* —On some small mountaintop he thinks. Little does he know the moment I'm king, dear Brother Steven is to be thrown into the deepest, darkest dungeon this castle holds.

AUGUSTY: Yes, there's nothing quite as unnecessary as a surplus of princes.

CRISPEN: Dealing with Steven will be only one of many items to attend to on that glorious day of days, Chamberlain Augusty.

AUGUSTY: Speaking of other items to be attended to, I have been secretly preparing the army for the planned invasion of Hollimer. Your Highness need only say the word and we are ready to go forward. Then we'll have two kingdoms to rule.

CRISPEN: Patience, Augusty. It might be prudent of me to marry Princess Angeleen before I overthrow her father. It would only be the polite thing to do.

   (CRISPEN and AUGUSTY share an evil laugh.)

AUGUSTY: Still, declaring war on Angeleen's homeland could possibly place a dark cloud over the honeymoon.

CRISPEN: Honeymoon? What care I of a honeymoon? This is purely a marriage of state—a joining of two countries in supposed peace and cooperation—that and nothing more. This is the official proclamation of both monarchs. But we readily know how financially strapped Interlocken is and that this marriage is to pump Hollimer's wealth into our deficit. So much for romance. I haven't met this woman, and I don't know her. Honeymoon? Please.

AUGUSTY: But love may come in time.

CRISPEN: Never. Just as I plan to toss Steven into the deepest hole in the castle, I intend to lock up Princess Angeleen in its highest tower.

AUGUSTY: And thus ridding you of two annoyances.

CRISPEN: Precisely.

AUGUSTY: With all of this arranging, should I be suspicious of what you have in mind for me, Your Highness?

CRISPEN: Your fate is secure, Chamberlain. As long as you agree with all I say and do what I order.

AUGUSTY: *(Bowing.)* Naturally, Your Highness.

> *(**CRISPEN** and **AUGUSTY** exit out stage right. BEAT. **THOR** and **SWAINE** peek around the left WALL, and then duck behind the nearby BANQUET TABLE. Halfway across, they poke their heads over the TABLE, look around, duck down again, and squat-walk the rest of the way across, behind the TABLES and out stage right. [Of course the audience can see their two helmets bob up and down over the TABLETOPS as they go along.] One of the **3 MINSTRELS** looks around the WALL as the **VIKINGS** exit. He or she glances back over to the other two. They all shrug their shoulders and go about their business. After another BEAT, **WALTER** reenters from stage left as **SIR DUKE LORD** [captain of the royal guard] enters from stage right and hurries over to **WALTER**.)*

SIR DUKE: Your Majesty, thank Heavens I found you.

WALTER: *(The flipping of **SIR DUKE'S** name is on purpose here.)* What is it, Sir Lord Duke?

SIR DUKE: Two fishermen of the village report spotting a Viking ship moored in the—moor.

WALTER: A Viking ship?

SIR DUKE: Yes, Sire. My troops have been combing the countryside trying to find them. We thought they might be bogged down in the—bog. But we found nothing. We're afraid they have gone into hiding whilst' they prepare an attack.

WALTER: Attack?

SIR DUKE: Yes, Sire.

WALTER: Why?

SIR DUKE: Well, um, it's what Vikings do, Sire. Attack, plunder, pillage, and so on and so forth.

WALTER: But why would they want to attack us? What did we ever do to them?

SIR DUKE: Uh—

WALTER: Perhaps they're simply hungry. We should invite them to the banquet tonight.

SIR DUKE: You Majesty, I don't believe food is what they're after. Well, naturally, they'll be after our food, but I believe they're after our—*everything*.

WALTER: Nevertheless, should you happen on these visitors, please extend an invitation to the festivities tonight.

SIR DUKE: I will, Your Majesty. If I have the opportunity—that is—if I'm not heavy in battle fighting for my life, I most certainly will. Come to think of it, I may have the perfect opportunity to invite the visitors to the festivities while hanging upside down on their mizzenmast just above the heaving fire they have made for my comfort. We'll have to see.

WALTER: Excellent. Thank you, Sir Lord Duke.

SIR DUKE: Yes, Your Majesty.

   (*SIR DUKE bows, but hesitates to exit.*)

SIR DUKE: *(Continued.)* Actually, Sire, it's Sir Duke Lord.

WALTER: Excuse me?

SIR DUKE: My name, Your Majesty. My name is Sir Duke Lord.

WALTER: It is? I thought it was Sir Lord Duke.

SIR DUKE: No. My mother was a duchess which made me a duke. Then my mother married a lord, and then you dubbed me a knight—Sir Duke Lord.

WALTER: I see. Fascinating. I'll do my best to address you properly.

SIR DUKE: Thank you, Your Majesty.

WALTER: Think nothing of it, Sir Lord Duke.

SIR DUKE: Uh, actually... It's nothing... Actually, addressing me as a captain would work just as well... Simply Captain, or Captain Sir Duke Lord which is my official title, although I can see where that might appear a bit pretentious... Never mind... I'll try to find the—yes—with your permission....

(*SIR DUKE bows once again and exits stage left.*)

WALTER: *(To himself.)* Vikings. My, my.

(*WALTER exits out stage right. As he passes the **3 MINSTRELS** tip their hats to him, then go back to their business of preparing for the show. **CYRIL** reenters from stage left. He's in a hurry, but stops when he sees the audience out of the corner of his eye again, and remembers something.*)

CYRIL: *(To the audience.)* Oh, to beg you pardon. We're in a bit of a crisis here. It seems the entourage sent to the shore of Interlocken to meet Princess Angeleen and her consort was diverted to a hush-hush classified matter. This is all well and good, but Her Majesty is concerned the princess will think ill of her new country what with having no one there to greet her properly and all. Consequently, the entire court is treading ever so lightly and ever so quickly to stay out of the queen's warring path.

(*CYRIL continues across the stage, but stops again before the **3 MINSTRELS**.*)

CYRIL: *(Continued.)* And how are things here? Have you need of anything?

(*CYRIL receives only blank looks from the **3 MINSTRELS**.*)

CYRIL: *(Continued.)* Would you like food or drink? Possibly something to wake you up?

(*Again, just blank looks from the **3 MINSTRELS**.*)

CYRIL: *(Continued.)* You must be conserving all your energy for the big show, eh? Deep in meditation preparing your whole being for the crowning performance, I hope. Well, carry on.

(*CYRIL backs up warily and addresses the audience again.*)

CYRIL: *(Continued.)* I'm not worried. Why would I be worried? *(CYRIL looks over to the **3 MINSTRELS** and lets out a little laugh.)* Oh, by the by, things are mysteriously disappearing from the castle; a gooseberry pie, an amulet of King Walter's, and a handheld mirror of Prince Crispen's. Fortunately, I'm not in charge of disappearing items. On the other hand....

(CYRIL looks back at the 3 MINSTRELS who now have their backs to the audience with their butts sticking up high. CYRIL sighs and mumbles as he exits stage left:)

CYRIL: *(Continued.)* Maybe there's an opening in moat dredging....

(BEAT. THOR and SWAINE peek around the right WALL, and then come into the room after seeing the coast is clear. SWAINE has a large AMULET around her neck. She's admiring it with a HANDHELD MIRROR. THOR is smacking his lips as he finishes eating the last bite of GOOSEBERRY PIE. His lips and that around his mouth have turned purple.)

THOR: I don't know, Swaine. This kingdom doesn't seem wealthy enough to tromp all over.

SWAINE: Oh, I don't know. I think it has potential. We haven't found their counting house yet. Who knows what treasures we'll come upon there?

THOR: And what if there is great treasure there? With only the two of us—

SWAINE: Don't bring that up. You're always bringing that up.

THOR: You're the one who got us kicked out of the lodge.

SWAINE: I know I was. And how you enjoy reminding me of it at every turn. Can we get back to why we're here, please?

THOR: *(Thinking.)* The king shouldn't be a problem.

SWAINE: No, but the queen will. Surely she is the leader of this kingdom. There are all those women around her all the time, and she's always giving orders. We'll cancel out both of them to be on the safe side.

THOR: And the princes?

SWAINE: We can dump Crispen in the swamp, but must we do anything to Steven?

THOR: Why not Steven?

SWAINE: He's cute and really sweet.

THOR: What?

SWAINE: Steven, he's—

THOR: Am I not enough for you?

SWAINE: Of course you are. Come on. We better get out of here before we're discovered.

THOR: No, no, no. I want to discuss this.

*(**SWAINE** begins to exit stage left. **THOR** follows her out as they continue to bicker.)*

SWAINE: This is ridiculous.

THOR: What is it? Is it his eyes?

SWAINE: Oh, for Pete's sake, Thor. You're so insecure.

THOR: I am not....

*(After **THOR** and **SWAINE** exit stage left, **PRINCESS ANGELEEN** [the betrothed] and **LADY VIVIEN** [**ANGELEEN'S** traveling companion] enter from stage right.)*

LADY VIVIEN: This kingdom's population must be sparser than first suspected, with not having a welcoming committee to meet us at the shore. And here, even at the royal castle, all appears vacant and empty.

PRINCESS ANGELEEN: It's for the best. This way we were able to view the countryside unabated of a special escort who has been instructed to show us only what the monarchy wants us to see.

VIVIEN: I must say, Your Highness, I admire how calm and collected you are with all of this. If I were soon to marry a man I never met, I'd be a blubbering mess.

ANGELEEN: It's my royal upbringing and blue blood properness. It's simply not in my makeup to be hysterical or uncouth. Besides, what good would my being upset do? It's not as if I've had any say over the smallest part of this. All I can do is hope the prince is a kind and gentle man.

VIVIEN: And what if he isn't?

ANGELEEN. Well, I can always immerse myself in charity work.

*(Enter **STEVEN** and **CYRIL** from stage left. Instantly, **STEVEN** and **ANGELEEN** lock eyes with a mutual and instant attraction.)*

STEVEN: *(Bowing.)* Ladies.

ANGELEEN: *(Curtsying.)* Sir.

STEVEN: You are new to the castle, are you not?

ANGELEEN: Aye.

STEVEN: Aye. May I offer my services?

VIVIEN: We seek out the prince.

STEVEN: You do? I'm the prince.

ANGELEEN: You are?

STEVEN: Yes, I am.

ANGELEEN: Oh, you have no idea how delighted I am to hear this. Honestly, I dared not to hope or build my expectations too high. But here you are. What a relief this is. What an utter relief.

STEVEN: Milady, you have no idea how happy I am to hear that I'm the source of your relief. But admittedly, I'm rather baffled as to why.

ANGELEEN: Why? The why is that you are the prince.

STEVEN: Never before has my mere princeliness brought forth such joy.

ANGELEEN: I must confess that I held my gigantic apprehension and terror with this marriage agreement within. But now that I see there was nothing to worry about, I am prepared to proceed with the wedding.

STEVEN: What wedding?

ANGELEEN: We are to be married.

STEVEN: We are?

VIVIEN: It's a done deal.

STEVEN: *(Comes the dawning.)* You're Angeleen.

ANGELEEN: Yes, and you're Prince Crispen.

STEVEN: Sorry to say, I'm not.

ANGELEEN: No?

STEVEN: No.

SCRIPT **Erstwhile...**

ANGELEEN: Oh, no, no, no. You said you were the prince.

STEVEN: I am the prince—*a* prince—one of two. I'm Prince Steven.

ANGELEEN: Prince Steven?

STEVEN: Yes, Your Highness.

ANGELEEN: Not Prince Crispen?

STEVEN: Afraid not.

ANGELEEN: But this is awful. The fates are too cruel. Are you sure you're not Prince Crispen? Not even a little bit?

STEVEN: Were that I were.

(ANGELEEN desperately grasps STEVEN'S shoulders.)

ANGELEEN: You simply have to be Prince Crispen!

VIVIEN: *(Mumbling to herself.)* So much for blue blood decorum.

STEVEN: Believe me, Your Highness; I'm just as distressed as you in knowing you're Princess Angeleen. Well, not that you are Princess Angeleen, but that Princess Angeleen is set to marry my brother.

ANGELEEN: *(To CYRIL for confirmation.)* He's Steven, not Crispen?

CYRIL: Sorry, Your Highness. This is Prince Steven, and has been Prince Steven the whole of his life to the best of my knowledge.

(ANGELEEN looks over to the 3 MINSTRELS who have been listening. They nod their heads "yes" as well.)

ANGELEEN: But this is disastrous. What are we to do? I cannot marry Crispen now. I'd rather rot in the swamp.

VIVIEN: Your Highness, please. You'll develop the vapors if you go on like this.

(To STEVEN and CYRIL as she takes ANGELEEN aside.)

VIVIEN: *(Continued.)* Will you pardon us... *(Then to ANGELEEN.)* Your Highness, not wanting to be especially critical right now, but isn't your behavior here a touch on the erratic side? It isn't proper for a princess to act so emotionally. You told me so yourself.

ANGELEEN: *(Calming herself with a deep breath.)* Lady Vivien, I realize my behavior is not that of a princess. Upon entering this castle I was a princess. But upon meeting Prince Steven, I am now a woman in love.

VIVIEN: In love?

ANGELEEN: Completely and rapturously.

VIVIEN: But again, Your Highness. Not to be overly critical here, but you just met the man. How can you be completely and rapturously in love with someone you've just met?

ANGELEEN: I know this is irrational, but isn't love irrational?

(STEVEN steps over to the women.)

STEVEN: Uh, excuse me, but I couldn't help overhear your conversation and would just like to say that I don't think it at all irrational to fall in love in a heart beat.

ANGELEEN: Thank you.

STEVEN: You're very welcome.

VIVIEN: All right. I'll concede that this is oh so precious with the two of you falling in love in a heat beat, and you are oh so adorable together, but what can be done about it? The princess is promised to Prince Crispen.

CYRIL: *(Aside to STEVEN.)* Something of a pessimist, isn't she?

STEVEN: The lady is being sensible, Cyril.

VIVIEN: My name is Vivien, Your Highness. Lady Vivien.

STEVEN: Oh, pleased to meet you.

(STEVEN kisses VIVIEN'S hand.)

VIVIEN: Charmed. And this is Her Royal Highness Angeleen of Hollimer.

STEVEN: Yes, we've met.

(As ANGELEEN has stuck her hand out, STEVEN obligingly kisses her hand as well.)

STEVEN: *(Continued.)* Most pleased to meet you both. May I introduce our court jester, Cyril.

VIVIEN: Yes, we gathered as much what with the jingle hat and all.

CYRIL: Factually, it's a hood.

VIVIEN: All right.

(There is a confused PAUSE.)

VIVIEN: Where were we?

CYRIL: Let me see. Princess Angeleen is in love with Prince Steven, but is to marry Prince Crispen, and so is distressed. Prince Steven is distressed that Princess Angeleen is distressed, and you, Lady Vivien, are perplexed at the suddenness of it all. And I am uncomfortable because my tights are beginning to creep up.

ANGELEEN: *(To STEVEN.)* So, my beloved, what say you of this? What I mean is how do you feel about my being in love with you?

STEVEN: Honestly, Your Highness, I find it not at all disagreeable.

ANGELEEN: This is encouraging.

STEVEN: However, Lady Vivien has introduced a valid concern. You're not betrothed to me. Regretfully you're not mine and I'm not yours. It's definitely a sheep in the middle of the road to everlasting bliss situation.

ANGELEEN: Oh, if only I was not who I am or you were who you are not.

STEVEN: *(A bit confused.)* Yes, if only.

ANGELEEN: Wait! That's the answer. I will simply stop being me. Princess Angeleen is to marry Prince Crispen. But if I am no longer Princess Angeleen, then I won't have to marry him because I won't be. *(To STEVEN.)* Can't you see, my darling? I cannot if I am not.

STEVEN: It's not a bad idea. What do you think, Cyril?

CYRIL: Yes, the idea has merit. I see but one hefty obstacle if not glaring flaw in staging such a deception.

STEVEN: What would that be?

CYRIL: The queen.

STEVEN: Oo, the queen.

VIVIEN: What are you talking about? What deception? What queen?

CYRIL: Her Majesty Tallulah has prepared this grand dinner to honor Princess Angeleen. She has commandeered the entire court to help in the affair. If we have this dinner and there isn't a Princess Angeleen to honor, the queen will be very disappointed. And trust me on this point; you don't want to disappoint the queen.

ANGELEEN: But I won't disappoint the queen because I won't be me being there.

CYRIL: *(Trying to figure out what **ANGELEEN** is saying.)* But you'll never get away with it.

VIVIEN: Get away with what?

ANGELEEN: *(Ignoring **VIVIEN**.)* But I can. It's perfect. No one knows who I am here. Except for you and you two, and those three over there—whoever they are. Otherwise no one knows I am me.

STEVEN: *(To **ANGELEEN**.)* My dear, it isn't that you cannot stop being you. It's just that someone will need to start being you when you stop. *(**STEVEN** thinks of what he just said, and then speaks aside to **CYRIL**.)* I'm beginning to sound just like her, aren't I?

ANGELEEN: That is the easiest part of the marvelous plan, my love. All we have to do is find another Angeleen.

   *(**ANGELEEN**, **STEVEN**, **CYRIL**, and even the **3 MINSTRELS** all look to **VIVIEN**.)*

VIVIEN: *(Still in the dark to what's going on.)* What?

ANGELEEN: Vivien, you could be me.

VIVIEN: Why would I want to be... Oh, no. Now wait a minute. I'm not finished being me yet.

ANGELEEN: Vivien, every girl dreams of becoming a princess. Here's your chance.

VIVIEN: But everyone will know I'm a fraud.

ANGELEEN: No they won't. They don't know who I am. They'll think the way you are is the way Princess Angeleen is. Please, Vivien. Please do this for me. Can't you see how desperately in love I am?

STEVEN: Please, Lady Vivien.

CYRIL: Yes, please. You can do this.

VIVIEN: I don't know.

ANGELEEN: If you become Princess Angeleen, you get to wear all my clothes.

VIVIEN: All of them? Even the gold, sparkly one?

ANGELEEN: Especially the gold, sparkly one.

VIVIEN: Maybe. Maybe it wouldn't be so difficult to pose as a princess at that. I mean, how hard can it be? All you have to do is smile and say "charmed" a lot.

ANGELEEN: *(With her ego a little bruised.)* Well, it takes a little more than that.

VIVIEN: No, it doesn't. I've watched you. There isn't much to it—just stand and curtsy and wave and smile. I can do that.

ANGELEEN: Vivien, dear, I believe you're not grasping the full scope....

STEVEN: *(Whispering to **ANGELEEN**.)* Sweetness, she's fancying to the idea. We shouldn't discourage it.

ANGELEEN: Oh. Yes. Yes. Of course.

   *(To **VIVIEN** giving her a big hug.)*

ANGELEEN: Oh, thank you ever so, Vivien. I love you for doing this for me.

VIVIEN: We'll need our personables brought into the castle.

CYRIL: *(To **VIVIEN**.)* Allow me to offer my assistance, Princess Angeleen.

VIVIEN: *(Getting into the swing of things now.)* Yes, you may go forth, peasant.

   *(**VIVIEN** struts out ceremoniously as she exits stage right with **CYRIL**. There is a moment before **ANGELEEN** speaks.)*

ANGELEEN: Poor Steven. What you must think of me.

STEVEN: What I must think of you? Princess, when Crispen was born the whole kingdom celebrated for weeks. People came from far and near to bestow gifts upon the heir apparent, and the day of his birth was declared a national holiday. When I was born, my parents smiled and the religious representation came to bless me, but that was it. And it's been that way ever since. Then suddenly here stands a princess willing to forfeit her right to the throne for the love of a second prince who has nothing to offer her but a mountain rising up from a swamp. What do I think of you? I think you are the loveliest, sweetest woman on the face of this earth, and I am the most fortunate man alive.

ANGELEEN: *(Coyly.)* I was hoping you were going to say that.

*(**ANGELEEN** jumps into **STEVEN'S** arms. He swings her around with delight and when they stop, he takes her hand.)*

STEVEN: Come. We'll see how Vivien and Cyril are doing.

*(**STEVEN** and **ANGELEEN** exit stage right. There is a BEAT until **THOR** and **SWAINE** peek around the left WALL and then enter. This time, **SWAINE** carries her helmet while wearing a WIMPLE. She is also wearing a lot of JEWELRY and bobbles that look out of place from the rest of the costume. **THOR** carries in a medium-sized, GOLD FRAMED MIRROR. He's admiring himself in it.)*

THOR: It's becoming very busy around here.

SWAINE: We need a plan.

THOR: Plundering and pillaging has always worked for us before. I say we stick with that.

SWAINE: Of course we'll plunder and pillage. But we should have a plan on how we're going to plunder and pillage.

THOR: We'll take the queen first. The rest should tumble all around us once the queen is seized.

SWAINE: Why, Thor, that's actually a good idea.

THOR: Why are you so surprised? I can come up with good ideas.

SWAINE: Yes, I know you can. You're wonderful.

THOR: I'm not just a big hunk of muscle and metal, you know.

SWAINE: I know. You're a wonderful specimen of a man.

*(**SWAINE** gives **THOR** a kiss on the cheek. **THOR** blushes. Then **SWAINE** hears something from offstage and the two quickly hide behind the **3 MINSTRELS** and the paraphernalia the performers have unpacked. The **3 MINSTRELS** will look back at **THOR** and **SWAINE** occasionally, but say nothing. **SIR DUKE** enters from stage left with **WALTER**.)*

SIR DUKE: I don't understand it, Sire. My men have combed the countryside thrice. There is nary a sign of Vikings anywhere.

WALTER: But that's good, isn't it?

SIR DUKE: Yes, Sire—and no, Sire. If we can't find them, it puts them in a position to pounce. The element of surprise and all.

WALTER: I see. Well, we'll simply have to hope they're not within pouncing distance.

SIR DUKE: Yes, Sire. To be sure.

WALTER: By the way, Lord—uh, Duke, uh—have you fetched the stone down from Loch Bowie Mountain?

SIR DUKE: Yes, Your Majesty. It's here in the castle. I secured it in a secret hiding place.

WALTER: Good, good. The stone is the most valuable possession Interlocken has.

SIR DUKE: Yes, Sire, I know....

*(**THOR** makes a noise behind the **3 MINSTREL'S** SACKS.)*

SIR DUKE: *(Continued.)* What was that?

WALTER: What was what?

SIR DUKE: Did you hear a noise?

*(**SIR DUKE** looks over to the **3 MINSTRELS** who have been standing like statues and watching. Suspicious, **SIR DUKE** begins to cross to the right until **STEVEN** escorts **ANGELEEN** in from stage right. **ANGELEEN** now wears what **VIVIEN** had on previously.)*

STEVEN: Good evening, Father.

WALTER: Steven, my boy. Isn't it a beautiful night for a party?

STEVEN: It is.

WALTER: And who is this lovely young lady on your arm? I don't recall seeing this enchanting vision at court before.

STEVEN: This is Lady Vivien. She is Princess Angeleen's traveling companion.

WALTER: Princess Angeleen is here? How marvelous.

STEVEN: Yes, she's up in her chambers changing for the evening.

WALTER: Has the princess met Crispen yet?

STEVEN: Not yet... Father, I know this sounds rather sudden, but Lady Vivien and I want to be married.

WALTER: Married? But—but—

ANGELEEN: Your Majesty, I understand your reservations with this being so spontaneous, and you may find it hard to believe our complete devotion to each other so soon, but rest assured our love is as genuine as any.

WALTER: No, my dear, I don't doubt your love at all. It's just that, well, when is it you plan to wed? Not tonight, I hope.

ANGELEEN: Oh no, Your Majesty. Not right away.

WALTER: *(Taking ANGELEEN'S hand and gently patting it.)* What a relief. I mean, take a little time to get to know one another. That will be best.

ANGELEEN: Yes, Your Majesty.

WALTER: My, my, you're such a delicately sweet... Oh dear, does your mother know about this, Steven?

STEVEN: No, Sire.

WALTER: Oo, I recommend not telling her until after this evening. She's a tad preoccupied at the moment. I'm sure she'll be more receptive to your pending nuptials once all of this is over.

STEVEN: Yes, Father. That's wise advice. Thank you.

WALTER: Well, come now. Let us go find our new princess.

(WALTER continues to escort ANGELEEN out stage right as STEVEN follows.)

WALTER: *(Continued.)* Come along Sir Lord Duke.

SIR DUKE: Actually, Sire, it's Sir Duke—never mind.

(Once the FOUR are out of the room, THOR and SWAINE struggle until they have dislodged themselves out from behind the SACKS, and then cross to center stage.)

THOR: What stone was he talking about? The king said something about a stone?

SWAINE: Yes, he said the Loch Bowie Stone. It must be some huge gemstone or something.

THOR: We have to find that stone.

SWAINE: If we could take that stone home with us, they would have to let us back in the lodge.

*(There is a commotion offstage left. **THOR** and **SWAINE** look off, then duck under the TABLECLOTHS of the BANQUET TABLES—**THOR** under the right TABLE, and **SWAINE** under the left TABLE. **TALLULAH** enters from the left with the **LADIES-IN-WAITING**. Each **LADY** carries festively decorated PLACE SETTINGS/COMPOTES of fruit and nuts.)*

TALLULAH: Very good, ladies. Now line up that I might see your table setting.

*(The **LADIES-IN-WAITING** flutter about to line up and hold out their PLACE SETTINGS for **TALLULAH** to inspect. **TALLULAH** starts at one end and makes her way down-the-line as if she were a general inspecting the troops.)*

TALLULAH: *(Continued.)* Uh, huh. Very good. Yes, yes. Oh, lovely. Yes, yes. Very nice....

*(And so on until she comes near the end. **TALLULAH** stops abruptly seeing the last PLACE SETTING which is not so lovely.)*

TALLULAH: *(Continued.)* Oh, my. Well, I know your heart was in it, dear... All right. Place your masterpieces about the tables—evenly spaced, naturally.

*(The **LADIES-IN-WAITING** scurry about again putting their PLACE SETTINGS on the TABLES as **TALLULAH** directs. At one point, **TALLULAH** steps close to the right TABLE and her foot presses down under the TABLECLOTH. **THOR** yells out from under the right TABLE and all stop and look about.)*

TALLULAH: *(Continued. Turning around.)* Was that something?

SWAINE: *(From under the left TABLE.)* No, it wasn't.

TALLULAH: Ah... Now, where are those decanters?

LADIES-IN-WAITING: Back in the kitchen, Your Majesty.

TALLULAH: Then we must fetch them at once. The time for the festival is quickly approaching. Come, ladies, hurry now.

> *(TALLULAH exits out stage left with her LADIES-IN-WAITING following. When all are gone, THOR and SWAINE crawl out from under the TABLES. THOR is nursing his hand. Almost immediately, SWAINE hears something else and motions to THOR to get back under the TABLE. THOR let's out a disgruntled "Augh!" before rolling back under the TABLECLOTH. CYRIL enters from stage right. Halfway across the stage, he stops, looks around as if sensing something amiss, shrugs his shoulders, crosses and exits stage left. This time THOR and SWAINE rise behind the BANQUET TABLES.)*

SWAINE: We have to find that stone. We're running out of time.

THOR: I know that, but we can't seem to get out of this room.

> *(Again, there is a commotion off stage left. THOR and SWAINE frantically look around for another place to hide, but it's too late this time to duck under the TABLES. Frantically they jump out the ARCH openings just as CRISPEN and AUGUSTY enter from stage left. They hear THOR and SWAINE holler [on their way down] then—splash! CRISPEN and AUGUSTY stop and look about for the source of the noise.)*

> **[SOUND CUE:** *SPLASH!***]**

CRISPEN: What was that?

AUGUSTY: I couldn't say.

CRISPEN: Mm.

AUGUSTY: I was told Princess Angeleen has arrived.

CRISPEN: And still no one has seen her. To be hiding like this, I can just imagine what she must look like. I have the distinct feeling I'll be saddled with the Moronic Hag from the edge of the Gallic Sea.

AUGUSTY: Certainly no, Your Highness.

CRISPEN: Certainly *yes*, Chamberlain. I'll have to set the stone masons busy on shoring up all the cracks and crevices in that high tower I lock the hag up in—for the sake of the commonwealth.

AUGUSTY: But, Your Highness, she *is* a princess, after all. I'm sure she's a real beauty.

CRISPEN: Well, whether you're sure or not, the only thing I'm sure of is that a lot of things are going to change around here once I'm king.

AUGUSTY: About those changes, Your Highness. Are you sure all of them are necessary? In point, Steven seems more than willing to stay out of your way.

CRISPEN: Steven? Two days ago you were delighting in having him boiled in oil. Are you switching sides here, Augusty?

AUGUSTY: Heavens no, Your Highness. I mean, I can be just as evil as you. I mean, whatever I do, I am following your wickedness. I mean—I'm here to serve His Highness.

CRISPEN: You better be certain of that. That pot of boiling oil is big enough for two, you know.

AUGUSTY: Yes, Your Highness. I mean, no, Your Highness. I mean—

CRISPEN: You better stop while you're ahead, Augusty.

AUGUSTY: Thank you, Your Highness.

> *(Entering from stage left are **VIVIEN** with **CYRIL** and **STEVEN** with **ANGELEEN**. We now see that **VIVIEN** is wearing the gown that **ANGELEEN** first had on with the exception of the small crown that still sits upon **ANGELEEN'S** head.)*

STEVEN: Ah, Crispen, you're here.

CRISPEN: Ah, Steven, who cares?

STEVEN: I should think you do. Don't you want to meet you forthcoming bride?

CRISPEN: *(Looking the women over.)* These are them? Which one is it?

STEVEN: *(Angrily.)* IT?!

> *(**CYRIL** quickly maneuvers himself between the two brothers to stop a possible fight.)*

CYRIL: Prince Crispen, this is Princess Angeleen and Lady Vivien.

> *(**CRISPEN** steps to **ANGELEEN** and bows.)*

CRISPEN: Well, I suppose you're attractive enough to be my queen.

> *(**STEVEN** quickly steps between the two and puts a protective arm around **ANGELEEN**.)*

STEVEN: Oh, no. This isn't Princess Angeleen....

(STEVEN moves ANGELEEN behind him while he takes VIVIEN'S arm and tugs her towards CRISPEN.)

STEVEN: *(Continued.)* This is Princess Angeleen.

CRISPEN: *(Confused.)* But the other one is wearing a crown.

(Realizing their error, ANGELEEN quickly removes her crown and gives it a backhanded toss to VIVIEN who just as quickly catches it and puts it on.)

VIVIEN: I'm Princess Angeleen, Your Highness. Lady Vivien so admired by crown, I allowed her to put it on, and then simply forgot she had it.

(A skeptical CRISPEN leans towards AUGUSTY who whispers to him.)

AUGUSTY: Still, hardly the Moronic Hag, Your Highness.

(CRISPEN stomps on AUGUSTY'S foot to shut him up. AUGUSTY lets out a little yelp, but otherwise remains contained.)

STEVEN: Have you nothing to say to your betrothed, Brother Crispen?

CRISPEN: Has she nothing to say to me?

VIVIEN: I understand your resentment to this arrangement, Your Highness. Please realize that I was pressured into this as well. It seems to me that the two people most affected by this union were the only two not informed of its creation. I come into this prearranged nuptial hopeful and willing to make the best of it. I'm pleased to see you are not altogether repulsive as well. I sincerely hope you see me in the same light.

CRISPEN: Well, uh, I....

VIVIEN: I fear you might have thought me to be akin to the Moronic Hag at the edge of the Gallic Sea.

CRISPEN: Well, uh, I....

VIVIEN: Steven, you failed to tell me how charmingly shy your brother is.

STEVEN: Believe me, Princess, Crispen's sudden lapse into this timidity is as surprising to me as it is you.

CRISPEN: Steven, you know I wouldn't weep a single tear should they find you face down in the moat.

STEVEN: Nor would I be especially upset were you sinking in the quicksand of the Loch Bowie Swamp.

VIVIEN: *(Aside to **ANGELEEN**.)* You were right. There's nothing to this.

ANGELEEN: *(In a whisper.)* Yes, you're performing remarkably well, Your Highness.

*(A smug **VIVIEN** crosses back and takes **CRISPEN'S** arm while **TALLULAH** and her **LADIES-IN-WAITING** enter from stage left. **WALTER** and **SIR DUKE** come in from stage right. The rest of the **ROYAL COURT** will wander in during the next exchange.)*

TALLULAH: Ah, we're all here. How delightful. And everyone so prompt, too. One might even say early. Actually, I wouldn't have minded a little stylish tardiness on everyone's part what with the roast boar still roasting. But how conscientious of you all. Why I'm just beside myself with happiness.

*(**STEVEN** leads **VIVIEN** over to **TALLULAH**.)*

STEVEN: Your Majesty, it is my pleasure to introduce you to Princess Angeleen.

*(**VIVIEN** curtsies before **TALLULAH**.)*

TALLULAH: Oh, how lovely. My how you've grown into a beautiful young woman. Odd how you look nothing like I remember, but then it has been a long time. You were but a child when we first met. Crispen, dear, you should be pleased.

CRISPEN: *(Less than thrilled.)* Uh, huh.

VIVIEN: Crispen is dubious, Your Majesty. Can you blame him? After all, I am a common stranger to him. But I'm hopeful in time we'll grow to appreciate one another.

TALLULAH: How wise, my dear. I dare say it was the same for me and King Walter.

*(**TALLULAH** and **VIVIEN** look over to **WALTER** who produces a big, silly grin in return.)*

TALLULAH: *(Continued.)* Yes, well—shall we sit? Before we dine, I believe Cyril has arranged for some entertainment... Cyril?

CYRIL: Yes, Your Majesty.

(As everyone occupies themselves with sitting behind the TABLES, STEVEN, ANGELEEN, and VIVIEN huddle to the side.)

STEVEN: *(To VIVIEN.)* You're doing wonderfully.

VIVIEN: Do you think so? I must confess I was so nervous meeting the queen, but she seems like a decent sort.

STEVEN: Mother is really a little lamb. She may put on airs of sternness, but all you have to do is be polite and "etiquettely" correct and you can have her in the palm of your hand. Crispen is the one that's surprising me. He's being almost civil.

VIVIEN: Truly? I must say, I'm quite attracted to him.

ANGELEEN: This is so wonderful, Vivien. I can't thank you enough.

(ANGELEEN gives VIVIEN a big hug, and then STEVEN escorts the two women behind the TABLES to their assigned seats. At the right TABLE—from the center—sits WALTER on his THRONE with ANGELEEN next to him, STEVEN is on the other side of ANGELEEN, and SIR DUKE on the other side of STEVEN. Other members of the ROYAL COURT will fill out the places continuing right. At the left TABLE—from the center—sits TALLULAH on her THRONE with VIVIEN next to her, CRISPEN is on the other side of VIVIEN, and AUGUSTY on the other side of CRISPEN. Other members of the ROYAL COURT will fill out the places continuing to the left.

Meanwhile, CYRIL has crossed over to the 3 MINSTRELS to confer. As all settle, CYRIL steps to center stage and looks back at the 3 MINSTRELS a bit apprehensively. They nod that they're ready.)

CYRIL: Your Majesties, royal Highnesses, and people of the royal court of Interlocken, it is with great pleasure that I give you the stylistic offerings of the 3 Wandering Minstrels.

(There is polite applause from ALL as CYRIL steps back, stage left. One of the 3 MINSTRELS hums a note, and the other two hum a note back—not the same note, but a note. Then the trio burst into an energetic song as they accompany themselves with tambourine and mandolin [optional].)

THE 3 WANDERING MINSTRELS:

> Oh, we welcome you, sweet princess.
> We're here to welcome you.
> To the bestest place
> In the human race.
> We hope you like us, too.

Dear princess what a honor.
Already we love you.
Please accept this song,
Join and sing along
In our welcoming to you... Hey!

*(The **3 MINSTRELS** end their song with outstretched arms. One has even dropped to one knee. So quickly was the song, **EVERYONE** looks around a bit surprised, and then applaud a little. When done, the **3 MINSTRELS** quietly pick up their **SACKS** and exit stage right. The applause stops with **EVERYONE** more surprised to think that the performance is over. **ALL** look a little stunned and bewildered.)*

TALLULAH: Um, Cyril.

CYRIL: Yes, Your Majesty?

TALLULAH: May I see you for a moment?

CYRIL: Of course, Your Majesty.

*(**CYRIL** crosses over to **TALLULAH**.)*

TALLULAH: About this entertainment....

CYRIL: I know, Your Majesty. They *did* come highly recommended.

TALLULAH: Did they? By someone they owe money to, no doubt.

CYRIL: I believe they have an encore in mind.

TALLULAH: Oh, they do? That would be nice. Would you go see to it, please?

CYRIL: *(Bowing.)* Absolutely, Your Majesty.

*(**CYRIL** quickly exits stage right.)*

TALLULAH: *(Trying to salvage the evening announcing.)* Well, there is still the roast boar.

*(**ALL** nod happily, appeased by the mention of food. There is under talk from the **ROYAL COURT** as the others speak in this sequence.)*

CRISPEN: *(Aside to **VIVIEN**.)* You needn't worry, Your Highness. When *I'm* the king, we'll have proper entertainment worthy of our blue blood.

VIVIEN: But I liked the song, my beloved. I'm enjoying myself very much.

CRISPEN: You are? *(Leaning over to **AUGUSTY**.)* Not much up in the ol' crow's nest, I fear.

AUGUSTY: That can be a blessing, Your Highness—to have a wife so easily pleased.

CRISPEN: I suppose. Not that it matters with where she's going.

> *(**CRISPEN** and **AUGUSTY** share a devious chuckle until **VIVIEN** tightly squeezes **CRISPEN'S** hand as she smiles at him. **CRISPEN** smiles back politely and slides his hand away from her, opening and closing it to regain circulation. **TALLULAH** leans over to **WALTER**.)*

TALLULAH: Walter, who is the pretty little mistress Steven seems most smitten with?

> *(**WALTER** leans over to **TALLULAH** while **STEVEN** and **ANGELEEN** cuddle and whisper into each other's ear, oblivious to the rest of the world.)*

WALTER: That is Lady Vivien, the princess' traveling companion. And yes, although it's been but a little while, they appear very devoted to each other. Eternal, everlasting, and all that.

TALLULAH: Really?

> *(**TALLULAH** steps out—in between the two **TABLES**—and down to center stage.)*

TALLULAH: *(Continued.)* Steven, may I see you and Lady Vivien for a moment, please?

> *(**STEVEN** rises and escorts **ANGELEEN** over to **TALLULAH**.)*

STEVEN: Yes, Mother?

TALLULAH: I see the two of you have struck up an endearing friendship.

STEVEN: Oh, it's much more than that, Mother. Lady Vivien and I plan to marry.

TALLULAH: Marry?

ANGELEEN: *(Curtsying.)* Yes, Your Majesty. It would please me very much to marry your son, Steven.

TALLULAH: It would?

STEVEN: As a matter of fact, Mother, I believe I have an idea on how we can salvage this evening's festivities—if I may be so bold to suggest.

TALLULAH: Yes, please. Be bold, Steven. Suggest away.

STEVEN: A wedding. Lady Vivien and I. What could be more joyous to set this evening apart from all the rest?

TALLULAH: Well, yes it would. But I'm afraid it's completely out of the question.

STEVEN: But why?

TALLULAH: A wedding takes weeks—months to plan. A royal wedding even more time.

STEVEN: Dear Mother, I love you for wanting to give me a proper wedding, but this is Steven here, not Crispen. It's not as if this marriage will mean anything.

TALLULAH: That's true. But there isn't anyone here who could marry you.

*(As **ALL** have been listening to the conversation at center stage, **AUGUSTY** rises to offer his services.)*

AUGUSTY: As a civil servant, I'm empowered to marry the couple.

*(**CRISPEN** scowls and moves with a jerk. You hear a clomp and once again, **AUGUSTY** lets out a little yelp as a pained expression crosses his face.)*

AUGUSTY: *(Continued.)* Maybe not. I'll have to look into it.

*(Bowing while wincing, **AUGUSTY** reseats himself.)*

ANGELEEN: Oh, what a shame. *(To **STEVEN**.)* How close we came, my love.

WALTER: *(Rising.)* I can marry them.

TALLULAH: *(Looking back.)* Did you say something, Walter?

*(**WALTER** steps out from behind the BANQUET TABLE and crosses over to the others.)*

WALTER: I'm the king of Interlocken, the ruling sovereign. I have the power to do anything.

STEVEN: That's right, he can. What say you now, Mother?

TALLULAH: But, for instance, there is the matter of the cake.

STEVEN: There's one downstairs.

TALLULAH: That says "Welcome Princess Angeleen" on it.

STEVEN: We *are* welcoming Princess Angeleen. One cake can serve two purposes. How economical of you, Mother.

TALLULAH: Steven, I know perfectly well what you're doing. You're... I... Well, if you two are sure this is what you want.

ANGELEEN: We are, Your Majesty! Oh, thank you!

   (**ANGELEEN** gives **TALLULAH** a big hug.)

TALLULAH: *(A bit flustered by ANGELEEN'S display of affection.)* My, my. Friendly little pixie, isn't she?

WALTER: *(Coaxing the couple to stage right.)* Come young people, over here.

CRISPEN: *(Standing indignantly.)* Hold on, now!

   (**CRISPEN** scrambles out from behind the left **TABLE** and crosses to the others. **VIVIEN** follows him and **AUGUSTY** follows her.)

CRISPEN: *(Continued.)* This is supposed to be *my* night, not Steven's.

AUGUSTY: But, Your Highness....

CRISPEN: But nothing. If Steven can suddenly marry, I can suddenly become king.

TALLULAH: Oh, now that is entirely out of the question.

CRISPEN: Why is it entirely?

TALLULAH: There is protocol and ceremony. There is history and tradition. There needs to be at least four days for the royal printers to make and send out the invitations.

CRISPEN: Protocol and ceremony and history and tradition all went out the window the moment you agreed Steven could marry. As for the invitations, everyone you would want at the coronation is already here.

TALLULAH: Now, Crispen... It isn't... Well... Walter, help me.

WALTER: Yes, dear. I think I know of a way to make everyone happy. Though we need to be careful that all previously signed treaties and laws are met. *(Thinking hard.)* Um, all right. I've got it. As king, I shall marry Steven and his lovely lassie here. Next I shall deed Loch Bowie and all its contents over to Steven. Then I shall marry Crispen to Princess Angeleen. Lastly, I shall crown Crispen as the new king of Interlocken. How does that sound?

CRISPEN: Why don't I get to be king until last?

WALTER: Because I'm still king for now and I say this is how it will go.

TALLULAH: But this could take all night.

WALTER: I promise to be most expeditious, my dear. We'll have all of this over by the time the roast boar is done.

TALLULAH: Well—

*(**SIR DUKE** has joined the group in front.)*

SIR DUKE: It isn't as if we have entertainment to watch or anything.

TALLULAH: *(Glaring at **SIR DUKE**.)* Oh, very well. I give up on all of you.

ANGELEEN & VIVIEN: *(Jumping up and down with glee.)* Hurray!

*(**WALTER** begins to situate everyone.)*

WALTER: All right, Steven, you stand here. Oh, I hope I remember how to do this... Lady Vivien by his side here. Have you a maid of honor?

ANGELEEN: Oh, Princess Angeleen, naturally.

WALTER: Yes. Of course. Princess, you over here by Lady Vivien's side. Steven, a best man?

*(**CRISPEN** begins to saddle up alongside **STEVEN**, but **CYRIL** hurries in from stage right and assumes the best man position.)*

CYRIL: That would be me.

TALLULAH: Cyril? The court jester? Really, Steven, has all thought of propriety completely left your brain?

STEVEN: Cyril is my best friend, Mother. It's only right he should be my best man.

TALLULAH: I give up. Do whatever you wish. But let it be known that I didn't have a hand in any of this.

Erstwhile... SCRIPT

WALTER: So noted, my dear. Thank you for being so gracious as always.

TALLULAH: *(Flattered.)* Well, I *am* a queen. Graciousness comes naturally.

(**WALTER** *steps before* **STEVEN** *and* **ANGELEEN**.)

WALTER: *(Continued.)* Now, let us stand to honor these two wonderful people who have decided to share their lives in love and happiness... Steven, my son, do you take this beautiful lass to be your wife?

STEVEN: I do.

WALTER: Oh, how marvelous. *(To* **ANGELEEN**.*)* And, my dear, do you take Steven to be your husband?

ANGELEEN: Oh, yes.

WALTER: Lovely, lovely... Then by the power vested in me as king of Interlocken, I now pronounce the two of you husband and wife.

(**STEVEN** *and* **ANGELEEN** *kiss sweetly. There is a moment of light applause, handshakes and hugs.*)

WALTER: Next. Steven, as promised to you five years ago—

CRISPEN: *(Amused.)* —As a consolation prize.

(**CRISPEN** *and* **AUGUSTY** *snicker together.* **WALTER** *is not pleased.*)

WALTER: Ahem... As I was saying—as promised to you, I hereby deed you the crown jewel of Interlocken—our precious Loch Bowie and all its privileges granted with ownership thereof.

(**WALTER** *removes the amulet he has been wearing around his neck and places it around* **STEVEN'S** *neck. There is more general applause, handshaking and hugs. Then* **WALTER** *steps over to* **CRISPEN** *and* **VIVIEN** *and continues to line everyone up like he did with the other marriage. This time,* **AUGUSTY** *stands as* **CRISPEN'S** *best man and* **ANGELEEN** *assumes the maid of honor position for* **VIVIEN**. **WALTER** *joins the hands of* **CRISPEN** *and* **VIVIEN** *much to* **CRISPEN'S** *irritation.*)

WALTER: Crispen, my boy, do you—

CRISPEN: Yes, yes, yes. I do, she does, happily-ever-after, and so forth. We're done.

WALTER: Uh, all right.

VIVIEN: We're husband and wife?

CRISPEN: Right.

*(Before **CRISPEN** can break away from her, **VIVIEN** smothers him with kisses until he backs away.)*

CRISPEN: *(Continued.)* All right already.

*(He shakes **VIVIEN'S** hand.)*

CRISPEN: *(Continued.)* Congratulations. Finally! I get to be king now.

*(**CRISPEN** quickly bends to one knee before **WALTER** and removes his crown—posturing to be dubbed and crowned again.)*

WALTER: Oh, you're ready. Uh....

*(**WALTER** begins feeling around in his pockets until **SIR DUKE** unsheathes his sword and presents it to **WALTER**.)*

WALTER: *(Continued.)* Thank you. This should do.

*(Dubbing **CRISPEN**.)*

WALTER: *(Continued.)* I, King Walter of Interlock, do hereby succeed my rightful right to the throne of Interlocken to my eldest and rightful heir. Prince Crispen, I hereby dub thee Crispen, king of Interlocken.

*(**CRISPEN** jumps up and grabs **WALTER'S** crown and plops it on his own head.)*

CRISPEN: Thank the Heavens. Glorious of all days, I'm king! And as king, I can decree anything I wish, correct? Good. Sir Duke Lord, I command you to seize Prince Steven and throw him in the deepest dungeon we have.

*(**ALL** are aghast.)*

SIR DUKE: What?

STEVEN: Me? What did I do?

CRISPEN: Nothing. But this will stop you from doing something.

VIVIEN: Dearest, this isn't very nice.

CRISPEN: And while we're at it, lock *dearest* here up in the highest tower.

TALLULAH: Crispen, this behavior is shameful!

CRISPEN: Oh, goodness. Whatever am I doing? Am I spoiling your party, Mother? If you don't like it, I'm sure we can find a lonely island to exile you to.

   (CRISPEN and AUGUSTY laugh.)

CRISPEN: *(Continued.)* You heard my order, Sir Knight. Take Steven to the dungeon. Take them all.

SIR DUKE: *(To WALTER.)* Do I have to?

CRISPEN: Of course you have to.

WALTER: Well, actually—technically—no he doesn't.

CRISPEN: What do you mean "no he doesn't?"

WALTER: Technically, as captain of the royal guard, Sir Duke Lord only answers to the king of Interlocken.

CRISPEN: Yeaaaaaah! I *am* king, and I ordered him to take Steven to the dungeon and he's not doing it!

   (CRISPEN stomps his foot and speaks to TALLULAH like a spoiled child.)

CRISPEN: *(Continued.)* Mother, he's not doing what I want him to!

TALLULAH: I know, dear. I'm confused as well. Walter, what are you talking about with this *technically* business?

WALTER: Oh, I'm so glad you asked that, my love. Technically, Sir Duke Lord doesn't have to obey Crispen's commands because technically, Crispen isn't king.

CRISPEN: What do you mean I'm not king? You just did the herebys and the thingy with the sword....

WALTER: I dubbed you king, yes. But technically, I didn't have the authority to dub you king or anything else for that matter because technically—at that moment—I was no longer king myself—technically.

CRISPEN: Yes, you were.

WALTER: No, I wasn't. At that moment the technical king of Interlocken was and is Steven.

CRISPEN: *(Outraged and flustered.)* What? How? Why?

---

34   SCRIPT **Erstwhile...**

WALTER: Steven is now owner of Loch Bowie. You see the founder of Interlocken, our savior and leader, Knight Howard of Celtania, made it most clear and decreed it into law that only the owner of Loch Bowie can be king of Interlocken. The owner is now Steven and it was Steven when I dubbed you king, Crispen. So, technically, I was no longer king to dub you king.

STEVEN: Father, I'm—

WALTER: —Speechless and grateful? I thought you would be, and you're very welcome.

TALLULAH: *(To WALTER.)* Darling, I didn't know.

WALTER: *(Sweetly taking TALLULAH'S hand.)* I know you would like me to explain further. I'd be delighted. I'm sure all of you have noticed my absentmindedness of late.

(**ALL** *readily nod their heads in concurrence.*)

WALTER: *(Continued.)* It was all a ruse.

TALLULAH: A what?

WALTER: My dear, I pretended to be addlepated to put my plan into action. What plan you ask? My plan to make Steven king and not Crispen. Now, how was I going to do this? How was I to deny my kingdom to the heir apparent; the rightful yet shamefully inept and mean-spirited Crispen and give it to my second son, the intelligent, fair, and compassionate Steven? There were two certainties I had to work with: 1. The king of Interlocken must be in possession Loch Bowie, and 2. In accordance to the Alliance with Hollimer, the king of Interlocken had to marry Princess Angeleen.

CRISPEN: Ah ha! This is where you slipped up, good ol' Dad. I'm the one who's married to Princess Angeleen.

STEVEN: Well, technically, Crispen, you're not.

CRISPEN: *(Now leery of anything beginning with "technically.")* Why not, technically?

STEVEN: Technically, you were married to Lady Vivien.

(*STEVEN takes ANGELEEN'S hand.*)

STEVEN: *(Continued.)* This is Princess Angeleen of Hollimer, and now my beautiful bride.

CRISPEN: *(To VIVIEN.)* You're not Angeleen?

VIVIEN: Um, no.

WALTER: But technically, you're not married to Lady Vivien either because when I married the two of you, I had already deeded Loch Bowie to Steven. So, I was no longer king of Interlocken and therefore not of legal authority to marry anyone.

AUGUSTY: If I may interject here, Sire. Or—apparently, formerly Sire—how did you know that Lady Vivien was truly Princess Angeleen and Princess Angeleen likewise was truly Lady Vivien?

WALTER: Cyril.

> *(**EVERYONE** but **CYRIL** and **WALTER** repeats Cyril?? with surprise.)*

WALTER: Cyril may not be the best court jester in the world, but he makes one heck of a good spy.

> *(**CYRIL** removes his hood and smiles. Suddenly **CYRIL** is an instant celebrity as the **LADIES-IN-WAITING** huddle around him awing and cooing.)*

LADIES-IN-WAITING: Why, Cyril, we had no idea you were such a figure of intrigue. You're so—so espionage-like.

TALLULAH: Why, Walter, I never... All this time I just thought you were a blithering idiot.

SIR DUKE: *(Taking his sword back from **WALTER**. To **STEVEN**.)* Your Majesty, I'd be more than happy to toss Prince Crispen into the dungeon for all-time. You just say the word and he's in there.

CRISPEN: By the stars, this can't be happening!

> *(Suddenly **THOR** and **SWAINE** rush in from stage right yelling a war cry and blazing swords. They hurry over and grab **TALLULAH**.)*

THOR: All right, Queenie. We have you good. *(**THOR** looks back to the others.)* Hand over the Sacred Stone of Loch Bowie, or we'll whack the ruling monarch here!

TALLULAH: Ruling monarch? Whatever gave you that idea?

SWAINE: Well, you've been running about all-day telling people to do this and do that.

TALLULAH: Yes, but I only hold dominion over the royal court, not the whole kingdom.

SWAINE: Oh... Sorry. We misunderstood.

(THOR and SWAINE look at each other, and then rush over and seize WALTER.)

THOR: All right, you people, hand over that gemstone, or your king is a goner.

WALTER: Excuse me, but technically I'm no longer king.

SWAINE: No longer king?

WALTER: Not for about five minutes now.

SWAINE: *(Seeing the crown on CRISPEN'S head.)* There's the crown. He's the king.

(THOR and SWAINE release WALTER and cross over to seize CRISPEN.)

THOR: All right, you people—

CRISPEN: *(Angrily wiggling to get away.)* Not me, you nitwits.

(CRISPEN points to STEVEN. SWAINE and THOR begin to cross over to STEVEN, but by this time the two are extremely discouraged and decide to give up at the same moment. THOR and SWAINE sigh in despair and toss their swords into the FIRE PIT. A tied SWAINE sits on the FIRE PIT embankment.)

SWAINE: Oh, forget it. This has been a fiasco from the start.

SIR DUKE: *(Siding up to STEVEN.)* Sire, do you want me to toss these pillaging plunderers into the dungeon?

STEVEN: I suppose that would be the thing to do, but I don't believe these two have really pillaged or plundered anything yet.

(WALTER crosses to THOR and SWAINE.)

WALTER: Excuse me, visiting savages. May I ask why you're seeking the Sacred Stone of Loch Bowie?

SWAINE: Because it's a precious gem worth a great deal, isn't it?

WALTER: Oh, I'm sorry. The Sacred Stone of Loch Bowie is only valuable to Interlockeneers. It isn't international currency for it's only a rock.

THOR: A rock?!

WALTER: Why, yes.

(WALTER gestures to SIR DUKE to fetch the STONE. SIR DUKE steps out stage right and is right back in carrying a large, heavy ROCK while WALTER speaks.)

WALTER: *(Continued.)* I had the Sacred Stone of Loch Bowie brought down from the mountain in case Steven's inheritance was disputed.

(EVERYONE glares at CRISPEN. SIR DUKE steps to the group of royalty and reads the inscription on the rock.)

SIR DUKE: It says here, "Whoever does claim the heights of this land shall rule all the eye can see below thee. As struck by and deemed to be law absolute: Sir Howard of Celtania."

THOR: No precious gems? No gold? No nothing? How can we return to the isle with nothing? They're already mad at us, and then we borrowed the ship. To return empty-handed, we'll be tossed out for sure.

SWAINE: We're already cast out, Thor. Have you forgotten?

THOR: And the fault belongs to?

SWAINE: Don't you dare start up with me, Thor. I warned the tribe I wasn't skilled in preparing the spoils of war. It's their fault for insisting I try something I'm not very good at.

ANGELEEN: Spoils of war?

SWAINE: Spoils. Booty. Case in point, a cow taken from the top part of Ireland. They ordered me to cook it.

THOR: Instead, she cooked the whole lodge.

ANGELEEN: Oh, dear. Do you mean to say you burned down your lodge?

(SWAINE buries her head in her hands. A sympathetic TALLULAH crosses and sits next to SWAINE on the FIRE PIT embankment.)

TALLULAH: *(Patting SWAINE on the knee.)* Not to fret, my dear. We can't be expected to excel in all things. I'm not particularly successful in the culinary arts myself. But I *am* exceptionally exceptional in scheduling and arranging dinners and festivals. All you need do is find your exceptional and build on it.

SWAINE: Well, I must admit I'm a fair hand at smashing, bashing, and dismembering.

TALLULAH: Well, yes, but... I'm sure there are dozens of other... a handful of... something else you're good at. We'll just have to explore all the possibilities.

SWAINE: We?

STEVEN: You can't very well go back empty-handed, and we can't let you go back with something of ours, so you'll just have to stay here.

THOR: But we tried to plunder you.

STEVEN: Yes, you did. But you failed. We'll have to find an *exceptional* you're good at as well.

THOR: You mean, you're not going to shackle us up in your dungeon?

STEVEN: Oh, I don't think so. You wouldn't like it down there. It's terribly dirty and damp—not at all pleasant.

SWAINE: You're going to make a very strange king, you know that?

STEVEN: Why, thank you very much.

*(The **3 MINSTRELS** hurry in from stage right carrying a small STRETCHER DEVICE. A large CLOTH covers whatever is on the STRETCHER. The **3 MINSTRELS** step back to the STAGE. One of the **3 MINSTRELS** whistles loudly so **ALL** stop their conversations and look over. With **EVERYONE'S** attention, one of the **3 MINSTRELS** whips off the CLOTH to reveal the ROAST BOAR with an apple in its mouth. **EVERYONE** is delighted and applaud and cheer. **STEVEN** and **ANGELEEN** encourage **ALL** to sit themselves and share in the goodies. In turn, **STEVEN** and **ANGELEEN** sit where **TALLULAH** and **WALTER** were seated previously on the THRONES. **WALTER** and **TALLULAH** guide **THOR** and **SWAINE** to a seat. **THOR** whips out his big knife and prepares to attack the ROAST BOAR that has been placed in front of them, but **WALTER** stops him and shows **THOR** the proper way to carve the BOAR. Meanwhile, **TALLULAH** is busy with **SWAINE**, pulling **SWAINE'S** hair up to see how it would look in a bouffant style, draping a sleeve of her royal cloak across **SWAINE'S** armor to see how that would look instead, and so on. Also, **SIR DUKE** happily puts the SACRED STONE OF LOCH BOWIE down and crosses to put an authoritative hand on **AUGUSTY'S** shoulder. In disgust, **CRISPEN** looks around trying to argue and gain anyone's attention on how unfair this all is. When he doesn't get the results he's after, he huffs across the stage until he trips over the SACRED STONE OF LOCH BOWIE and goes sprawling. **VIVIEN** is quickly by his side.)*

VIVIEN: Oh, did poor Crispen fall down and get a boo-boo?

(**CRISPEN** whimpers "yes" like a little boy.)

VIVIEN: *(Continued.)* Here, let me kiss it better.

(**VIVIEN** *scoops* **CRISPEN** *up in her arms to smother him once again with kisses. His arms and legs swing about helplessly. Finally,* **CYRIL** *crosses to center stage and poses with one foot on the SACRED STONE OF LOCH BOWIE.*)

CYRIL: Well, there you have it. What? You were expecting something other than a happy ending? After all, this *is* a fairy tale, and a pretty good one at that. It had everything; castles, moats, crowns, kings, queens, princes, princesses, everlasting love, sibling rivalry, good and evil, danger and peril, mystery, espionage and intrigue, dominate government practices, social expectations and obligations of those supporting royal blood and pedigree, relationship issues—and a roast boar. What else could you ask for? (**CYRIL** *looks over to the* **3 WANDERING MINSTRELS**.) All right. Next time I promise to book better entertainment.

(**CYRIL** *steps back to the BANQUET TABLE as the* **3 WANDERING MINSTRELS** *strike up the same song they sang earlier. All are happy and gay while* **CRISPEN** *continues to be smothered by* **VIVIEN'S** *kisses.*)

End of ERSTWHILE...

the cronus offense

The Cronus Offense
a Drama
by Joan Garner

Play Information and Suggestions

Director's Notes

Overall Tone — **The Cronus Offense** studies ethics within conditions of desperation and tension and individual reaction to these foibles. As a result, an atmosphere of extreme tension should permeate throughout the performance.

Essence of Play — This play explores the external and internal conflict introduced during competition. Externally, there is the competition of the games to gain power and material items. Internally, there is the conflict in choosing the right path and the struggle of following social demand or standing alone with ones principles.

Moral of Play — On reflection, right and wrong is not as black and white as often inferred. Does the wrong for many supersede over the right of one? Is "to win at all costs" justifiable or wrong?

Symbolism — Uniforms of repetition symbolizes conformity and unity. The wings emblems symbolize the wish to be free of dependency, an angelic view of sacrifice, and the brave lifting of an oppressed nation to the heights of godly power.

Attention Required for Special Characters — Because this is an ensemble piece, attention to one specific part over another isn't addressed here. Characters shouldn't be especially bad or particularly good.

Scenes and Moments Needing Special Attention

- The audience will probably be confused during the first few minutes of this play with not knowing what's going on. That the play takes place in the future and in an unknown setting might increase their confusion. This is why it's important for **SPARROW** and **ROBIN** to project a desperation and doomed tension. The audience should be more comfortable recognizing a familiar situation in this unfamiliar environment.
- When **FALCON** returns "from the dead," **MEEKER** must be as baffled as the audience. Later, when **GRAVES** plan is disclosed, **MEEKER** needs to be angry.

Dialogue and Accents — This play takes place in the staging area (locker room) of an Olympics arena. Accents of any sort are perfectly acceptable. A mixture of accents within the team, or an absence of accents is also acceptable.

Director's Notes

Character Traits to Enhance Performances

- Obviously **MEEKER** is judgmental with an air of superiority. He or she should always stand straight and strong. An occasional disapproving hand on the hip could help show this feeling of superiority.
- Hopefully, **MEEKER** will be the emotional reflection of the audience.
- **SPARROW** is flighty and nervous, but should not be overtly so that it becomes distracting. A nervous habit of twisting parts of clothing, or often standing on one foot and then the other would be a good visual.
- **CARTER** needs to move in and out in a "sneaky way." A weasel in appearance and reaction would contribute to the character.
- **GRAVES** and **JAEGER** appear smug the more their plan reveals itself.

Movement of Players/Staging

A traffic jam may occur when the large group scrabbles up the steps to see what has happened to **FALCON**. To avoid a possible bottleneck, block which character goes up first, second, and so on. Rehearsal of this piece of blocking will produce a smooth sequence that only looks chaotic.

Character Analysis

FALCON—Defeated and depressed, **FALCON** is forever whining while dragging from one place to another.
RAVEN—Determined. Not the best, but is always in there fighting.
SPARROW—Fatalist. Flighty, nervous, and unintentionally humorous.
ROBIN—Loyal. Concerned and considerate. Intelligent and practical.
SANDPIPER—Confident. Something of a superior attitude that's not entirely unjustified.
FINCH—Complainer. A competitor at heart, but prone to point out everything that isn't just perfect.
HERON—Competitive. Perhaps lacking in people skills.
JAEGER—Meek (in the beginning). Later calculating and mechanical.
MEEKER—Pious. Self-righteous, but sincere and compassionate.
GRAVES—Demanding. Authoritative and a natural leader.
CARTER—Unbending. Annoying and suspicious of everything.

Production Notes

Design Concept

A stylized, futuristic design is appropriate for this play. A clean, sleek look of the set and costumes will work best. Think simple.

Production Notes

Costume Narrative

ATHLETES

(FULL PRODUCTION) Basic white uniform consisting of white, short sleeved T-shirt with light green accent pattern down the middle. Side bird emblem applied to white T-shirt breast area. White, long pants with light green accent pattern down the middle. Light green upper-armbands. Light green canvas spats over white athletic shoes. Clean-cut hairstyles.

(GOOD REPRESENTATION) White, short sleeved T-shirt. Light green gymnast T-shirt over white T-shirt. Side bird emblem applied to white T-shirt breast area. Light green, upper-thigh length shorts. Light green upper-armbands. Ankle-high, white crew socks with white athletic shoes. Clean-cut hairstyles.

(MINIMAL REPRESENTATION) White T-shirt and white, long pants. Side bird emblem applied to T-shirt breast area. White wrist sweatbands. Clean-cut hairstyles.

STEWARDS

(FULL PRODUCTION) Basic white uniform consisting of long sleeved T-shirt for the first layer, a light blue, short-sleeved T-shirt for the second layer, and a gymnast cut white T-shirt on top acting like a vest. Full bird emblem applied to bottom portion of vest. White, long pants. Light blue socks with light blue canvas deck shoes. Clean-cut hairstyle.

(GOOD REPRESENTATION) White, short sleeved T-shirt. Light blue, no-sleeved T-shirt over white T-shirt acting like a vest. Full bird emblem applied to bottom portion of vest. Light blue, mid-thigh length shorts. Light blue knee-high crew socks with white canvas deck shoes. Clean-cut hairstyle.

(MINIMAL REPRESENTATION) White, short sleeved T-shirt and white shorts. Full bird emblem on T-shirt. White crew socks and white canvas tennis shoes. Clean-cut hairstyle.

STAFF

(FULL PRODUCTION) Under outfit same as ATHLETES only with violet accent pattern reversed (on sides instead of middle). White, mid-thigh length overcoat with long lapels and violet accents. Side bird emblem on left bottom portion of overcoat. Violet canvas spats over white canvas deck shoes. Hair of no particular style.

(GOOD REPRESENTATION) White, short sleeved T-shirt. Violet gymnast T-shirt over white T-shirt. White, long pants. White windbreaker with side bird emblem on breast pocket area. White socks and white canvas deck shoes. Hair of no particular style.

(MINIMAL REPRESENTATION) White, short sleeved T-shirt with side bird emblem applied to breast area. White, long pants. White sweater. Hair of no particular style.

CARTER

(FULL PRODUCTION) White, long sleeved, waist-length vest-coat with red collar. Ultra Olympics emblem over breast part of exaggerated, double-breasted lapels. Red pants. White boots. Hair of no particular style.

(GOOD REPRESENTATION) Red, long sleeved turtleneck sweater under black, long sleeved windbreaker. Ultra Olympic emblem on breast-pocket area of windbreaker. Black, long pants. Black boots. Hair of no particular style.

(MINIMAL REPRESENTATION) Black, long sleeved turtleneck shirt with Ultra Olympics emblem on breast pocket area. Black pants. Black socks and shoes. Hair of no particular style.

Production Notes

Costume Narrative

Costume Illustrations

STEWARD'S EMBLEM

ATHLETE & STAFF'S EMBLEM

CARTER'S EMBLEM
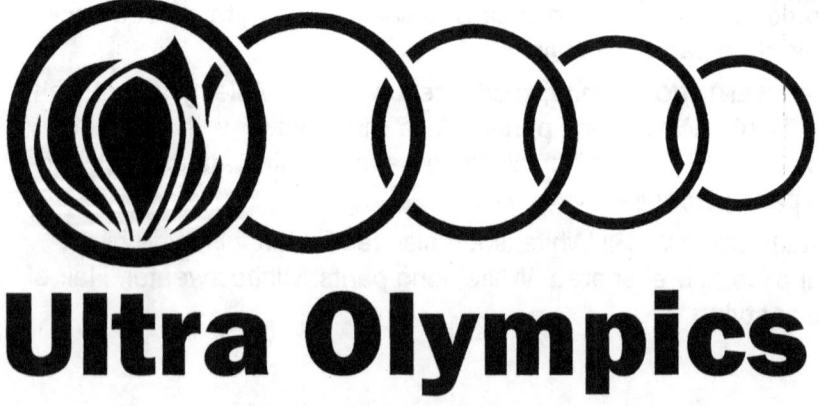
Ultra Olympics

UNIFORM EMBLEMS

64 PLAYESQUE • Volume 1 (Teacher Ideas Press)

Production Notes

Costume Illustrations

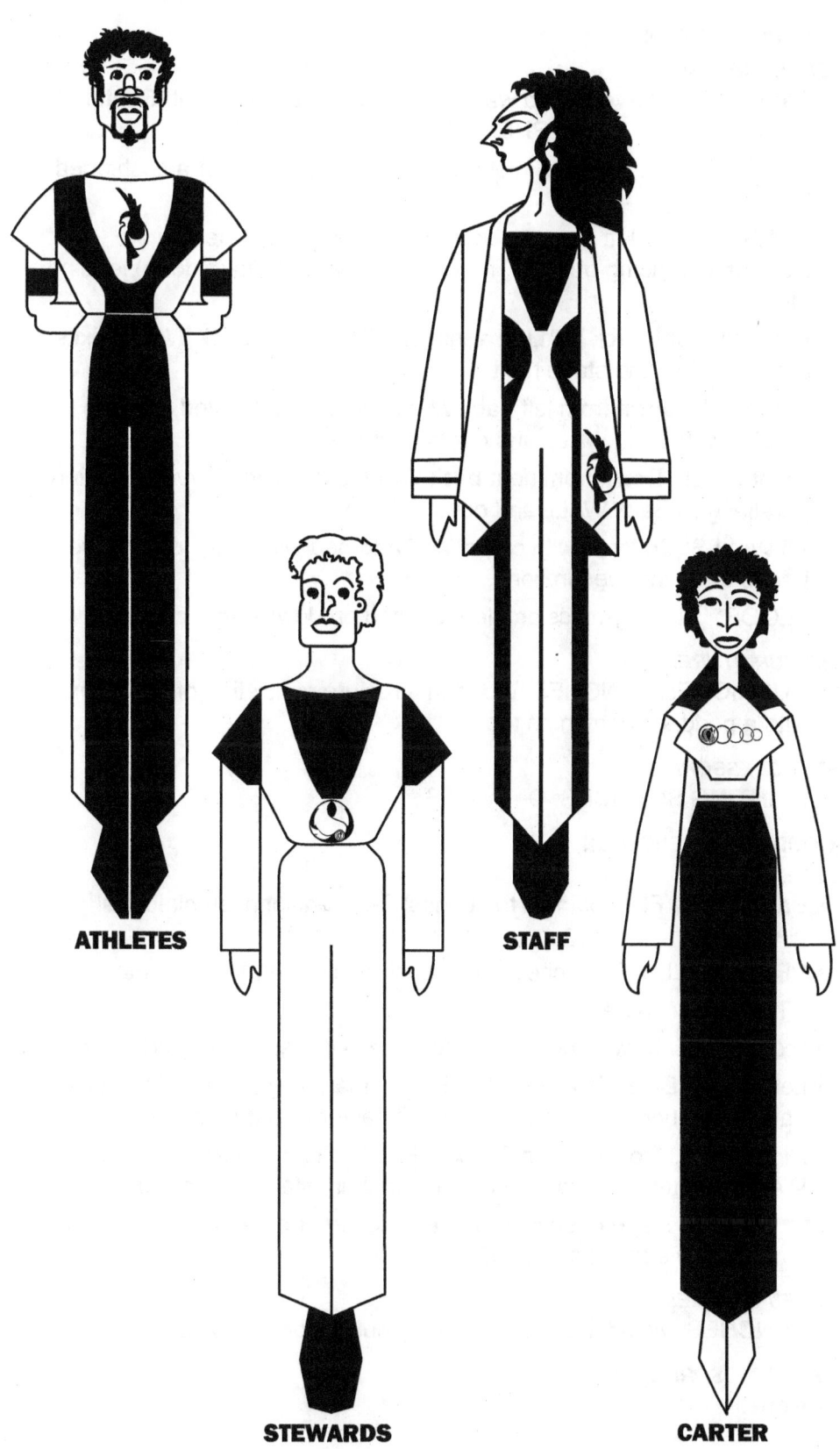

ATHLETES

STAFF

STEWARDS

CARTER

Production Notes

Set Design Narrative

(FULL PRODUCTION)

SET ELEMENTS:

- Back WALL: Curved, solid wall extending out left and right. Center of Back WALL has 3 inset PREP STALLS.
- PREP STALLS: 3 walled inlets with built-in shelves over a cushioned bench.
- STAIRS: Stage left along back WALL. Three or four steps up to platform extending out left. Three or four steps down (hidden) leading offstage behind.
- Left and Right Back WALL Extensions: Down from back WALL. Exits out stage left and stage right.
- Left WALL: Down from left back WALL extension. Curved, running parallel with Back WALL and out to offstage.
- Right WALL: Down from right back WALL extension. Curved, running parallel with Back WALL and out to offstage.
- All WALLS: Covered with carpet and adorned with metal decorative bands and other decorations.
- FLOOR: Ultra Olympics emblem painted on downstage, center.

SET FURNITURE:

- CUSHIONED BENCHES: Wooden structure consisting of seat (bench) with a padded cushion on top.

SET ACCESSORIES:

- LIGHTING SCONCES: On WALLS.

(GOOD REPRESENTATION)

SET ELEMENTS:

- Back WALL: Flats painted to suggest 3-dimensional architectural elements.
- PREP STALLS: 3 benches set against the Back WALL at center.
- STAIRS: Eliminated.
- Exit SPACE: Down from back WALL. Exits out stage left and stage right.
- Left WALL: Down from left exit SPACE. Flats angled from Back WALL, painted to suggest 3-dimensional architectural elements.
- Right WALL: Down from right exit SPACE. Flats angled from Back WALL, painted to suggest 3-dimensional architectural elements.
    - *When stage directions suggest exiting or entering by the stairs, simply exit out stage left.*

SET FURNITURE:

- BENCHES: Wooden structures long enough for two to sit on.

SET ACCESSORIES:

- None.

Production Notes

Set Design Narrative (MINIMAL REPRESENTATION)

SET ELEMENTS:
- Right and Left EXITS: Although nothing else needs to be part of the set, you do need exits out stage left and right.

SET FURNITURE:
- BENCHES: 3 benches of any sort up center stage.

SET ACCESSORIES:
- None.

Lighting and Sound Requirements

LIGHTING:
- Standard Lighting. For FULL PRODUCTION, individual track lighting in each PREP STALL and in the STAIRWELL could be a good design touch.

SOUND:
- None.

Prop List
- GAUZE, discarded packages and wrappings. JOINT BRACES, ointment tubes, and other "sports medicine" items.
- Sorted CLOTHING.
- ICE PACK package.
- ELECTRONIC TABLET (for **GRAVES**).
- LISTENING DEVICES (for **STEWARDS** and **STAFF**).
- FENCING EQUIPMENT: foil, gloves, protective helmet, vest and so forth.

Production Notes

Set Design Floor Plan

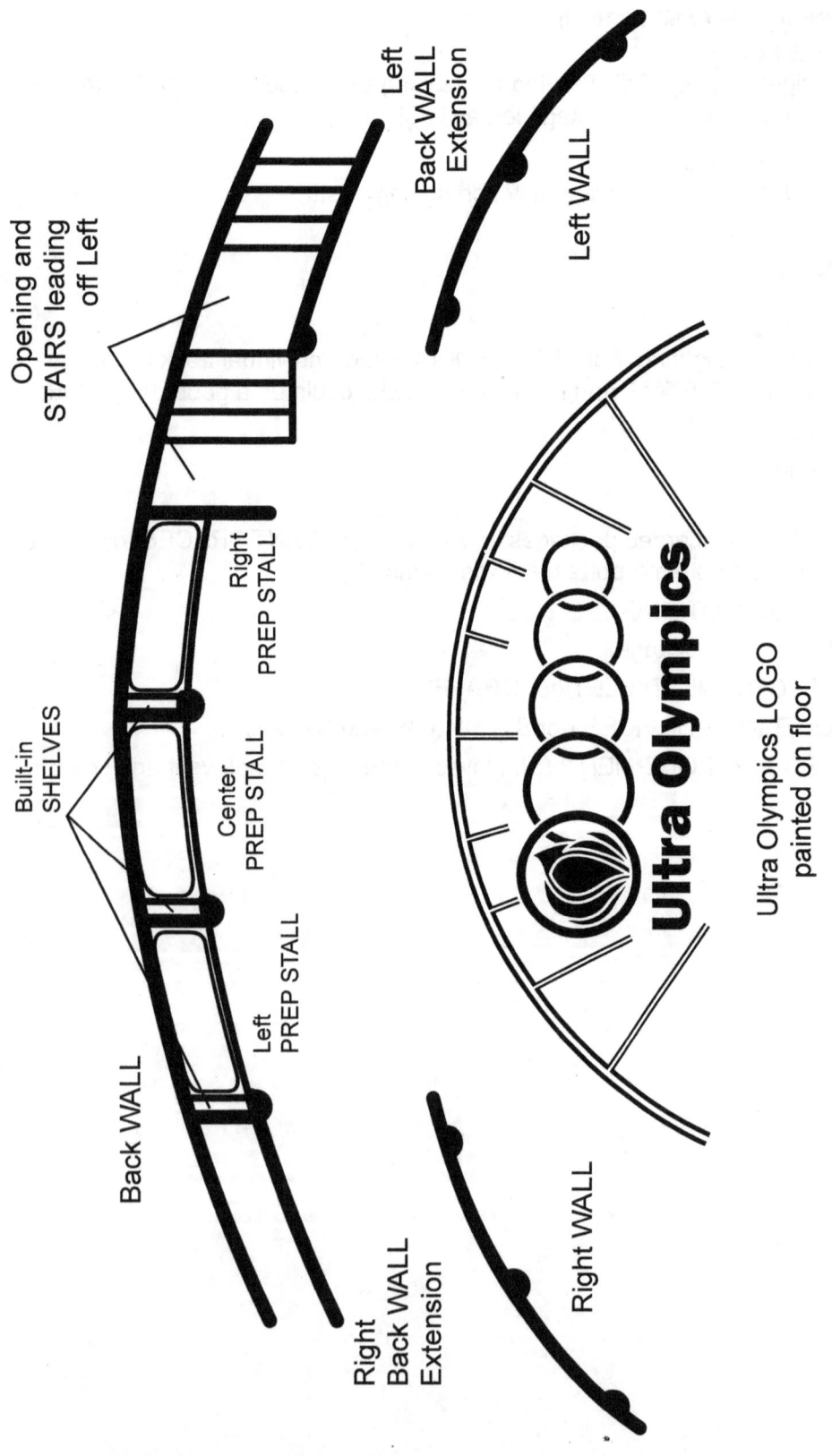

The Cronus Offense
a Drama
by Joan Garner

CAST OF CHARACTERS *(by category)*

THE ATHLETE PLAYERS
FALCON
RAVEN
HERON
SANDPIPER

THE STEWARDS
ROBIN—Falcon's Steward
SPARROW—Raven's Steward
JAEGER—Heron's Steward
FINCH—Sandpiper's Steward

THE STAFF
MEEKER—Physician
GRAVES—Trustee
CARTER—Inspector

(This script is void of gender identification to allow freedom of casting the most suitable actor for the part. It also accommodates an all male or all female cast.)

SET

The bottom level of the Ultra Olympics Stadium. Upstage left is a half-exposed staircase showing three to five steps leading up and out left. Within the subtle concave curve of the back wall are three PREP STALLS. A PREP STALL is a three-walled inlet with built-in shelves and a CUSHIONED BENCH. The structural elements suggest these STALLS continue out to the right and left, and the corridor might continue in a full circle.

The overall design is clean and stark, familiar but with some indistinguishable items. It's futuristic in feel, yet absent of electronic communications equipment, monitors, and such.

AT RISE

- Ultra Olympic Stadium.
- Morning. In the future.

(Of the PREP STALLS, the one to the right has strewn GAUZE, empty and discarded PACKAGES and wrappings, JOINT BRACES, and CLOTHING. The other two STALLS are tidier.

*The corridor is empty until **PHYSICIAN MEEKER** hurries through from stage right to left. After a BEAT, **PLAYER FALCON** stumbles down the STAIRS. Out of breath and in agony, **FALCON** crosses to the right PREP STALL and sits in defeat. When the he or she hears others coming down the STAIRS, **FALCON** rises and hurries out stage right.*

***STEWARDS ROBIN** and **SPARROW** enter flying down the STAIRS, and then abruptly halt. **ROBIN** and **SPARROW** exchange dirty looks as both are visibly upset. **ROBIN** crosses out stage left. **SPARROW** paces nervously. When **ROBIN** reenters from* *stage left, they exchange another look. **ROBIN** continues out stage right until **SPARROW** speaks.)*

SPARROW: This is disastrous.

ROBIN: Yes.

SPARROW: You know how disastrous this is.

ROBIN: I know.

SPARROW: How could we be this ill prepared?

ROBIN: Where did Falcon go?

SPARROW: Our best Athlete—both heats lost. Who over-evaluated that one? That's what I'd like to know. I could do a better job of selection. This is ridiculous.

ROBIN: Falcon *is* our best Athlete.

SPARROW: If Falcon is the best we have, we're finished.

ROBIN: No, we're not.

SPARROW: Where is this ringer everyone has been whispering about?

ROBIN: I wish I knew.

SPARROW: If we can't get something happening fast, it's going to be all over before it even gets started. It's disastrous.

ROBIN: I need to find Falcon.

SPARROW: Why bother?

ROBIN: It's my job.

SPARROW: Listen, the only thing you can do at this point is tell your Player they did their best and give them a consoling pat on the back. You both know it means absolutely nothing, but it's all you can do. I suggest you cut your losses and move on to a more promising prospect.

ROBIN: You're a cruel one, Sparrow.

SPARROW: I'm practical, Robin. It's all for the perks, and you're only fooling yourself by claiming some greater, noble cause. They call it a Stewardship, but you're simply a glorified lackey. You bolster their enormous egos, comfort them when they cry, and wipe away the blood when they're hurt. Why would anyone do it if it wasn't for the possibility of receiving the free houses and exotic travel and so on?

ROBIN: We do it for pride. We do it for the empire.

SPARROW: Some empire. They've stuck us on the bottom level, that's what they think of our empire. We're so far down; we can't hear the crowd in the arena. I think we're even under the sewer. We even have to walk up a flight of stairs to get to the sonic lift tubes. No monitors or visuals. No holding lounges or warm-up equipment. We just have benches and shelves. Oh yeah, we're a part of some impressive empire, all right.

ROBIN: It doesn't matter if the empire is impressive or not. Players are here representing those who haven't the talent to take part in the games, and that includes us.

SPARROW: Are we paraphrasing from the recruiting manual now?

ROBIN: Why am I even speaking to you?

(Enter **PLAYER SANDPIPER** and **STEWARD FINCH** from stage left.)

SANDPIPER: What's the problem?

SPARROW: Problem? We're losing everything in sight, that's the problem.

SANDPIPER: I haven't lost yet.

SPARROW: What stage are you at?

FINCH: The Uranus.

ROBIN: We're already at the Uranus?

SPARROW: I told you it was over.

ROBIN: Sandpiper, what are you playing for?

FINCH: The serum for Anabelom disease.

SPARROW: Hey, my cousin had that. It was awful. You've got to get that serum, Sandpiper.

SANDPIPER: Yes, yes. Not to worry, little Sparrow.

(**SANDPIPER** exits up the **STAIRS**.)

The Cronus Offense *SCRIPT* 3

SPARROW: *(Mocking with contempt.)* "Not to worry, little Sparrow." Why are all Intellectual Players pompous jackasses?

FINCH: Exaggeration, Sparrow.

SPARROW: Who asked you, Finch?

ROBIN: Finch, have you seen Falcon?

FINCH: No—sorry... I have to get back up top. Excuse me.

    *(**FINCH** exits up the STAIRS. Passing **FINCH** on their way down the STAIRS and into the corridor are **PLAYER HERON** and **STEWARD JAEGER**. Their pace is heavy as they cross to sit in the left PREP STALL.)*

SPARROW: *(Watching the two enter and sit.)* Oh, no. What did we lose?

HERON: The Carnac Channel water rights.

    *(**SPARROW** sighs with disappointment.)*

HERON: *(Continued.)* I'll get it back during the Rhea.

SPARROW: Sure, sure—you'll get it. You always do.

JAEGER: *(To **SPARROW**.)* Isn't Raven's match coming up? What are you doing down here?

    *(**SPARROW** nods agreeing and exits up the STAIRS.)*

ROBIN: Have either of you seen Falcon?

HERON: Not for awhile.

ROBIN: I need to find Falcon.

HERON: Try the facilities.

ROBIN: That's a good idea. Thanks.

    *(**ROBIN** exits stage left. There is an awkward moment as **HERON** and **JAEGER** sit in silence.)*

HERON: It isn't your fault.

JAEGER: How can it not be my fault? I didn't have the correct information and profiles for you. You can't win without all that.

HERON: You only had one day to prepare—just one day. Besides, I always lose the first set. It's a psychological failing. But, I'll get it back—trust me.

JAEGER: I'm sorry.

HERON: Don't be. I'll get it.

*(**FALCON** enters from stage right. **FALCON** leans against the frame of the right PREP STALL. **ROBIN** reappears from stage left and immediately crosses to **FALCON**.)*

ROBIN: Where did you disappear to? Are you all right? Come sit down.

*(**ROBIN** helps **FALCON** sit down in the right PREP STALL.)*

ROBIN: *(Continued.)* How are the legs? Are the legs cramping? Here, put your legs up. That should help.

*(**ROBIN** takes **FALCON'S** legs and swings them up to rest on the bench.)*

ROBIN: *(Continued.)* There. Isn't that better?

FALCON: My side is killing me.

ROBIN: Your side? I'll get the doctor. You just take it easy. *(**ROBIN** calls out.)* Has anyone seen Meeker?

VOICE: *(From offstage left.)* The doc's around the corner.

ROBIN: We need the doctor over here.

VOICE: *(From offstage left.)* Meeker, you're needed over here.

ROBIN: *(To **FALCON**.)* Can I get you something? *(Grabbing a WATER BOTTLE.)* Do you want some water?

FALCON: No.

ROBIN: Tell me what I can do.

FALCON: You can go away.

ROBIN: Come on. Don't be that way.

*(**PHYSICIAN MEEKER** enters from stage left.)*

MEEKER: Someone need me?

(**ROBIN** *jumps up and crosses over to lead* **MEEKER** *back to the right PREP STALL.*)

ROBIN: Over here, Doc. Falcon's in distress.

MEEKER: We're all in distress today, Robin.

(**MEEKER** *sits next to* **FALCON**.)

MEEKER: *(Continued. To* **FALCON**.*)* What's you're problem?

FALCON: My side. It's not letting up.

MEEKER: You're breathing wrong. You know better than that.

FALCON: I know. I couldn't get enough air.

MEEKER: What did you place?

FALCON: Fifth.

MEEKER: Then your problem is part breathing, part anger, and part humiliation.

(**MEEKER** *pulls an ICE PACK PACKAGE off the shelf, snaps off the seal, and presses it to* **FALCON'S** *side.*)

MEEKER: *(Continued. To* **FALCON**.*)* Hold this there for a few minutes. Breathe slowly and focus.

(**MEEKER** *rises and takes* **ROBIN** *aside.*)

MEEKER: *(Continued. To* **ROBIN**.*)* This Player's finished.

ROBIN: We can't be. We have the long-distance and the sprint left to run.

MEEKER: Falcon is done, Robin. You better petition for a substitute right away.

ROBIN: We haven't any substitutes.

MEEKER: I know, but petitioning will give us a little time to figure out what to do.

ROBIN: Figure out what to do? Nothing can be done. It's not like we have options here. Are you a miracle worker as well as a doctor?

MEEKER: Hardly.

ROBIN: Have you heard tell of a ringer?

MEEKER: Yes. Do you know anything about that?

ROBIN: No. I was hoping you did.

*(Enter **TRUSTEE GRAVES** from stage left. **GRAVES** is checking the readings on an ELECTRONIC TABLET in hand.)*

ROBIN: Trustee Graves, what are you doing down here?

GRAVES: I heard an inspector was snooping around in our quadrant.

MEEKER: An inspector? Are they insane? How can anyone be suspicious of this team? We're losing everything in sight.

ROBIN: Surely the committee doesn't suspect us of cheating. How can we be cheating?

GRAVES: There's a rumor about a ringer.

ROBIN: Do we have one?

GRAVES: Introducing a ringer in the middle of the Ultra Olympics is against the rules.

MEEKER: Then a ringer is already in place.

GRAVES: No, a ringer isn't already in place—and keep your voice down. I told you an inspector was lurking in the corridors.

MEEKER: So, how are we doing? Is it all over?

GRAVES: It's pretty grim, I won't lie to you. We've lost the Uranus.

ROBIN: The whole game?

GRAVES: The games we did win only allowed us to keep what we already had. We've gained nothing.

MEEKER: What do we have to do?

GRAVES: *(Looking at the ELECTRONIC TABLET in hand.)* Sandpiper and Raven must win or we forfeit all offensive challenges in the Cronus Events.

ROBIN: Without offensive challenges in the Cronus, we'll be the ones gobbled up by everyone else.

GRAVES: It's the risk everyone accepts in entering these games.

ROBIN: Have we lost the water rights?

GRAVES: Robin, try to grasp the gravity of our situation. If we lose any more games, challenges in the Cronus will pour in and the victor will consume our entire nation.

MEEKER: I don't believe this. And we were so strong coming in.

GRAVES: You can't predict a calamity like this.

FALCON: *(From over in the right PREP STALL.)* Why don't you just say what you're all thinking? I failed. I'm the one who's going to bring our country to ruin.

GRAVES: *(Back to **FALCON**.)* You're not the only one who's losing, Falcon.

ROBIN: What will we do if we're challenged? Who would we even put in the Cronus?

GRAVES: The strategy would obviously be entering an Intellectual Player —Sandpiper, possibly. Fortunately for us, the team challenged in the Cronus gets to select the game. Yes, I think our best alternative is going with Sandpiper.

ROBIN: I'd feel so much better if we had a ringer.

> *(**INSPECTOR CARTER** enters from stage left. **CARTER** speaks when entering after overhearing the end of the conversation with **GRAVES**, **ROBIN**, and **MEEKER**.)*

CARTER: Would you now? You know it's against the rules to be saving a ringer for the final game of Cronus. It means your team's disqualification and loss of everything.

MEEKER: We've already lost everything. Disqualifying us at this point would be an act of mercy.

CARTER: *(Smiling smugly.)* You're playing this well.

MEEKER: Playing what?

CARTER: Pretending you haven't a ringer.

MEEKER: We don't have a ringer.

CARTER: And the sincerity in your voice—very effective.

MEEKER: *(Angrily.)* Listen, you moron....

GRAVES: Doctor, please—

(GRAVES speaks to CARTER while holding MEEKER at bay.)

GRAVES: *(Continued.)* Inspector Carter, I wasn't aware badgering an Olympic team was a part of your duties.

ROBIN: *(To CARTER.)* How can we be staging this? Clearly our Players are done in.

CARTER: Yes, your Athletes, perhaps—but your Intellectuals... Which one is it? Heron or Sandpiper?

GRAVES: And just how can Sandpiper or Heron be the ringer? They're in the games and playing.

(HERON rises and crosses to the group.)

HERON: And I've lost my first match.

CARTER: Of course you lost your first match. It's the classic hustler maneuver; lose early to lull your opponent into a false sense of confidence and superiority. Then when the stakes are high enough, suddenly the mediocre talent turns into a stellar professional.

HERON: Then I can't win for winning. I must win my next match or we walk home. But if I do win, I'm tagged as the ringer and we're disqualified. The results are just the same—we walk. What's my move here, Inspector?

(Suddenly ROBIN presses the LISTENING DEVICE close to the ear.)

ROBIN: Oh, wonderful. *(Calling back to FALCON.)* Falcon, we're up.

FALCON: Already?

ROBIN: Afraid so.

(FALCON slowly rises and steps heavily up the STAIRS and out as the others watch on.)

MEEKER: *(Yelling after FALCON.)* And breathe properly this time.

ROBIN: *(Crossing to the STAIRS.)* Oh, yeah—we're definitely cheating.

(ROBIN exits up the STAIRS.)

MEEKER: I understand the Ultra Olympics began to give smaller governments an equal opportunity to amass commerce and technology, but nothing has changed. The wealthier the state, the better the finances to recruit the best and build state-of-the-art facilities for training.

CARTER: This is true. But there are no guarantees that big money will produce a capable Player for the Cronus. And it's equally plausible that a small sovereignty like yours could be hiding one that can.

MEEKER: But we're not.

CARTER: *(Still skeptical.)* Of course you're not.

   *(**CARTER** bows slightly with a grin and exits back out stage left. **MEEKER** waits until **CARTER** is gone before speaking.)*

MEEKER: It still isn't fair.

HERON: Is anything at all fair? I can't think of one at the moment.

   *(**JAEGER** jumps up and crosses to the others. **JAEGER** has been listening to the LISTENING DEVICE attached to the ear.)*

JAEGER: Hey—hey, something's wrong.

HERON: What?

JAEGER: *(Listening.)* It's Falcon.

   *(**ALL** with listening devices begin to listen to them.)*

GRAVES: Falcon has collapsed.

MEEKER: Oh, great.

   *(**MEEKER** charges up the STAIRS. **HERON** and **JAEGER** follow. **GRAVES** remains remarkably calm while continuing to listen to the LISTENING DEVICE. **GRAVES** paces for a BEAT, and then crosses to sit in the left PREP STALL. After another BEAT, **JAEGER** steps back down and crosses to **GRAVES**.)*

JAEGER: I faded back.

GRAVES: I see.

JAEGER: No one noticed—they were all rushing up to see Falcon.

GRAVES: No doubt.

JAEGER: Apparently they just stepped out of the tube when Falcon fell. Someone said Raven and Sparrow were already there.

GRAVES: Good.

JAEGER: Do you want to pull Sandpiper?

GRAVES: No.

JAEGER: I thought a show of unity would underline our desperation—

GRAVES: —Or cause a greater suspicion.

JAEGER: That's possible. Yes, I didn't think of that.

GRAVES: Which is why I'm the Trustee and you're not.

JAEGER: *(Listening to the DEVICE.)* Nothing yet. I thought there would be something.

GRAVES: It's too soon. Word needs to get back to the others Trustees. And then they'll need to confer, access our pitiful showing, and decide just how vulnerable we are....

JAEGER: Yes. Right. I'm just anxious... I didn't think Falcon would go down this fast.

GRAVES: Riding in those sonic tubes to the top probably didn't help. It makes it a bit tricky with Carter accusing us of having a ringer.

JAEGER: But we couldn't time this. Nor could we be sure Falcon would drop.

GRAVES: *(Looking at the ELECTRONIC TABLET.)* Here we go—our first Cronus challenge.

JAEGER: Should I go change?

GRAVES: —second—third challenge. Yes, go, go.

*(JAEGER exits out stage right. **RAVEN**, **HERON**, and **SPARROW** come down the STAIRS. Their gate is slow and sad.)*

SPARROW: *(After a BEAT.)* Well, let's pack up and go home.

GRAVES: Why?

SPARROW: Why? We just lost a Player. Under the Unforeseen Misfortune rule, we can pull out "per selfsame." Nothing lost, nothing gained. We can get out with the shirts still on our backs.

*(**SANDPIPER** and **FINCH** hurry down the STAIRS.)*

FINCH: We heard about Falcon and came right down.

GRAVES: What are you doing here? You can't leave in the middle of a match.

SANDPIPER: Oh, I won. How's Falcon?

RAVEN: We don't know.

GRAVES: *(To RAVEN.)* And you... What are you doing down here?

RAVEN: Don't get upset, I won as well. I can't believe you're only thinking of the games.

GRAVES: Raven, do you want to quit?

RAVEN: What?

GRAVES: Sparrow proposes we claim Unforeseen Misfortune and pull out of the games. Do you want to quit?

RAVEN: It isn't a matter of wanting to quit. Realistically, we should— I guess.

GRAVES: What about everyone else? Heron? Sandpiper?

HERON: I don't know, Trustee. It's going to be hard to focus knowing Falcon—

GRAVES: —you weren't focusing to begin with.

FINCH: Now wait just one minute....

GRAVES: All right, all right. I know we're all doing the best we can. I apologize, it's just that—it wasn't supposed to happen like this. We have our best Players in the games. You're all the best. Falcon was the best.

SANDPIPER: Was?

   (ROBIN and MEEKER enter from the right.)

FINCH: Where's Falcon?

MEEKER: In the emergency unit. We followed the medics down.

SPARROW: And?

MEEKER: Early prognosis is that Falcon died of internal bleeding aggravated by a herniated lung. I'll attend the autopsy performed after the games.

SPARROW: Hold it. Falcon's dead?

MEEKER: It just doesn't figure. For a rupture of that extent, the walls of the lungs have to be paper-thin. How is it possible an Athlete Player is cleared to participate in the Ultra Olympics with such a condition? A runner must have a healthy heart and lungs—who signed off on the physical exam? *(To GRAVES.)* It's inconceivable to believe no one knew about this. You had to have known.

*(BEAT. **ALL** wait for **GRAVES** to respond.)*

GRAVES: The question on the table is whether to continue or not.

SPARROW: You set Falcon up, didn't you?

*(**CARTER** enters from the left.)*

CARTER: This is what I'm thinking.

FINCH: Don't you ever announce you presence?

HERON: What do you want?

CARTER: I want to know what this team is up to.

GRAVES: The only thing this team is "up to" is deciding where to go from here. And that is a private matter, thank you.

CARTER: Everyone is wondering what this team is doing here. The minimum number of Players a team can have is four. You have four. Only the best Players enter. So far, your Players have performed subpar. The other teams offer resources worth competing for. What do you have? What are you doing here?

GRAVES: Our being here isn't a great mystery. We're trying to get what we don't have. Unfortunately, the day hasn't gone as well as we had hoped.

FINCH: Universal understatement.

CARTER: And what are we going to find when examining your fallen Player, Trustee?

HERON: Not fallen Player, Inspector Carter; dead Player. If you're after the truth, why don't you start by using it yourself?

CARTER: Dead? I didn't know. My sincerest condolences.

SANDPIPER: And we're supposed to believe you feel bad about this?

CARTER: I suspect you won't believe anything I have to say at the moment, so I'll leave you alone. Remember, I'm your contact. You'll need to let me know if and when you pull out—arrangements and documents need preparing.

 (**CARTER** *crosses to the STAIRS, but turns back to the* **GROUP** *before leaving.*)

CARTER: *(Continued.)* Keep in mind, if after the games, it's discovered that you've violated Olympic laws in anyway, all that you have gained will be stripped from you.

 (**CARTER** *exits up the STAIRS.*)

GRAVES: To continue, we have a vote pending whether we go or stay. We're all to vote and the majority calls it. That's fair, isn't it?

 (*The* **GROUP** *looks to one another and nod in agreement.*)

GRAVES: All right, then. Sandpiper?

SANDPIPER: Stay.

GRAVES: Finch?

FINCH: If Sandpiper stays, I stay.

GRAVES: Raven voted to go. Sparrow?

SPARROW: I go with Raven.

GRAVES: Such loyalty. I respect that. Doctor, I assume you wish to get out before something happens to another Player.

MEEKER: You assume correctly.

ROBIN: I vote go.

GRAVES: And, I vote stay. Heron?

HERON: Stay.

GRAVES: That makes four to go and four to stay. We have a tie.

HERON: What about Jaeger? Jaeger gets to vote.

(*JAEGER enters from the right now wearing an ATHLETE'S uniform and carrying FENCING EQUIPMENT.*)

JAEGER: Thanks for remembering me, Heron. After my pathetic contribution to the cause, I presumed no one would notice I was missing. I vote stay.

RAVEN: *(To JAEGER.)* What are you made up for?

JAEGER: The Cronus Offense. I'm Falcon's substitute. Since I'm already registered as Heron's Steward, it's all perfectly legal and within the rules.

ROBIN: *(To JAEGER.)* You're the ringer.

JAEGER: I'm the ringer.

FINCH: *(Referring to the FENCING FOIL JAEGER has.)* You any good with that?

JAEGER: The best.

GRAVES: Strategy is eighty percent of these games. You study the opponent and find out their strengths and weaknesses and most importantly, what they're after. Then you supposedly give it to them. We have experienced significant losses and the other competitors are flying overhead like vultures. We already have six Cronus challenges since Falcon went down.

JAEGER: And their representation in the fencing category is far inferior to me.

FINCH: So we gobble them up. It's the perfect Cronus Offense. Brilliant.

MEEKER: And what was Falcon in all this? the sacrificial lamb?

JAEGER: Falcon was a superb athlete. We fully expected the Player to add to our winnings.

GRAVES: But two weeks ago, doctor's diagnosed Falcon with Anabelom disease of the right lung. The disease itself is terminal; apply extreme physical exertion to the diseased area and it can rapidly turn fatal.

JAEGER: In fact, there was a fifty-fifty chance that Falcon would survive the day. We simply prepared for either outcome.

MEEKER: So you were gambling with a human life.

GRAVES: Doctor, I know you think of yourself the righteous conscious of this team, but while you're here judging our methods, consider this:

(*GRAVES holds the ELECTRONIC TABLET out for MEEKER to see.*)

GRAVES: *(Continued.)* Within the few minutes we've been talking, twelve more competitors have issued Cronus challenges. Here when we're at our weakest and most vulnerable, the locusts are swarming in. It's the way these games have been set-up. The rewards go to the opportunist. It's nature at its most brutal and pure form.

    *(**CARTER** hurries into the room from down the STAIRS. **CARTER** overheard the strategy of the team.)*

CARTER: I knew it. You had a ringer all along.

GRAVES: It's perfectly legal to substitute one person with another as long as they are a registered participant of the team. Jaeger is registered.

CARTER: As a Steward.

GRAVES: There's nothing in the rules disallowing a Steward from playing in the games. Believe me; we've checked it out thoroughly. Now, I would appreciate it if you would inform our first Cronus challenger our game is fencing.

CARTER: Do you really expect the Blue Planet to continue with the Cronus when they find out what you've done?

GRAVES: They're the challenger. They can't back out now. That's our prerogative.

CARTER: Unless you have broken the rules.

GRAVES: Which we haven't.

CARTER: This stinks to high Heaven.

JAEGER: Just a minute. *(To **GRAVES**.)* Did you say our first challenge is with the Blue Planet?

GRAVES: Yes.

JAEGER: That's the planet Earth.

GRAVES: What of it? Their resources are plentiful. When we take over, it's all ours.

JAEGER: My parents are from Earth. I was born there. We were once a satellite of Earth. We can't take it all away from them.

RAVEN: Their taking it all away from *us* doesn't seem to be a problem for *them*. After all, they were the first ones to go for the kill.

JAEGER: Still....

GRAVES: This is ridiculous. Jaeger wasn't trained to—

MEEKER: —Have a conscious.

CARTER: I need a decision here. What are you going to do?

JAEGER: I'm not playing the Cronus against Planet Earth.

GRAVES: You have to!

JAEGER: I'm not going to!

GRAVES: *(Irate.)* Fine! Just fine!

CARTER: Are you declaring Unforeseen Misfortune and getting out?

GRAVES: Absolutely not.

CARTER: I need an answer, or I'll announce your forfeiture myself.

GRAVES: All right... *(Looking at the **GROUP** and thinking hard.)* Sandpiper, what do you think?

SANDPIPER: I can do it.

GRAVES: Are you sure?

SANDPIPER: Yes. Let's go.

GRAVES: *(To **CARTER**.)* Is this acceptable to you, Inspector?

CARTER: Yes, I can accept that. Sandpiper is a registered Player in good standing. This would be legal and likely go unquestioned among all involved in the Ultra Olympics.

GRAVES: *(Sarcastically.)* What a relief.

   *(**MEEKER** takes **GRAVES** aside.)*

MEEKER: Are you insane? You're risking the lifestyle of millions. Our empire is in the fate of a spontaneous and desperate decision? You don't have the authority.

GRAVES: I am the Trustee of the team on behalf of the empire. I have all the authority and right to make such a decision.

MEEKER: Perhaps according to procedure, but what of moral rectitude? Trustee, you can't do this. I beg you; get out before we lose everything.

GRAVES: You're problem hasn't anything to do with moral rectitude. You're only afraid Sandpiper is going to lose.

MEEKER: All right, I'm terrified!

   *(BEAT as **ALL** react quietly to **MEEKER'S** true colors.)*

GRAVES: Doctor, You had a vote like everyone else. You lost.

MEEKER: Know that I plan to file a formal protest over this.

GRAVES: Then do so and let me get on with the matter at hand.

   *(**GRAVES** steps back to the **GROUP**.)*

GRAVES: Sandpiper says the Cronus is ours. What do you say?

HERON: If Sandpiper says go, then we go.

   *(The **GROUP**, but for **MEEKER** agree.)*

CARTER: Then I'll tell the others you accept their Cronus challenges?

GRAVES: We accept.

CARTER: Very well. I need Trustee Graves and Player Sandpiper to come with me. The rest of you can follow or stay behind as you wish.

   *(**CARTER** escorts **GRAVES** and **SANDPIPER** up the **STAIRS**. The **GROUP** follows but for **MEEKER**, **ROBIN**, and **JAEGER**.)*

JAEGER: If it's any comfort, Falcon knew that Anabelom was taking over and willingly took part in the ruse.

MEEKER: *(Bitterly.)* How noble of our fallen Player.

ROBIN: *(To **JAEGER**.)* And you? We could have used you from the beginning.

JAEGER: It wasn't in the plan.

ROBIN: And your dropping out was?

   *(**FALCON** appears from stage right.)*

FALCON: Of course it was.

(MEEKER, ROBIN, and JAEGER look over to find FALCON alive.)

MEEKER: *(Chuckling.)* Unbelievable.

(ROBIN crosses to FALCON.)

ROBIN: But Falcon, I saw you. You were dead. The medics pronounced you dead.

FALCON: I stopped breathing. There's a difference.

ROBIN: Is there? Would you care to explain it to me?

MEEKER: Any more surprises, you two?

FALCON: Do you really want to know?

ROBIN: Well, I do.

FALCON: I had to die to create an opening for Jaeger.

JAEGER: Everyone is so suspicious at these games. To have such a pathetic team like ours enter the Ultra Olympics, it's automatically assumed we'd try something shady—introduce a ringer most likely—so we gave them one.

FALCON: And what better time to slip in a ringer—

ROBIN: —Than bringing in a substitute for a dead Player?

FALCON: Exactly.

ROBIN: Then you're not dying of Anabelom disease.

FALCON: But I am—until we get the serum.

MEEKER: *(To FALCON.)* And you agreed to this at the risk of your own life.

FALCON: The risk would be far greater not to go forward with the plan.

JAEGER: Once Carter's suspicions were confirmed that we had a ringer—me—I was to drop out with some excuse.

ROBIN: The excuse that your parents were from Earth and you couldn't go up against the planet you were born on.

JAEGER: Or whichever planet or power was the first to challenge us.

FALCON: The last I heard, over thirty universal governments were challenging us. It's a pity we can only accept six.

MEEKER: With Sandpiper.

JAEGER: Who is the genuine article.

ROBIN: We're talking about our Sandpiper who placed sixty-first coming into the games?

FALCON: But who has been playing below potential for years.

JAEGER: Because Carter thinks the ringer was exposed already, we placed the true ringer in the Cronus Offense.

FALCON: And we get it all.

JAEGER: How else could we launch the Cronus Offense? Simply playing for itemized wins would not have gotten us what we needed and wanted.

ROBIN: I don't know. It still seems wrong. Someone is going to find out and we'll lose everything we get.

MEEKER: Then there is the practical view of this. Should Sandpiper win, how does our little empire reign over six superpowers of the universe?

FALCON: Oh, we know that. We're not going to claim Zeus and have total control or dominance over anyone. We want to be in a position to do a little bargaining. We'll let them keep their sovereignty as long as we get whatever resources and technology we want.

JAEGER: For a very, very long time.

MEEKER: And what if our leaders change their minds? What if they're seduced by all this power?

JAEGER: Then I suppose we truly do become Zeus, the God of Gods.

MEEKER: Then may the God of Gods help us all.

FALCON: But that's not going to happen.

MEEKER: And how do you know this isn't going to happen? If all these lies were told to us in a matter of minutes, how do you know you're not being lied to as well?

(FALCON and JAEGER look at each other with wavering confidence. Then JAEGER turns to leave.)

JAEGER: I'm going up top.

ROBIN: I'll go with you.

(JAEGER and ROBIN exit up the STAIRS.)

MEEKER: *(To FALCON after a BEAT.)* So, how did they fake your death?

FALCON: What does it matter?

MEEKER: I could reveal this entire deception.

FALCON: But you won't.

MEEKER: Why not?

FALCON: Because to spite this deception, it's for the greater good of the empire and its people. And because Trustee Graves directed us to fill you in on everything—

MEEKER: —Knowing that because I'm the self-righteous conscious of this team as Graves has said—

FALCON: —You'll stop anything from getting out of hand.

MEEKER: But now my life is on the line. Power corrupts and produces extreme action. There will be those wanting to silence me for what I know about this.

FALCON: What do you want? Do you want what is right and just? Well, you have it. This is in your hands now. Go upstairs and stop the whole thing. You can if you want. Go on, right now.

(MEEKER doesn't move.)

FALCON: *(Continued.)* But you won't. You hypocrite.

MEEKER: Are you finished?

FALCON: Am I? What are you going to do? Are we finished?

MEEKER: I don't know.

FALCON: Well, there is much to think about... I need to disappear again. Excuse me and bless our beloved empire.

MEEKER: Yes, bless our beloved empire.

*(Before **FALCON** exits.)*

MEEKER: Falcon, you're very brave—doing all this when you're ill. I don't think I could.

FALCON: Sure you could. You do what you have to do, as the saying goes. It seems we're in something of the same predicament here. You blow the whistle and we're both doomed. Isn't it interesting how your perspective changes when your life is on the line like this? You're in the same place I was a few weeks ago. Hard to know what to do, isn't it? Well, good luck.

MEEKER: Good luck to you.

*(**FALCON** exits stage right. **MEEKER** looks around dazed and a little frightened.)*

MEEKER: What do I do?

[LIGHTING CUE: *LIGHTS FADE TO BLACK.***]**

End of THE CRONUS OFFENSE

It's Nothing
a Farce
by Joan Garner

Play Information and Suggestions

Director's Notes

Overall Tone — As in all plays or movies labeled "farce," it's essential the PLAYERS play their parts with earnest purpose. Events may appear ridiculous or outrageous to the observer (aka, the audience), but it's real to the characters, and if their reaction is not of the utmost sincerity, the absurd circumstance will not be as comical.

Essence of Play — There are no bad guys here—perhaps one misguided ex-girlfriend—but no out-and-out villains. Among all the chaos and misfires, there needs to be an undercurrent of love and caring. These are ordinary and good people during trying times.

Moral of Play — Great thought wasn't exercised in establishing the moral of this play. Although there's probably one in here—somewhere—this author concentrated more on the gags and laughs.

Symbolism — Again, this isn't high drama—just a lot of fun.

Attention Required for Special Characters — If anything needs to be noted here, it would simply be that **WILLY** and **TINA** are your average teenagers. They're not angry or spoiled, or even witty like many teens in TV situation comedies whose only purpose is to stand there and spout back sarcastic one-liners. They're just good kids.

Scenes and Moments Needing Special Attention — Timing is everything. Doors opening and closing; people coming and going; carefully block and rehearse this action or the play won't be as humorous as it could be.

Dialogue and Accents — This play isn't placed in a specific location. It's assumed that it takes place in a suburb near the performance. With this in mind, the dialogue pattern of the area is perfectly acceptable.

Character Traits to Enhance Performances — Hopefully reaction and dialogue reveals these traits, but just in case a PLAYER misses them: **JOHN** would constantly rub the stress out of his neck. **TERRA-COTTA** fidgets and constantly adjusts her dress. **CINDY** might put her hand to her hair and smooth it back thinking it out of place.

Director's Notes

Character Traits to Enhance Performances

WILLY'S posture is not good. He would hunch over some and have most his weight on one leg or the other. **TINA** would be more demure and unnoticeable up until the time she defends her big sister. **GREG** uses expressive gestures with his hands as if he were trying a case before a jury.

Movement of Players/Staging

When the entire cast is onstage, movement may become difficult (especially when including the flower sprays). A method to ease this possible crashing into one another is to keep those coming out of the right door to the right and the same with the left door. Also, lining the PLAYERS up like a broken chorus line of dancers may prove the best blocking when placing everyone waiting to hear **CINDY'S** answer to **GREG'S** second proposal.

Character Analysis

JOHN CAULFIELD—**JOHN'S** a good dad and husband. **JOHN** always tries to do for his family. However, he doesn't handle crisis well. Fortunately for him, his wife helps him from coming unglued.

NICOLE CAULFIELD—**NICOLE'S** a cool mom. You get the sense she doesn't take any nonsense from anyone, but is supportive and loving. She has all the qualities others would like to have.

WILLY CAULFIELD—He's probably a gangly and awkward kid who likes weird things and teasing his little sister. **WILLY** hates dressing up—you know, your typical teen boy.

TINA CAULFIELD—She's probably a petite and pretty kid who likes talking on her phone. **TINA** likes dressing up—you know, your typical teen girl.

CINDY CAULFIELD—**CINDY'S** a little Jekyll and Hydish who can be calm one minute and freaking-out the next. But you can tell her heart is large and intent sincere.

BESS MASTERS—**BESS** is the ultimate in cool. If you study this script, you'll discover that—although this is an ensemble piece—**BESS** is the lead. She's a strong figure, but one who also goes with the flow.

ADELLE CAULFIELD—On first glance, you might suspect **ADELLE** is the head of a successful family run business more than being just a matriarch. Maybe she's both. Confident and poised, **ADELLE** complements the family.

Character Analysis

GREG WELLS—**GREG'S** a nice guy who thinks too much. He knows his heart tells him he's in love with **CINDY**, but his brain hasn't processed all of it yet.

HUNTER WELLS—**HUNTER** is **BESS'** counterpart; the ultimate cool. Taking a second-seat to the core of the story, he's still a necessary part to the overall madness.

TERRA-COTTA—**TERRA'S** a woman with a single purpose in life—fabulous. This makes her vocation as a wedding coordinator ideal for her. If only she were near to ideal in fulfilling her duties as wedding coordinator….

PAULA HICKS—**PAULA'S** delusional and only hears what she wants to hear, and accept what she wants to accept. In other words, she's over-the-top which makes her a great character to toss into the thick of things.

Production Notes

Design Concept   This is a present-day farce and as farces go, the more realistic looking the set, the more absurd and humorous the outcome. So, it's recommended this design be as representative and current as possible.

Costume Narrative   **THE MEN**
(**FULL PRODUCTION**) Black tuxedo with bow tie and cummerbund. White, long sleeved shirt. Jewel studs. Black socks. Black patent leather shoes. Hairstyles can be however the PLAYERS have their hair, but well-groomed.

(**GOOD REPRESENTATION**) Black or gray suits with matching colored neckties. White, long sleeved shirts. Black or gray socks and shoes. Hairstyles can be however the PLAYERS have their hair, but well-groomed.

(**MINIMAL REPRESENTATION**) Dark blazers and pants. White, long sleeved shirts. Conservative ties. Dark socks and shoes. Hairstyles can be however the PLAYERS have their hair, but well-groomed.

WILLY CAULFIELD
Besides wearing the tuxedo or suits in the beginning, he changes into a simple short sleeved T-shirt with some form of logo on it, jeans, and socks and athletic shoes.

Production Notes

Costume Narrative

* If the men wear suits or blazers, the following may act as alternative dialogue when JOHN refers to the studs on his tuxedo.

Divert from script here. *(Page 7 of SCRIPT.)*

ADELLE: Either one. I'm in both.

(***JOHN*** *comes out of the right BEDROOM DOOR. He now has on his suit pants and white shirt. He's trying to tie his necktie.*)

JOHN: Mother—glad to see you.

(***JOHN*** *bends down and kisses* ***ADELLE*** *on the forehead. She pats his arm.*)

ADELLE: Hello, darling. How are you holding up?

JOHN: If I could just get this thing tied, I'd be a happy man. Whoever invented these anyway?

ADELLE: Here, let me.

(***ADELLE*** *turns and begins to fix* ***JOHN'S*** *tie.*)

BESS: *(To* ***JOHN****.)* Don't you wear a tie to the office every day?

JOHN: Nicole always does it for me.

ADELLE: —The secret to a long-lasting marriage. *(Finishing with the tie.)* There you go.

JOHN: Bess, will you do something for me?

BESS: Sure, what is it?

JOHN: Will you find that plaster woman? I need to talk to her.

ADELLE: *(Standing.)* I'll get her.

BESS: (Standing.) It's all right. I can.
Pick-up Script from here....

Production Notes

Costume Narrative

THE WOMEN

(FULL PRODUCTION) Tasteful, long evening gowns with matching accessories and shoes. Hairstyles can be however the PLAYERS have their hair, but **NICOLE** and **CINDY** will have their hair up unless their hair is short.

(GOOD REPRESENTATION) Nice dresses of the season (should match the season when the performance takes place—summer dresses, winter dresses, and so forth); conservative cut yet flattering. Hose, high heels or pumps. Hairstyles can be however the PLAYERS have their hair, but **NICOLE** and **CINDY** will have their hair up unless their hair is short.

(MINIMAL REPRESENTATION) Same as GOOD REPRESENTATION.

TERRA-COTTA—Although the other women *may* be in evening gowns, **TERRA-COTTA** should dress in a severely tailored, two-piece suit with a tight-fitting skirt, hose and pumps for all three production approaches.

PAULA HICKS—Knit or cotton shirt with jeans or slacks with athletic shoes or sandals.

CINDY CAULFIELD

(FULL PRODUCTION) White, wedding dress with train and veil with matching hose, shoes and accessories. Robe large enough to cover dress. Hairstyle up.

(GOOD REPRESENTATION) White, knee-length gown and veil with matching hose, shoes and accessories. Robe large enough to cover dress. Hairstyle up.

(MINIMAL REPRESENTATION) Neutral colored dress with matching hose, shoes and accessories. Robe large enough to cover dress. Hairstyle up.

The Wedding Portrait (with a couple of "guests" included)

98 **PLAYESQUE** • Volume 1 (Teacher Ideas Press)

Production Notes

Set Design Narrative

SET ELEMENTS:
- Back WALL painted black. Stage left, white trellis with sky blue painted behind it.
- Hall WALL with two doors set in center*. Stage left picture window large enough to see trellis through it. Wallpapered with wainscoting.
- Black dividing WALL between the two doors behind hall WALL to separate the two rooms.
- Left stage WALL and right stage WALL down from hall WALL to create exits. Wallpapered with wainscoting.

SET FURNITURE:
- Accessory table between bedroom doors (center).
- Small accessory table stage left.
- Two side chairs on either side of the "phone table" stage left.

SET ACCESSORIES:
- Landscape painting hanging on hall WALL between the two bedroom doors (center).
- Telephone (stage left).
- Large houseplant (stage right).

There's a lot going in and out and slamming of the two bedroom doors. It's suggested to securely attach the Hall WALL to the set. The sturdier the better.

(FULL PRODUCTION)
Walls of plywood. Real doors and door frames. Paned picture window (no glass). Authentic trellis adorned with vines and flowers. WALLS with wallpaper and wainscoting. Carpeted floor. Actual furniture and accessories.

(GOOD REPRESENTATION)
- Flats painted to look like interior walls. Doors and door frames secured to flats. Paned picture window. Trellis and flowers painted on back WALL.
- WALLS with wallpaper and wainscoting painted on. Rug on floor. Actual furniture and accessories.

(MINIMAL REPRESENTATION)
- Left stage and right stage exits. When exiting into bedrooms, exit out stage right.
- Stools stage left.

Production Notes

Lighting and Sound Requirements

LIGHTING:
Standard lighting.

SOUND:
- Recording of "O Fortuna."
- Glass breaking. (Break glass in box, or recording.)
- A telephone ringing. (Either a live line, or recording.)
- Loud crash. (Things running into each other and toppling over.)

Prop List

- GLASS OF ICED TEA.
- NECKTIES, BELTS, etc. (to tie **PAULA** up with).
- WEDDING CAKE.
- CART WITH WHEELS with CAKE on top.
- Several FLOWER SPRAYS.

Set Design Floor Plan

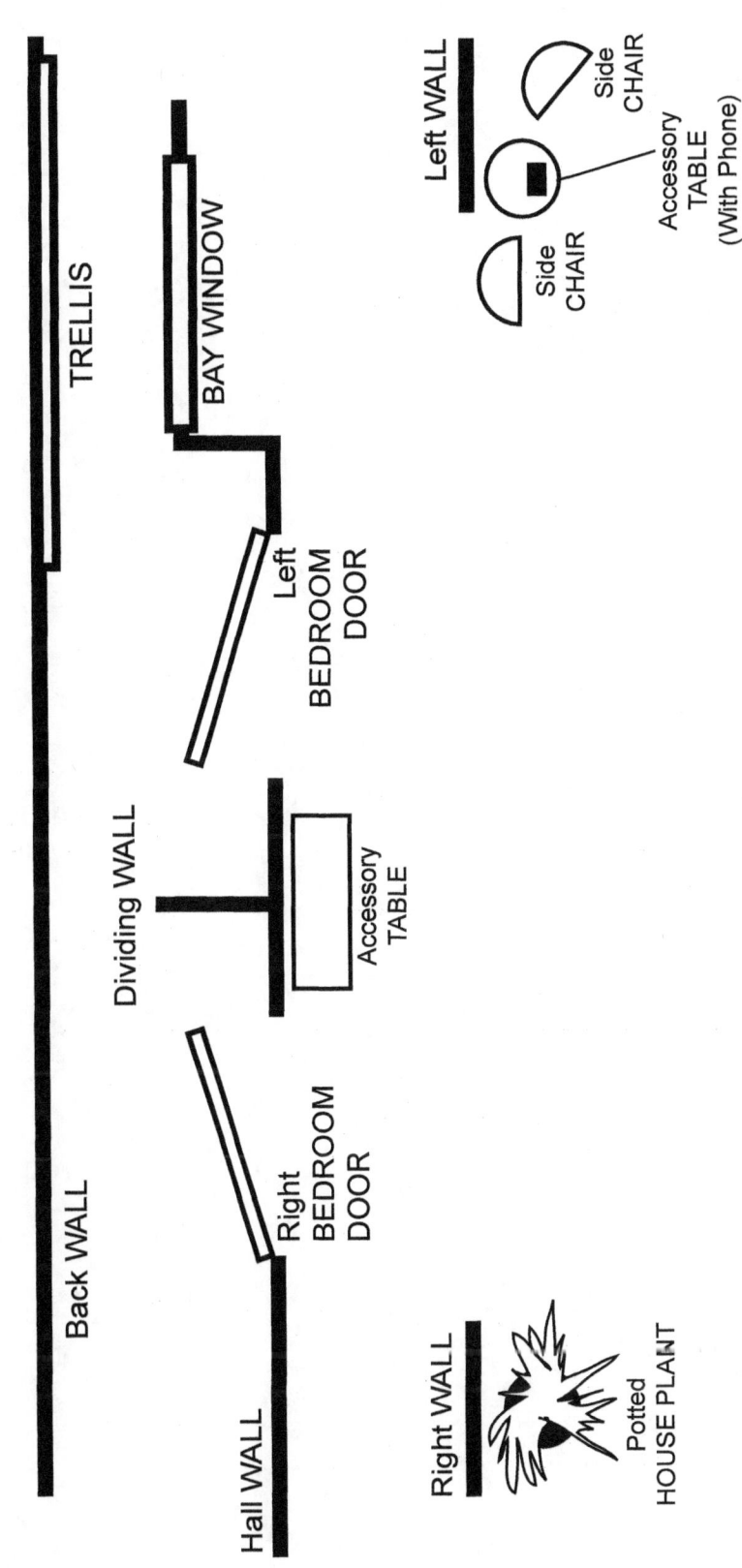

(© 2006 Joan Garner) **It's Nothing Play Information and Suggestions**

It's Nothing
a Farce
by Joan Garner

CAST OF CHARACTERS *(in order of appearance)*

JOHN CAULFIELD—The Father
WILLY CAULFIELD—The Brother
NICOLE CAULFIELD—The Mother
BESS MASTER—The Aunt
TERRA-COTTA—The Wedding Coordinator
TINA CAULFIELD—The Sister
CINDY CAULFIELD—The Bride
ADELLE CAULFIELD—The Grandmother
GREG WELLS—The Groom
HUNTER WELLS—The Best Man
PAULA HICKS—The Ex-girlfriend

SET

The hallway leading to two BEDROOMS in the Caulfield house. The back WALL is comprised of two DOORS in the center. Between the DOORS is a small accessory table with a landscape painting above it. Extending out left in the back WALL is a large picture window that shows bushes and a TRELLIS of vines and flowers. This trellis blocks the view of the rest of the backyard. Down from the PICTURE WINDOW is another wall that heads out left. In front of the wall is a small table with a telephone on top. Two CHAIRS sit on either side. The hall extends out to the right in the same manner. The furnishings are nice and tasteful, perhaps a little conservative upper middle class.

AT RISE

• The Caulfield home.
• Saturday Morning. Present-day.

(All is quiet. Suddenly Carl Orff's "O Fortuna" blares into the hall.)

[SOUND CUE: *RECORDING OF CARL ORFF'S "O FORTUNA"* **]**

The right BEDROOM DOOR opens and **JOHN CAULFIELD**, *a good-looking man in his mid-forties steps out from behind. At the moment he's wearing jeans and a knit shirt, socks, but no shoes. He yells out to the left, but can't be heard over the loud music. Just as abruptly, the music stops and* **JOHN** *is then heard finishing his sentence.*

JOHN: —That off! *(He lowers his voice a few decimals.)* What in blue blazes is going on out there?

VOICE OFFSTAGE: It's nothing!

JOHN: The music needs to be turned down.

VOICE OFFSTAGE: We're on it. Everything's cool, man.

JOHN: *(To himself.)* "Everything's cool, man?" *(Yelling back to the right BEDROOM DOOR.)* Willy, get out here.

*(**WILLY CAULFIELD** enters from the right BEDROOM DOOR. **WILLY** is a typical sixteen year old boy who expresses his individuality with his odd hairstyle. **WILLY'S** fully dressed in a tasteful tuxedo.)*

WILLY: Yeah, Dad?

JOHN: We're did you find that record guy?

WILLY: He's an events D.J., Dad.

JOHN: Well, he sounds like he's 1000 years short of a millennium.

WILLY: He's Kenny Dawkins' cousin.

JOHN: Can Kenny's recommendation be trusted? I mean, are you and Kenny Dawkins—what is it now? tight?

WILLY: Tight? He's a freshman, Dad. Get real.

*(**WILLY** exits back behind the right BEDROOM DOOR.)*

JOHN: *(Grumbling as he also goes back behind the right BEDROOM DOOR.)* I never liked that phrase.

*(**JOHN** closes the right BEDROOM DOOR behind him. After a BEAT, we hear a bloodcurdling scream from behind the left BEDROOM DOOR. **JOHN** is immediately out of the right BEDROOM DOOR again. His socks are off.)*

JOHN: *(Continued.)* What's that? What's wrong?

*(**NICOLE CAULFIELD** pokes her head out from the left BEDROOM DOOR. **NICOLE** is a pretty woman in her early forties.)*

NICOLE: Calm down, John. It's nothing. Cindy just popped a fingernail.

JOHN: Popped? My Heavens, is she okay? Quick, get some ice. How badly is she bleeding?

NICOLE: *(Calming **JOHN**.)* John, John, it's fine. She popped one of her false fingernails. She accidentally hit her finger on the dresser and the false fingernail flew across the room.

JOHN: *(Greatly relieved.)* Oh... Gees, I though she hacked off her hand or something.

NICOLE: No, no. She's just a little edgy. You know—nervous bride.

JOHN: This is supposed to be the happiest day of her life for crying out loud. You're not supposed to freak out on the happiest day of your life.

NICOLE: John, this is Cindy we're talking about. She freaks out if someone leaves a glass ring on the coffee table. Today has to be perfect or the rest of her life will be ruined—as will our's.

JOHN: No kidding. Will you come out here, please? I feel like I'm talking to the door.

NICOLE: I can't come out, I'm not dressed.

JOHN: So?

NICOLE: So, there are strangers roaming all over the house. I don't want them to see me in just a slip.

JOHN: A slip, huh? *(Sweeping a finger over his chest.)* It is that black one with the lace that goes across here?

NICOLE: Down Tiger... Why aren't you dressed?

JOHN: I keep hearing things.

   (There's a loud crash offstage left.)

   [SOUND CUE: *CRASHING SOUND OF BREAKING GLASS.*]

JOHN: *(Continued.)* See? *(He hollers offstage left.)* What was that?

   *(Enter **BESS MASTERS** with a GLASS OF ICED TEA in her hand. **BESS** is a little younger than **NICOLE**, but equally attractive. She wears a tasteful dress.)*

BESS: It's nothing.

JOHN: What do you mean "nothing?" I definitely heard a "something."

BESS: All right. You know the fluted champagne glasses for the reception?

It's Nothing SCRIPT

JOHN: Yeah.

BESS: Well, some of them no longer flute.

JOHN: Oh, great. I'm not paying for it. You go back and tell them I'm not paying for anything they break.

BESS: I think they're aware of their little whoopsie.

JOHN: It's a flaming whoopsie and I'm not paying for it.

*(Enter a flustered **TERRA-COTTA** from stage left. **TERRA-COTTA** is a nervous but enthusiastic woman. She wears a business suit with straight skirt and high heels.)*

TERRA-COTTA: Of course not, Mr. Caulfield. It's totally our responsibility. I wouldn't dream of charging you for our little boo-boo. We have plenty more—not to worry. It's going to be wonderful, you'll see.

JOHN: *(Grumbling again as he heads back behind the right BEDROOM DOOR.)* Well, I'm not paying for it. That's all I can say.

NICOLE: It's all right, Miss—Cotta. Mr. Caulfield gets a bit loony when he's financially extended.

BESS: And John is rather extended with this wedding.

TERRA-COTTA: Oh, I understand. Daddy can't say no to his little girl. But it's going to be a beautiful wedding. I promise.

NICOLE: I know it will. I have every confidence.

TERRA-COTTA: Oh, thank you. You have no idea how much I value your confidence. Thank you. Thank you.

*(**TERRA-COTTA** happily bounces back out stage left.)*

BESS: Where did you find that one?

NICOLE: John keeps asking me the same thing.

(The TELEPHONE on the ACCESSORY TABLE rings.)

[**SOUND CUE:** *TELEPHONE RINGING.*]

NICOLE: *(Continued.)* Could you get that, hon? I banned all the cell phones from the bedroom and we're a little busy in here.

BESS: No problem.

(NICOLE slips back behind the left BEDROOM DOOR while BESS crosses to answer the TELEPHONE.)

BESS: (Continued. Answering the TELEPHONE.) Caulfield Asylum for the composed and placidly challenged... Oh, Mrs. Wells, hello. This is Bess Masters. I'm Nicole's sister... Nicole, the mother of the bride... That's right. Yes, well, I call her "dear" too... U huh... U huh... Funny you should mention that. No, he's not. Not yet. Why?... No, I haven't heard anything... Sure, I'll keep my eyes open for him, but shouldn't you be here, too?... Oh, I hope everything goes well... Yes, I'll tell them... Bess, Bess Masters... I understand. Mrs. Wells, are you sure everything is all right? You sound a little unnerved... Good—Bess. Bess Masters... No problem. I'll see you soon.

(BESS hangs the TELEPHONE up as NICOLE sticks her head out of the left BEDROOM DOOR again.)

NICOLE: Who was that?

BESS: Claudia Wells.

NICOLE: Where are they? They should be here.

BESS: Dr. Wells had an emergency.

NICOLE: Emergency?

BESS: Well, it's hard to schedule a baby delivery. Although, I guess that's precisely what they're doing now-a-days.

(CINDY CAULFIELD sticks her head out the left BEDROOM DOOR alongside of her mother. CINDY is a pretty young woman who will make a striking bride when the curlers are out of her hair and her make-up is on.)

CINDY: What's wrong?

NICOLE: Dr. Wells is delivering a baby.

CINDY: A baby? But it's Saturday.

NICOLE: Well, you know how it is, dear. You always come down with something awful on the weekends.

BESS: I'd hardly call a baby "something awful."

CINDY: Couldn't another doctor deliver it?

BESS: I didn't ask. I can call back and get Dr. Wells out of the delivery room if you like.

CINDY: *(Whining.)* Mamma, they can't be late. It's my wedding.

(WILLY comes out of the right BEDROOM DOOR. His tie is undone.)

WILLY: Speaking of late, where's Greg?

CINDY: Greg? He's not here?

BESS: Uuuuu....

CINDY: Mother!

NICOLE: Yes, dear. We need to get dressed.

(NICOLE coaxes CINDY back behind the left BEDROOM DOOR.)

CINDY: But, Mother....

(The left BEDROOM DOOR closed behind the two.)

BESS: Nice timing with the Greg Alert.

WILLY: Hey, Aunt Bess.

BESS: Hey, Willy.

WILLY: You look great.

BESS: Why, thank you, Willy. What do you want?

WILLY: Some champagne.

BESS: Right. Try again.

(BESS gives him her GLASS OF ICED TEA and kisses him on the cheek. He grins and goes back behind the right BEDROOM DOOR. The TELEPHONE rings and BESS crosses to answer it again.)

[SOUND CUE: *TELEPHONE RINGING.* **]**

BESS: Hello... Yes, Mrs. Wells, this is Bess again. Thank you for remembering my name. Oh, that's super. I know Cindy will be happy to hear it... Well, no. But it's only been a few minutes. I'm sure he's just held up somewhere... Twenty minutes. Good. I'll be looking for you. Bye. Bye.

(**BESS** *hangs up the TELEPHONE.* **ADELLE CAULFIELD** *enters from stage left. She hesitates at the left BEDROOM DOOR.* **ADELLE** *is an attractive, older woman also nicely dressed.*)

BESS: *(Looking over.)* Hi, Adelle.

ADELLE: *(Looking over to* **BESS**.*)* Oh. Hello, Bess. You look lovely as usual.

BESS: So do you.

ADELLE: Yes, but I bet it didn't take you two and a half days to get the same results. *(She looks back at the left BEDROOM DOOR.)* Are they all in there?

BESS: Uh huh.

ADELLE: I suppose they're expecting me to go in and dispense some grandmotherly tidbits of wisdom.

(*BEAT.*)

BESS: Would you like to sit down for a moment?

ADELLE: *(Quickly jumping on the invitation.)* I'd love to.

(**ADELLE** *sits off to the left with* **BESS**.*)*

BESS: It's a lovely day for a wedding.

ADELLE: Oh, gorgeous. And everything is done up like a Disney theme park out back. I can just imagine what this is costing John. It surprises me he hasn't asked for his inheritance early... There is this strange woman running all over the place, though. She told me her name—Stucco something?

BESS: That would be Terra-Cotta, the wedding coordinator.

ADELLE: Oh, well that explains a lot... So, what's the betting pool up to now?

BESS: Which one? the one betting on how long the marriage lasts, or the one betting on whether the wedding even takes place?

ADELLE: Either one. I'm in both.

(**JOHN** *comes out of the right BEDROOM DOOR. He has on his tuxedo pants and white shirt now. No socks or shoes yet. He's trying to attach a stud to his sleeve.*)

JOHN: Mother—glad to see you.

(*JOHN bends down and kisses ADELLE on the forehead. She pats his arm.*)

ADELLE: Hello, darling. How are you holding up?

JOHN: If I could just get this stud in, I'd be a happy man. Who wears these things anymore?

ADELLE: Here, let me.

(*ADELLE takes the stud away from JOHN and attaches it to his sleeve.*)

JOHN: Bess, will you do something for me?

BESS: Sure. What is it?

JOHN: Will you find that plaster woman? I need to talk to her.

ADELLE: *(Finishing with JOHN'S sleeve and standing.)* I'll get her.

BESS: *(Standing.)* It's all right, I can.

ADELLE: *(Glaring a little at BESS.)* Please, let *me* get her.

BESS: *(Catching onto ADELLE'S inference.)* Oh. Okay. Yes. I can really use your help, ADELLE. Let's go together to fetch the sandstone woman.

ADELLE: *(Relieved.)* Thank you.

(*BESS and ADELLE exit out stage left. JOHN begins to head back to the right BEDROOM DOOR when there is another blood-curdling scream from CINDY behind the left BEDROOM DOOR. JOHN rushes over and knocks on the left BEDROOM DOOR.*)

JOHN: What in blue blazes is going on in there?

TINA: *(From behind the left BEDROOM DOOR.)* It's nothing, Daddy.

JOHN: She has to stop screaming like that before she gives me a heart attack.

(*TINA CAULFIELD comes out of the left BEDROOM DOOR, closing the DOOR behind her. TINA is a fourteen year old pixie—year's ahead of her age in maturity and wisdom.*)

TINA: Cindy broke a strap on her shoe.

JOHN: The shoes that cost me two hundred bucks? For two hundred bucks you should be able to plow fields in those shoes.

TINA: Gosh, Daddy, you sounded a little Jewish just then.

JOHN: How do you know how a Jewish person sounds?

TINA: When I'm interested, I pay attention.

JOHN: Well, in case you didn't know, your great-great-great grandmother was Jewish. So I guess that makes us all a little Jewish.

TINA: How can you be "a little Jewish?"

JOHN: I tell you what—one day soon we'll sit down and discuss religion, culture, and the state of the world—just not today. It's your sister's day.

TINA: Like I wasn't aware of that.

*(A slightly miffed **TINA** starts to head back into the left BEDROOM DOOR.)*

JOHN: Hey, can you keep a secret?

TINA: *(Turning back.)* What?

JOHN: When Cindy's married and off on her honeymoon, I'm having a home entertainment center installed in the basement.

TINA: *(Crossing to **JOHN**. Now she's excited.)* For true, Daddy?

JOHN: I know you and Willy have had to take a backseat for months with all of these wedding plans, so your mother and I thought....

TINA: *(Giving **JOHN** a big hug.)* Oh, Daddy, you're awesome.

JOHN: Keep it a secret, now.

TINA: I will. This is amazing.

*(**TINA** crosses and opens the left BEDROOM DOOR, but before she goes back inside, she turns to **JOHN**.)*

TINA: *(Continued.)* Daddy, I love you.

*(**TINA** closes the left BEDROOM DOOR behind her. **JOHN** puffs up quite pleased.)*

JOHN: Score one for the ol' man.

(TERRA-COTTA enters from stage left. BESS and ADELLE follow her in. TERRA-COTTA is a bit leery as she approaches JOHN.)

TERRA-COTTA: You wanted to see me, Mr. Caulfield?

JOHN: *(Distracted as he zeroes in on BESS' shoes.)* Yes, I did. We may have to delay the ceremony a little.

TERRA-COTTA: *(Trying to stay calm.)* A little? How little little?

JOHN: Well, I'm pretty sure we can get the ball rolling as soon as the groom arrives.

TERRA-COTTA: *(Really trying to stay calm.)* The groom isn't here?

JOHN: *(Breaking his focus on BESS' shoes.)* No. Is that a problem?

TERRA-COTTA: *(Really really trying to stay calm.)* Is he expected soon? How long of a delay are we talking about?

JOHN: I don't know.

TERRA-COTTA: I see.

JOHN: So, is this going to mess things up?

TERRA-COTTA: Well... The hot dinners just arrived. They're timed to stay hot one hour—just enough time for the ceremony to finish with a fifteen minute allowance for congratulatory mingling. The ice sculpture is guaranteed to stay hard for two hours. It's already been one. And the Reverend has another wedding to perform in ninety minutes. Naturally, it's across town... Mess things up?

(TERRA-COTTA whimper and exits back out stage left in an unsteady stride. BESS looks after TERRA-COTTA with a smile.)

BESS: You just made her day.

(When she turns back to the room, BESS notices JOHN noticing her shoes.)

BESS: *(Continued.)* John, what is it with my feet?

JOHN: How much did your shoes cost?

BESS: Excuse me?

JOHN: They look pretty sturdy. What's your shoe size?

BESS: Suddenly you have a foot fetish? Does Nicole know about this?

JOHN: Nooo. Cindy broke a strap on her shoe. I thought she could borrow yours.

BESS: Oh. Apart from the bride wearing white and my shoes being brown, these are heels. A bride usually wears pumps. If she should happen to step on her train, a pump will pull the gown, but not necessarily tear it. Are there any other fashion tips I can offer?

JOHN: There's no need for sarcasm. I was just trying to help.

ADELLE: Yes, dear. You're a good father.

(*TINA comes back out from behind the left BEDROOM DOOR.*)

TINA: Aunt Bess, have you seen Justin?

JOHN: *(To TINA.)* What about the shoe?

TINA: What shoe?

JOHN: Cindy's busted strap on her shoe.

TINA: Mom fixed it.

JOHN: Then there's no more catastrophe?

TINA: No, Daddy. You better get dressed.

JOHN: *(Grumbling again as he exits back behind the right BEDROOM DOOR.)* That movie was right. The most worthless member of the wedding party *is* the father of the bride.

(*As JOHN goes back behind the right BEDROOM DOOR, WILLY comes out. He now has his coat off.*)

TINA: So, Aunt Bess, have you seen him?

BESS: Seen who-him?

TINA: Justin!

BESS: Who's Justin?

WILLY: Lame boyfriend of the week.

BESS: Well, what does he look like?

WILLY: A total geek.

TINA: He is not.

WILLY: Is too.

TINA: Is not.

ADELLE: Children, make nice. This is your sister's big day.

*(Another scream from **CINDY** behind the left BEDROOM DOOR.)*

BESS: Cindy agrees.

*(**JOHN** flies out from behind the right BEDROOM DOOR again. He now has on his cummerbund.)*

JOHN: I swear I'm experiencing cardiac arrest right here and now.

*(**NICOLE** comes out of the left BEDROOM DOOR. She's now fully dressed.)*

NICOLE: It's nothing. Tina, honey, go help your sister with her hair.

TINA: Okay, Mom.

*(**TINA** exits back behind the left BEDROOM DOOR. **WILLY** goes back behind the right BEDROOM DOOR.)*

JOHN: So, what is it now?

NICOLE: She's upset with her hair.

JOHN: What's wrong with her hair?

NICOLE: It's clumping.

JOHN: It's what?

NICOLE: It's supposed to be flowing and it's clumping. You wouldn't understand.

*(**CINDY** comes out from left BEDROOM DOOR. She now has on her gown.)*

CINDY: Mother, I can't stand it. It's all wrong.

JOHN: I think your hair looks very nice.

CINDY: My hair? This isn't about my hair.

JOHN: Then what's it about this time?

CINDY: This time? This time? Daddy, how could you be so cruel?

*(**CINDY** bursts into tears and runs back in, slamming the left BEDROOM DOOR behind her. Poor **NICOLE** slumps a bit with a weary sigh.)*

BESS: Want me to field this one, sis?

NICOLE: Would you? Bless you.

BESS: Adelle, want to help?

ADELLE: Help? Me? But... Oh, all right.

*(Following **BESS** into the left BEDROOM.)*

ADELLE: *(Continued.)* If we're not out in ten minutes, send in a rescue party.

*(**BESS** and **ADELLE** exit behind the left BEDROOM DOOR.)*

JOHN: Nicole, why don't you write down everything I could possibly say to set Cindy off, and I'll try to censor my replies.

NICOLE: I'm sorry, sweetheart. But we knew Cindy would most likely go ballistic with all of this. That's why we took out that insurance policy.

JOHN: *(Chuckling.)* Well, if Greg doesn't show up soon, we may have to put in a claim.

NICOLE: He's still not here?

JOHN: I don't think so.

NICOLE: That's not good.

JOHN: No, sh....

*(There is another scream from **CINDY** behind the left BEDROOM DOOR. **JOHN** and **NICOLE** look at each other warily, then **JOHN** takes **NICOLE'S** hand and they hustle it out stage left. The hallway is silent for a moment until **PAULA HICKS** enters from stage right. **PAULA'S** pleasant looking enough, but there's something "off" about her. **PAULA** sneaks in, looks back and forth, scoping*

out the place as not to be detected. Still looking about nervously, she crosses to the right BEDROOM DOOR and taps softly on it.)

PAULA: *(Whispering.)* Greg. Psst, Greg... Greg, honey....

*(Getting no response, **PAULA** broadly faces the DOOR and starts pounding madly, hollering for **GREG**. **WILLY** opens the DOOR and **PAULA** jumps into his arms while calling out **GREG'S** name. [**WILLY** now has on his jeans and his tuxedo shirt is not tucked in.] **PAULA** quickly breaks from her embrace when she realizes **WILLY** is not **GREG**.)*

PAULA: *(Continued.)* You're not Greg.

WILLY: I know.

PAULA: I need to see Greg.

WILLY: He's not here.

PAULA: I really need to see him.

WILLY: Okay, but he's not here.

*(**BESS** comes out from behind the left BEDROOM DOOR with **TINA**.)*

BESS: What's this?

PAULA: Please, I need to see Greg.

BESS: He's not here.

PAULA: All I need is five minutes—two.

BESS: What part of "he's not here" didn't you understand?

*(Not listening to **BESS**, **PAULA** goes back to the right BEDROOM DOOR and knocks again.)*

PAULA: Greg, sweetness, I'm coming in.

BESS: "Sweetness?" Who are you?

PAULA: *(To **BESS**.)* Greg's fiancé. *(To the BEDRROM DOOR.)* Greg, honey, here I come.

*(**BESS** steps over and stops **PAULA** from going into the BEDROOM by grabbing **PAULA'S** collar.)*

BESS: Hold it. What do you mean you're his "fiancé?"

PAULA: What part of "fiancé" didn't you understand?

BESS: Greg is engaged to my niece. You might have noticed all the wedding decorations around here. They're getting married today.

PAULA: Not after I talk to him.

BESS: Greg has proposed to you, too? He said, "What's your name, please marry me?"

PAULA: Not in those exact words.

BESS: Well, what exact words did he use?

PAULA: Greg is just a little confused right now. But I know once I talk to him, he'll realize what a mistake marrying this Cindy woman would be, and come to his senses and marry me.

TINA: You're crazy.

PAULA: Was I talking to you, little girl?

BESS: All right. I think—whoever you are—you're the one who's mistaken here.

> (**PAULA** ignores **BESS** and crosses to the right BEDROOM DOOR again. She knocks calling for **GREG**, and exits behind the right BEDROOM DOOR.)

WILLY: What a loony.

BESS: She's obviously delusional.

TINA: She's going to ruin Cindy's wedding, Aunt Bess.

BESS: Not if we can help it. Are you two up for some covert action?

WILLY: Cool!

TINA: Sure.

BESS: Do whatever you have to do, but get that woman in a closet in there and keep her there. Move the dresser in front of the door or something, just fix it so she can't get out. We'll sort this all out when Greg shows up. Go, go, go.

(BESS hustles WILLY and TINA in and closes the right BEDROOM DOOR behind them as ADELLE and CINDY come out of the left BEDROOM.)

ADELLE: What's going on out here?

BESS: You don't want to know.

(Now all hear PAULA screaming and pounding again inside the right BEDROOM. TINA quickly reappears from the right BEDROOM, a little ruffled and out of breath.)

TINA: Mission accomplished.

CINDY: What mission?

BESS: Cindy, I don't quite know how to—this woman claims she's engaged....

CINDY: Paula Hicks.

TINA: You know her?

CINDY: We try not to talk about it. Greg had one date with her before he met me, but the idiot claims Greg is her soul mate and won't leave him alone.

ADELLE: Can't you get the police to issue a restraining order or something?

CINDY: You have to be dealing with a stalker to get one of those. Paula doesn't exactly stalk, it's more like—lurks. We thought our getting married would send a clear enough message that... Where is he?!

ADELLE: Come on, sweetie. Let's finish getting you ready. Greg will be here when we're done. I promise.

CINDY: *(Surprisingly becoming calmer.)* This is not going well, Grandma.

ADELLE: I know, but it will be all right.

(CINDY goes back behind the left BEDROOM DOOR when ADELLE says her next line before going in as well.)

ADELLE: *(Continued.)* I don't know how, but it will....

BESS: We have to find Greg.

TINA: What can I do, Aunt Bess?

BESS: Go back in there and help Willy with that woman. Try to shut her up if you can.

TINA: Can we tie her up and gag her?

BESS: Well, no not that—

(**PAULA** *suddenly becomes louder with her banging and yelling.*)

BESS: *(Continued.)* All right. Whatever it takes.

TINA: Willy's going to love this.

BESS: How nice.

(**TINA** *exits behind the right BEDROOM DOOR.*)

BESS: *(Continued.)* If I were a groom about to marry, where would I be? Here? Obviously. A bar? Possibly. Siberia? Probably.

(*From behind the right BEDROOM DOOR, we hear* **PAULA'S** *banging and yelling, and then suddenly the yelling is muffled, and then silence.*)

BESS: *(Continued. Looking over.)* Way to go, Willy.

(**BESS** *exits out stage right. After a BEAT,* **GREG WELLS** *appears on the other side of the PICTURE WINDOW. He is very handsome in his tuxedo.* **GREG** *cups his hands over his eyes to look inside. And then* **HUNTER WELLS** *steps up behind* **GREG**. *He looks equally dashing in his tuxedo.* **HUNTER** *grabs* **GREG** *and pulls him offstage left. After another few seconds,* **HUNTER** *pushes* **GREG** *into the hallway from stage left.*)

GREG: *(Mad.)* Will you cut it out?!

HUNTER: I'll cut it out when you stop acting like a two-year-old.

GREG: I'm not acting like a two-year-old. I'm acting like a responsible adult who has realized the error in his thinking and seeks to rectify the situation.

HUNTER: Oh, get off it. You're just scared and want to run.

GREG: Well, see? Here is yet one more example of how you and I see things differently.

HUNTER: Enough with the platitudes. You're not a lawyer yet and you're going through with this marriage.

GREG: Am not.

HUNTER: Are too.

    (**BESS** *comes back in from stage right.*)

BESS: Oh, thank Heavens, you're here.

GREG: Bess, how are you today?

BESS: Uh, I'm just fine, Greg. How are you today?

GREG: Fine.

BESS: *(A bit leery.)* This is good.

GREG: Bess, I need to speak to Cindy.

HUNTER: *(Under his breath.)* Don't do this.

GREG: *(Under his breath back to* **HUNTER**.*)* Shut-up. I know what I'm doing. *(To* **BESS**.*)* May I see Cindy, please?

BESS: But it's bad luck to see the bride right before the wedding.

HUNTER: See?

GREG: *(Mocking.)* See?

HUNTER: *(Mocking the mock.)* See?

GREG: *(Mocking the mock mock.)* See?

BESS: What's going on?

    (**GREG** *crosses to the left BEDROOM DOOR.* **TERRA-COTTA** *enters from stage right with a large FLOWER SPRAY on an easel.*)

TERRA COTTA: Excuse me.

    (**TERRA-COTTA** *puts the FLOWERS down to the left, and then slinks back out stage right as* **GREG** *knocks on the left BEDROOM DOOR.*)

GREG: Cindy, it's Greg. May I come in?

CINDY: *(From behind the left BEDROOM DOOR.)* No! Are you nuts?

GREG: Come on, I really need to see you.

BESS: *(Aside to HUNTER.)* What's this all about?

HUNTER: The end of the world as we know it.

GREG: *(Knocking on the BEDROOM DOOR again.)* You either come out here, or I'm coming in. These are you only choices.

CINDY: *(From behind the BEDROOM DOOR.)* You can't see me, it's bad luck.

GREG: Well, figure something out because we're going to talk and it's going to be right now.

BESS: You tell her, Greg. Take charge. Cherish these last few minutes believing *you're* going to be the dominant one in this marriage.

> *(**CINDY** comes out from behind the left BEDROOM DOOR. She has a robe over her wedding gown to hide it. **TERRA-COTTA** reenters from stage right with another large FLOWER SPRAY on an easel. All look on as she goes about her business, then exits back out stage right. After she leaves, **CINDY** turns her attention back to **GREG**.)*

CINDY: This had better be good.

GREG: *(To **BESS** and **HUNTER**.)* Will you give us some privacy, please?

HUNTER: Greg, don't do this.

CINDY: Don't do what?

GREG: There's been a development.

HUNTER: That's putting it mildly.

BESS: Greg, just spit it out.

GREG: All right! I don't want to get married.

(Dead silence.)

CINDY: What?

GREG: I don't think it's in our best interest... I feel it isn't the most opportune time for the two of us to become husband and wife. I believe we should spend more time getting to know each other. There's also law school and the softball tournament is coming up. It really isn't the most opportune time.

    *(Remarkably, **CINDY** remains calm. She looks over to **HUNTER** and **BESS** and then back to **GREG**.)*

CINDY: You have two more years of law school. It isn't like you're studying to take the Bar Exam right now. The softball tournament isn't until next month, and we've known each other for over three years. How much longer do you think it's going to take?

GREG: I don't know....

CINDY: Greg, this is a very opportune time. It's probably the most opportune time of our lives. If you don't want to get married, it's not because of timing, it's because of me. You don't want to marry me. That's it, isn't it?

GREG: All right, then. Yes, it's you.

BESS: Whoops.

HUNTER: *(Taking **BESS** by the arm.)* I think we should excuse ourselves.

BESS: Yes, I....

CINDY: *(Firmly.)* You're staying.

BESS: *(To **HUNTER**.)* We're staying.

CINDY: *(To **GREG**.)* So what is it about me you don't want to marry?

GREG: Shouldn't we be discussing this in therapy or something?

CINDY: Greg, we have 150 guests arriving as we speak—half of them belong to your side of the family. All of them are expecting flowers, candles, and a relative singing a terrible rendition of "Feelings" as the bride is escorted down the aisle. And one key ingredient to this blissful scene is the groom. As a matter of fact, the groom is a very big essential ingredient.

GREG: I know, and I'm sorry....

    *(**JOHN** and **NICOLE** reenter from stage left.)*

JOHN: Sorry? Sorry about what?

CINDY: Apparently, the wedding's off.

JOHN: What?

HUNTER & BESS: She said the wedding's off.

JOHN: Oh, no, no, no, no, no. No off wedding. With what this is costing me, there's no off wedding. Is that clear?

> (**WILLIE**, **TINA**, and **ADELLE** sneak out from behind their respective BEDROOM DOORS to huddle together in the back and watch. Also, during the next sequence, **TERRA-COTTA** will slink in from stage right with three more large FLOWER SPRAYS, excusing herself as she steps around people, depositing the FLOWERS in different "empty" spots in the hallway, finally exiting stage left.)

CINDY: If Greg has a problem marrying me, then I definitely have a problem marrying him.

NICOLE: Now, everyone, I'm sure this is just a small misunderstanding.

CINDY: What's there to misunderstand? He doesn't want to marry me.

JOHN: *(In a daze.)* I don't believe this. 40 grand down the tubes.

> (**JOHN** sits in one of the CHAIRS next to the ACCESSORY TABLE.)

JOHN: *(Continued.)* 40 smackers. 40 enchiladas. 40 big ones—pouf—out the window.

WILLY: Well, why doesn't Greg want to marry my sister?

TINA: Yeah, why not? She's pretty and smart, and isn't at all like Stephanie's big sister.

ADELLE: Who's Stephanie?

TINA: Just a friend from school. *(To **GREG**.)* And she treats her just awful.

WILLY: Who?

TINA: Stephanie's big sister treats her, Stephanie that is, just awful.

WILLY: Oh.

CINDY: Thank you, Tina.

TINA: *(Crossing and putting a supportive arm around **CINDY**.)* You're very welcome.

HUNTER: Look, I still think this would be better if we left these two alone to work this out.

CINDY: Work what out? If he doesn't love me anymore, it's over. Period.

NICOLE: Oh, I'm sure it isn't as final as all that.

GREG: Mother Nicole, you know how I love your optimism, but at the moment it's most inappropriate.

CINDY: *(Now getting miffed.)* Most inapp—Hunter, you have my permission to knock some sense into your brother.

WILLY: Cool! Fight!

   (TERRA-COTTA reenters from stage left with yet another FLOWER SPRAY.)

TERRA-COTTA: Fight? Oh, my Heavens, no. There can't be a fight. It isn't in the agenda—which, by the way—is very behind schedule.

JOHN: Well, it's about to get behinder.

TERRA-COTTA: But the hot dinners are getting cold and the ice swan is rapidly melting in the punch bowl. Its beak is dripping, dripping, plop, plop, slowly diluting the raspberry punch.

JOHN: So, take it and stick it in the freezer.

TERRA-COTTA: I beg your pardon.

JOHN: Take the melting swan out of the diluted punch and stick it in the freezer.

TERRA-COTTA: Yes, that would be a good idea except we have 200 individual parfaits in the freezer. Excuse me.

   (TERRA-COTTA sits her FLOWER SPRAY down.)

JOHN: And what's with all the flowers? They're supposed to go out back under the tent.

TERRA-COTTA: Canopy.

JOHN: Whatever. Why are you putting them in here?

TERRA-COTTA: It's nothing—something to do with too many zero's on the order form. Under the canopy is full, and so is the rest of the house, and—

JOHN: I'm not paying for—

TERRA-COTTA: *(Starting to unravel.)* —Of course not, Mr. Caulfield. Our error, our expense.

JOHN: That's right.

TERRA-COTTA: That's right!

(PAULA bursts out from behind the right BEDROOM DOOR, struggling to get her bindings off [which happen to be several NECKTIES around her ankles, legs, wrists, and one important TIE over her mouth]. Once the one NECKTIE around her wrists is off, she quickly removes the one over her mouth.)

PAULA: *(Puffing and trying to catch her breath from the struggle.)* Ha! Try to get rid of me, will you? Well, it's not going to work. You can't mess with fate, people. It's our destiny and no matter what you try to do, it's going to be.

ADELLE: What's going to be?

PAULA: Greg and I, that's what.

GREG: Paula, for crying out loud....

JOHN: Who the heck is this?

BESS: Greg's old girlfriend.

GREG: She's not my girlfriend, old or otherwise.

BESS: She thinks she is.

PAULA: *(Making herself presentable and coaxing.)* Greg, honey. You know you belong to me. We're soul mates.

GREG: Oh, I'm so sick of hearing about this soul mate business.

CINDY: Greg, you told me *we* were soul mates.

GREG: Well, *we* are.

CINDY: But you're sick of hearing about it.

GREG: *(Pointing at PAULA.)* Just from her!

TERRA-COTTA: Who is she?

EVERYONE: *(Answering TERRA-COTTA loudly.)* Nobody!

ADELLE: All right, all right—everyone except Greg and Cindy into the bedrooms. This is the authority of age speaking. Come on—vamoose.

(ALL But GREG and CINDY exit [the MEN behind the right BEDROOM DOOR and the WOMEN behind the left BEDROOM DOOR] with each mumbling the following as they exit:)

NICOLE: This is unreal.

TERRA-COTTA: But I have to check on the....

ADELLE: You can do that later.

TINA: When it's my time, I'm going to elope.

PAULA: Greg and I are going to have a simple wedding—just the immediate family.

BESS: What planet do you live on?

WILLY: This is the best wedding I've ever been to!

HUNTER: Glad we could oblige.

JOHN: 40 thousand dollars up in smoke....

(CINDY waits for the BEDROOM DOORS to close.)

CINDY: You wanted to talk?

GREG: Yes, I did.

CINDY: And?

GREG: This is very difficult.

CINDY: *(Sarcastically.)* Oh, you poor dear. Here, I'll make it easier for you. I'll ask the questions and all you have to do is answer. That's simple enough, isn't it?

GREG: Sure. That's good. Ask whatever you want and I'll answer anything.

CINDY: Is there a specific quality about me that you've apparently just discovered you can't stand?

GREG: I wouldn't put it that way, exactly, but yes there is... Cindy, you're an amazing woman. You're beautiful and kind. You love people, and you have this wonderful laugh.

CINDY: Uh huh. I can see where this would drive you up the wall.

GREG: You didn't wait for the "but."

CINDY: The "but?"

GREG: There's a "but." You have all these great qualities, *but*....

CINDY: But what?

GREG: You're—contrary, Cindy.

CINDY: Contrary?

GREG: Yes, that's the only word I can think of to describe you.

CINDY: Contrary.

GREG: Yes.

CINDY: What are you talking about?

GREG: Well, you kinda' have your priorities mixed up. What you think is important and what you think is not important is all backwards—more or less. Like right now, for instance.

CINDY: What about right now?

GREG: I show up minutes away from when we're supposed to be married and tell you I don't want to go through with it. And here you stand, calm and rational about it all. But two days ago when the umpire threw me out at home plate, you practically tore the stands apart. You get very upset if the dish isn't rinsed off enough to go into the dishwasher, but two months ago when that car crashed into the neighbor's living room, you took charge of the scene and helped everyone through it. At first I thought this behavior a little odd, and then I fell in love with you and I thought I could live with this minor problem. But, gees, Cindy, I'm just afraid you're going to give me an ulcer before our first wedding anniversary.

*(There is a long pause as **CINDY** merely stars at an uncomfortable **GREG**. After a moment, **TERRA-COTTA** slinks out from behind the left BEDROOM DOOR.)*

TERRA-COTTA: Excuse me. I don't mean to interrupt, but I need to check on the wedding cake.

*(**TERRA-COTTA** exits out stage left.)*

GREG: Would you like to sit down? Maybe you should sit down.

CINDY: There's one thing I'm not clear on, Greg. Is it you don't want to marry me because you no longer love me?

GREG: I didn't say that.

CINDY: Then you still love me.

GREG: Of course I do.

CINDY: And this is what's so terrible.

GREG: You're not... That's not what I said. You're twisting my words around. You should be the lawyer, you're very good.

CINDY: Greg, I got upset when that umpire threw you out because it was like someone was attacking you. Besides, you were safe—it was so obvious. I protect the people I love. I guess I go overboard at times, but I don't like to see anyone unhappy. If I start to holler about the dishes it's because I want everything to be perfect for you.

GREG: But everything doesn't have to be perfect for me.

CINDY: But this is who you fell in love with. If I change or act differently, then I won't be the same person, and you won't love me anymore.

GREG: Babe, that's not it at all. I don't ever expect you or me or our lives to be perfect. How boring would that be? It can just be. Come what may, and all that. And I would want you to just be you, and I can just be me. And maybe we can raise a couple of just bes' that will look just like us, and maybe experience a few bumps in the road. But that will be okay, because there will be more better times than not. I promise... How does that sound?

CINDY: Sounds pretty good to me.

GREG: All right, then. Miss Caulfield, will you marry me—before the ice swan melts altogether?

(TERRA-COTTA enters from stage left rolling in a WEDDING CAKE on a CART.)

TERRA-COTTA: Well, here's one thing that's turned out right. Isn't it lovely? I thought seeing this beautiful cake would lift your spirits.

*(Suddenly there are several screams and the **WOMEN** come busting out from behind the left BEDROOM DOOR. The **MEN** also come out from behind the right BEDROOM wanting to know what all the screaming is about. Major mayhem as the FLOWER*

*SPRAYS are knocked all over the place. **TERRA-COTTA** fiercely protects the CAKE from being destroyed. **NICOLE** rushes to **JOHN**, **TINA** heads for **WILLY**, and **BESS** wraps herself up in **HUNTER'S** arms for protection while **PAULA**, screaming the loudest and running around the most, hops straight into **GREG'S** arms.)*

JOHN: What is it?! What's going on?!

*(**ADELLE** is the last to come out from behind the left BEDROOM DOOR. She's not as flustered as the others.)*

ADELLE: *(Looking back into the left BEDROOM DOOR.)* Poor little fellow. The entire ruckus must have driven him inside.

GREG: *(To **CINDY**.)* Well, Cin? What do you say?

JOHN: *(To **ADELLE**.)* Drove who inside?

CINDY: *(To **GREG**.)* It's difficult to say anything while you're carrying another woman in your arms.

ADELLE: A little mouse.

GREG: *(Nearly dropping **PAULA**.)* Oh, Paula, go bother Hunter.

ADELLE: *(To **JOHN**.)* He's probably more scared of us than we are of him.

BESS: *(To **PAULA**.)* No, you don't. I already have dibs on Hunter.

PAULA: *(To **GREG**.)* But, sweetest lips, we're in love.

WILLY: *(To **TINA**.)* Gees, it's just a little mouse.

GREG: *(To **PAULA**.)* Go away, you lunatic, I'm proposing here.

TINA: *(To **WILLY**.)* A Stewart Little little mouse I can handle, not a real one.

HUNTER: *(To **GREG**.)* Didn't you already do that?

GREG: I'm trying it again.

NICOLE: But I thought the wedding was off.

JOHN: Maybe not. If there is a God in Heaven, don't let it be off.

CINDY: Daddy, please be quite—the rest of my life is on he line here.

BESS: Should we all go back in the bedroom?

TINA: Not with that mouse in there.

GREG: Nobody has to leave. *(He takes **CINDY** by the hand.)* Cindy, while the fact remains you'll probably drive me crazy, the truth is—the absolute truth is, I can't picture my life without you. *That* would be absolute madness. So, if you can forgive my doubts and own failings, will you marry me?

*(Suddenly **ALL** are silent and listening intensely.)*

CINDY: Yes, Greg, I'll marry you.

(Hurrahs, laughter, sighs of relief, and so on explode all around.)

TERRA-COTTA: Marvelous! The wedding's back on. If we hurry, we might be able to make up the time.

*(**TERRA-COTTA** begins shuffling **EVERYONE** out stage left.)*

TERRA-COTTA: *(Continued.)* Come on. Dad, Mom, bridegroom, bride. Lovely, lovely—one and all. Hup, hop, hup, hop....

*(ALL manage to exit stage left leaving **TERRA-COTTA** by herself.)*

TERRA-COTTA: *(Continued.)* Whew, that was a close one. Who says I'm not the best wedding coordinator in town? *(She looks over and sees the **WEDDING CAKE**.)* Oh, the cake. We can't start without the wedding cake.

*(**TERRA-COTTA** gets behind the CART and rolls it out stage left. There is a loud crash-like sound offstage left.)*

[SOUND CUE: *LOUD CRASH.***]**

*(After a BEAT, **TERRA-COTTA** returns to the hallways. She has icing and cake all over her face and chest as if she has taken a nose dive into the **WEDDING CAKE**.)*

TERRA-COTTA: *(Continued. Calling out stage left.)* Not to worry. It's nothing!

*(**TERRA-COTTA** wearily exits stage left.)*

End of IT'S NOTHING

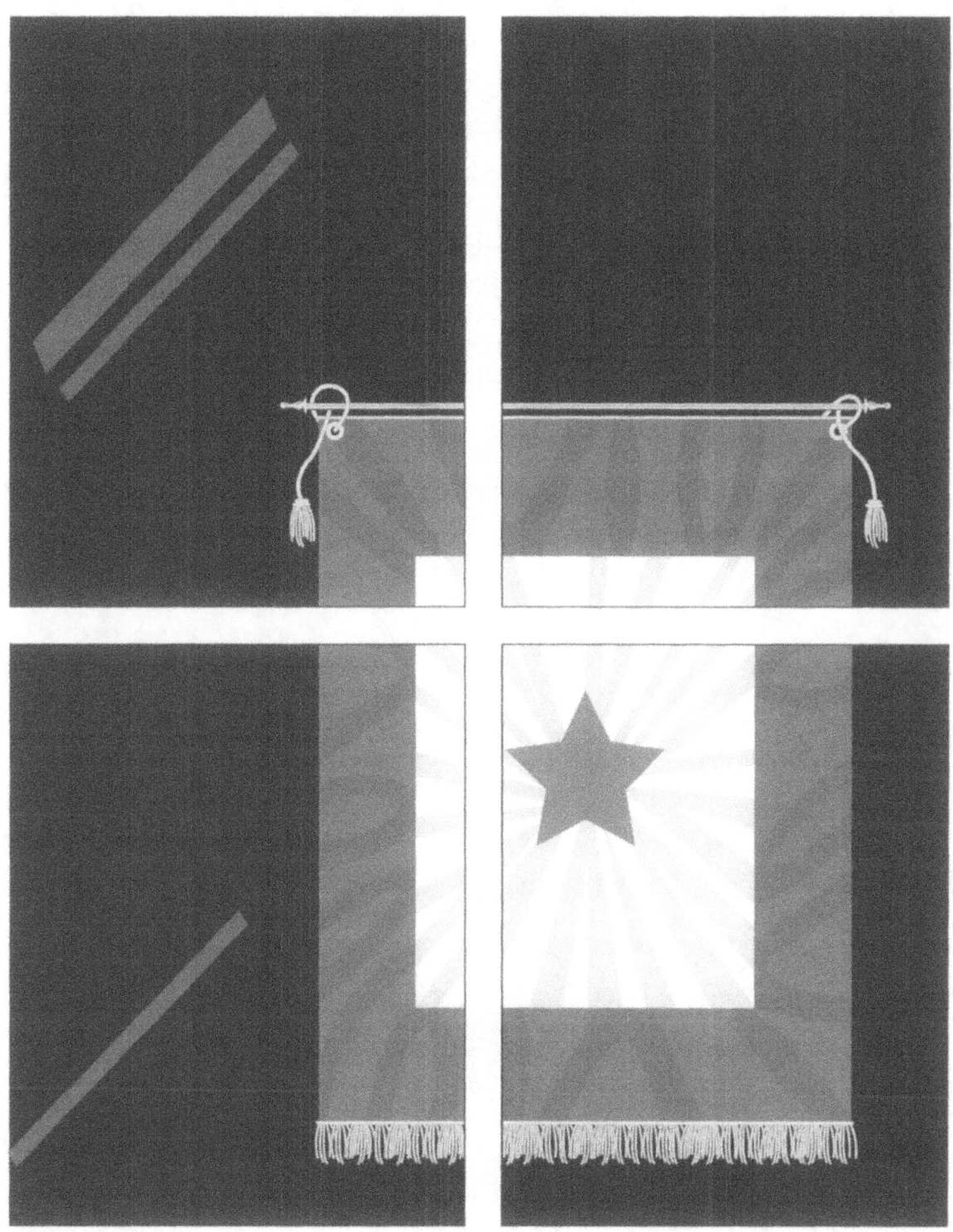

Americana

Americana
a Drama
by Joan Garner

Play Information and Suggestions

Director's Notes

Overall Tone — This is a feel good play where the plot concentrates more on situations than character interaction. Though set in the middle of World War II, it's a pure and innocent era—possibly one of the best and most respected and admired decades in U.S. history. A retrospect of genuine Americana.

Essence of Play — The essence of AMERICANA is the essence of the American Way. Granted the "American Way" has many meanings, but here it's the way most families live. That is, they exist in their own private little world. The rest of the planet may be annoyingly intrusive at times, but as long as global affairs do not directly affect the nucleus, the family forges on content.

Moral of Play — There is good in most people, events, and things. It may be hard to find at times, but it's there if you're willing to look beyond the obvious.

Symbolism — Ironically, AMERICANA is nearly all symbolic. It's a wish and a yearning for yesteryear. And, ironically, it shows how every era wishes for its own yesteryear. Specifically, the following visuals are symbolic of:

—The Bungalow HOUSE: Harmony with function. A simpler time.
—The ORCHARD: America's past identity as an agricultural country.
—ICE CREAM: The emphasis on ice cream is intended. First, it's a familiar and nationally liked food. Second, it's a comfort food needed and cherished during this time. Finally, it's a luxury food making it a special treat.

Also, each character demonstrates a key ingredient that identifies the United States during World War II. Here is the obvious and maybe not so obvious symbolism:

MASON: Youth During War
LAVONNE: The Home Front
GLORIA: Religion and Home Front War Effort Participation
JACK: The Military
ALICE: National Security
NOREEN: Work Supporting the War
OWEN: Local Official and the Older Generation's Support
PENNY: "What We Were Fighting For"
TED: The Promise of the Next Generation
ELLA: Motherhood and Apple-Pie
HANS: The Enemy

(© 2006 Joan Garner) Americana Play Information and Suggestions

Director's Notes

Attention Required for Special Characters

ALICE JENNINGS could prove a difficult character to portray. She must be likable yet distant and guarded at the same time. One way to show this is to have **ALICE** react with kindness and compassion at first (as an automatic reflex), but then stop herself and move away from the situation.

Though the youngest at five years old, **MASON** is an important character. He often introduces the scene and motivates scene progression. Because of this significant contribution, it might be beneficial assigning someone to work specifically with the young fellow playing **MASON**.

Dialogue and Accents

Taking place in the western United States, dialects are more generic and without distinctive inflections. Also, these are simple people so the dialogue isn't especially sophisticated. Of course **HANS** will have a broken German accent.

Character Traits to Enhance Performances

MASON—Because of his age, it may be best to let the PLAYER behave naturally. Trying to impose anything different from what he's accustomed to could produce an insincere, unwanted result.

LAVONNE—A "huggy" and "touchy" person when speaking to others, **LAVONNE** would press an arm with a hand or rest it on a shoulder, etc.

GLORIA—Unaccustomed to change, **GLORIA** might rub her arms in a nervous habit when confronted with unpleasantness (aka, **HANS** coming onto the scene).

JACK—A one time extrovert, his experience and injuries have humbled and slowed him. **JACK** will start out quickly with assertiveness and confidence, but will then pull back or gasp for breath when his injuries kick up. He'll then commit to a weaker movement and stance.

ALICE—A good person but restricted. As mentioned above, **ALICE** would instinctively move towards people to help but then stop playing her assigned part. This action needs to be subtle and undetectable by the other characters.

NOREEN—Pretty enough to be a model, graceful movement will enhance this observation.

OWEN—Bubbly, **OWEN** moves quickly—uncharacteristic of an elderly man.

PENNY—**PENNY** moves purposefully. She takes **TED'S** arm whenever they're near, hand combs her hair occasionally to make herself presentable, and often checks the height of her bobby socks.

TED—Basically wanting to get anywhere fast, and because of his history of abuse, **TED** may move nervously when trying to get his point across. He gestures a bit more broadly to stress how important his message is.

Director's Notes

ELLA—The rock, **ELLA** would probably sway in a comfortable gate as she walks, thinks a moment on how and where she sits before she does, and with hands folded, bows her head when intently listening to serious matters.

HANS—Because of his terminal illness, **HANS** will teeter when standing, hunch over when speaking, and probably take careful, short steps towards anyone.

Scenes and Moments Needing Special Attention

The sequence with **HANS WELLER** is a bit tricky. Initially a possible harrowing situation, it's quickly realized there's no real danger and then the scene turns into one of the lightest. The actions of **HANS** and **OWEN** may be amusing, but all the PLAYERS need to maintain the seriousness of the events at hand.

Movement of Players/Staging

Each of the major PLAYERS has their own special moment. Placing each front and center will help them project their message.

It may be difficult placing the entire ensemble on stage at the end of ACT I. An effective staging direction is grouping two or three lesser PLAYERS together and away from the principle action. This scene helps in part because **TED**, **JACK**, and **HANS** are stage right while the others stand stage left. It also helps that **LAVONNE** and **OWEN** are up on the PORCH (center) when the focus moves to them.

Character Analysis

MASON—A happy little boy. On his mind throughout the play is riding his bicycle in the Victory Parade. Little else excites him until **JACK** enters to fill his impressionable mind with war stories and heroics.

LAVONNE—The cornerstone of the story. She is a natural born leader and good woman. In a stressful situation, she carries on and overcomes whatever obstacles are placed before her. Though she may be hurting inside, she'll try not to show it.

GLORIA—An unhappy woman. **GLORIA** still broods over her husband's death feeling she was cheated. She's a nice and giving neighbor, but not one to forget past and continue with her life.

JACK—A genuinely nice man. A victim of the horrors of war, he's attempting to set his life straight again, but things have changed and frustration overtakes him at times. Because of his circumstance, there is the feeling that **JACK** may be doomed to wander aimlessly the rest of his life yet there is hope in his attitude.

ALICE—A "proceed with caution" manner that perplexes those around her. Later it's revealed she's a quiet hero in her own right. Even though she tries to play her part, others like **LAVONNE** and **JACK** can see her goodness through the facade.

Character Analysis

NOREEN—An intelligent and stunning young woman. More than any other character in the play, she belongs in a big city with a career. Since this is 1944, she'll most likely marry and have children as expected.

OWEN—Your typical old fashioned, good-natured gentleman who lives a simple life. A friendly soul, tragedy could happen right in front of him and it would only mildly effect him.

PENNY—A pretty young woman who has her life well planned. She has accepted her station in life and is willing and able to follow it through. Only when this well planned life is challenged does she have problems.

TED—An impatient young man who wants to contribute to the world yet feels held down by family obligations. To spite his father's abuse, he has become a thoughtful and caring individual.

ELLA—Your typical rural housewife. She does the fall canning and is an expert quilt maker. She is gentle in nature and follows the crowd. She's the little old lady everyone loves.

HANS—A sympathetic young German man whose life has been limited to a dull existence of a prisoner of war. One can't help but think he might have been a poet or teacher if he had lived a normal life.

Production Notes

Design Concept

It's believed the best look for this play is *realistic fake*. Exterior sets are difficult to pull off because everyone knows they're inside in an auditorium. This author has found the best approach to this problem is to try to make everything look as realistic as possible while keeping superficial characteristics. In other words, the HOUSE should be constructed with building materials (that is shingles, siding, posts), but the grass will obviously be fake (outside carpeting or Astroturf?). Real branches and bushes may represent the ORCHARD, but the back WALL might be painted a flat sky blue. All props and costumes should look as authentic as possible, and if there's room, a nice touch would be to build a small living room and kitchen inside the HOUSE (seen from the two HOUSE WINDOWS). Viewing the women inside the kitchen doing the dishes and conversing in low tones while the primary action takes place outside will add a realistic feel of the production.

Because costuming for this play isn't as expensive or difficult to create as in other productions, the following **Costume Narrative** *concentrates on suggestions for a* **(FULL PRODUCTION)**. *However, most costume change suggestions will keep an item or two from the previous ensemble to help budget matters.*

Production Notes

Costume Narrative

MASON
(FULL PRODUCTION)

ACT I & ACT II Scene 1 *(Friday Evening)*
White, long sleeved shirt. Khaki colored shorts. White socks. White canvas shoes. Short hair.

ACT II Scene 2 *(Saturday Evening)*
Red, white, and blue striped knit shirt with long sleeves. Khaki colored shorts. Red, white and blue striped socks. Brown shoes with laces. **JACK'S** sailor's cap. Short hair.

ACT II Scene 3 *(Sunday Morning)*
White, long sleeved shirt. Light yellow sweater vest. Brown, long pants. White socks and brown shoes with laces. Short hair.

LAVONNE
(FULL PRODUCTION)

ACT I & ACT II Scene 1 *(Friday Evening)*
Light blue tailored dress with short sleeves and no collar. Full apron of bold floral pattern with ruffled edges. Nude nylon stockings (with seam down the back of the leg). Black pumps. Semi-long bobbed hair.

ACT II Scene 2 *(Saturday Evening)*
Dark blue dress with large, squared white lace collar. White lace facing on left and right pockets at the waist. Dark nylon stockings (with seam down the back of the leg). Black pumps. Semi-long bobbed hair.

ACT II Scene 3 *(Sunday Morning)*
Dark purple two-piece suite with long sleeves. Dark nylon stockings (with seam down the back of the leg). Black pumps. Semi-long bobbed hair.

GLORIA
(FULL PRODUCTION)

ACT I & ACT II Scene 1 *(Friday Evening)*
FIRST ENTRANCE: Bright yellow, small floral patterned puffy short sleeved blouse. Bib overalls. White socks and brown oxford shoes with laces. Bandanna/turban over the hair of same material as blouse. Shoulder length hair.
SECOND ENTRANCE: Teal dress with white polka-dots. Square collar trimmed with white rick-rack. Nude nylon stockings (with seam down the back of the leg). Black pumps. Shoulder length hair.

JACK
(FULL PRODUCTION)

All of Play
Army service uniform of a sergeant. (See page 142 for instructions on **JACK'S** patches, badges, and medals.) Tan shirt with long sleeves and buttoned breast pockets. Tan pants. Tan tie tucked into shirt. Metal and cloth belt. Brown socks and brown shoes with laces. Tan cap. Short hair.

Production Notes

Costume Narrative

ALICE
(FULL PRODUCTION)

ACT I & ACT II Scene 1 *(Friday Evening)*
Dark blue dress with white ruffled collar. Dark nylon stockings (with seam down the back of the leg). Black pumps. Curled hair.

ACT II Scene 2 *(Saturday Evening)*
Dark gray, two-piece suit. Dark nylon stockings (with seam down the back of the leg. Black pumps. Curled hair.

NOREEN
(FULL PRODUCTION)

ACT I & ACT II Scene 1 *(Friday Evening)*
Black and gold dress with brocade black top and flowing gold skirt. Nude nylon stockings (with seam down the back of the leg). Slippers. Black high heels. Long curled hair.

ACT II Scene 2 *(Saturday Evening)*
Lavender blouse with puffy long sleeves. Dark lavender cloth vest. Brown straight skirt. Dark nylon stockings (with seam down the back of the leg). Black pumps. Long curled hair.

ACT II Scene 3 *(Sunday Morning)*
Rose silk blouse with long sleeves. Brown straight skirt. Dark nylon stockings (with seam down the back of the leg). Black pumps. Long curled hair.

OWEN
(FULL PRODUCTION)

ACT I & ACT II Scene 1 *(Friday Evening)*
White long sleeved shirt. Tan tweed pants. Suspenders. Gaudy red short tie. Black socks and black shoes with laces. Glasses. Short hair (balding).

ACT II Scene 2 *(Saturday Evening)*
White long sleeved shirt. Blue striped suit vest and pants. Gaudy blue short tie. Black socks and black shoes with laces. Glasses. Short hair (balding).

ACT II Scene 3 *(Sunday Morning)*
White long sleeved shirt. Blue striped suit (with jacket but not the vest) and pants. Gaudy green short tie. Black socks and black shoes with laces. Glasses. Short hair (balding).

PENNY
(FULL PRODUCTION)

ACT I & ACT II Scene 1 *(Friday Evening)*
White blouse with round collar. Dark green jumper. Dark green bobby socks. Brown shoes with laces. Semi-long hair.

ACT II Scene 2 *(Saturday Evening)*
Dark green blouse with white collar. Dark colored pants with cuffs. Dark green bobby socks. Brown shoes with laces. Semi-long hair.

Production Notes

Costume Narrative

ACT II Scene 3 (Sunday Morning)
White blouse with round collar and puffy short sleeves. White long sleeved sweater. Dark green jumper. White bobby socks. Brown shoes with laces. Semi-long hair.

TED
(FULL PRODUCTION)
ACT I & ACT II Scene 1 (Friday Evening)
White long sleeved shirt. Dark red sweater. Dark brown pants. Black socks and shoes with laces. Short hair.

ACT II Scene 2 (Saturday Evening)
White long sleeved shirt. Dark brown pants. Black socks and black shoes with laces. Short hair.

ACT II Scene 3 (Sunday Morning)
White long sleeved shirt. Dark brown suit coat and pants. Blue tie. Black socks and black shoes with laces. Short hair.

ELLA
(FULL PRODUCTION)
ACT I & ACT II Scene 1 (Friday Evening)
Black and white print dress. Dark nylon stockings (with seam down the back of the leg). Black pumps. Glasses. Hair pulled back.

ACT II Scene 2 (Saturday Evening)
Burgundy dress with brown trim. Dark nylon stockings (with seam down the back of the leg). Black pumps. Glasses. Hair pulled back.

HANS
(FULL PRODUCTION)
ACT I & ACT II Scene 1 (Friday Evening)
German World War II uniform consisting of gray jacket with high collar and gray pants. The uniform is stripped of all ranking and Nazi insignia, but has the letters "PW" or "POW" painted on back of the jacket. Black socks and black shoes with laces. Round cap. Short hair.

Production Notes

Costume Illustration

(Costume Illustrations reflect ACT I and ACT II, Scene 1 Costuming.)

MASON

LAVONNE

NOREEN

ALICE

Production Notes

Costume Illustration

(© 2006 Joan Garner) **Americana Play Information and Suggestions**

Production Notes

Costume Illustration

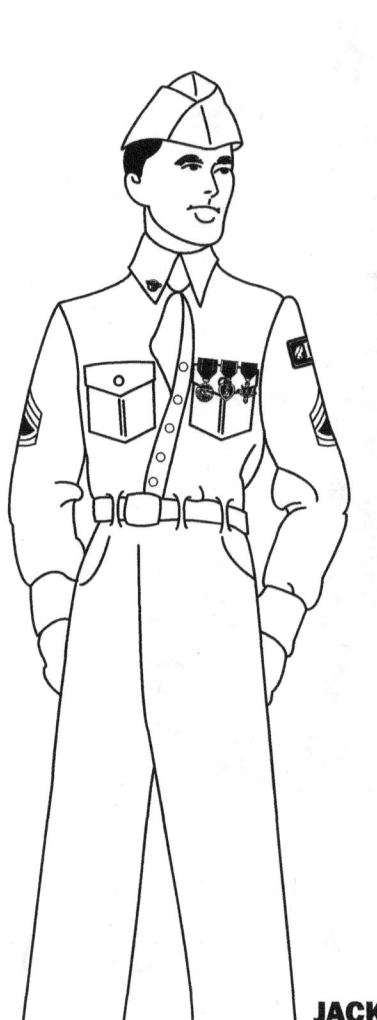

JACK

ELLA

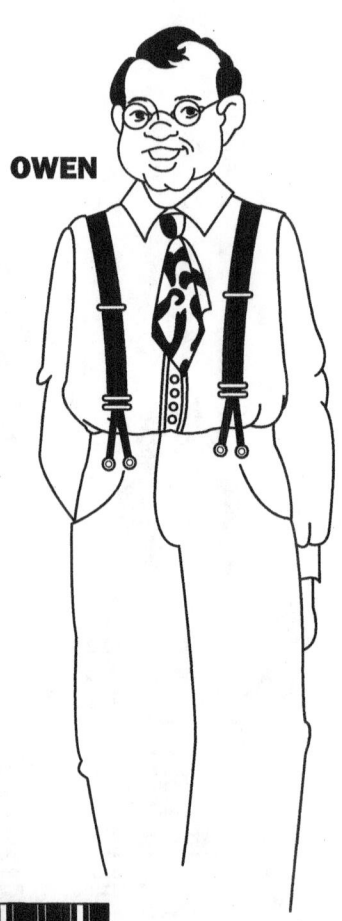

OWEN

EUROPEAN, AFRICAN, and MIDDLE EASTERN CAMPAIGN Medal

JACK'S UNIFORM INSIGNIA

SERGEANT FIRST CLASS Army Ranking

II Corps Insignia

RUPTURED DUCK Honorable Service Lapel Button

DISTINGUISHED SERVICE CROSS Medal

PURPLE HEART Medal

Production Notes

Set Design Narrative

(FULL PRODUCTION)
SET ELEMENTS:
- Back WALL: Painted sky blue.
- HOUSE: Bungalow style of the 1930's. Brick or wood siding. Appearance of continuing second story of house optional.
- FRONT DOOR: Wood. Probably with paned glass window inserted.
- SCREENED DOOR: Wood decorative frame around edges and through the center. Screen inserted between.
- LIVING ROOM WINDOW and KITCHEN WINDOW. Paned style windows that can be raised. CURTAINS inside pulled back on either side of bold if not gaudy floral pattern. Roll-up BLIND in KITCHEN WINDOW. A BANNER (red with white rectangle inside and blue star on the white rectangle) adorned with gold rod, fringe and cording.
- PORCH: In front of HOUSE. Stretching all the way across the HOUSE. Wood slatted floor. Wood decorative posts and railing. Wood slatted steps (three to five). Wood latticework along bottom of PORCH. Tile or asphalt shingled roof.
- FLOWER BEDS: Brick border with dirt inside. No flowers.
- STONE PATHWAY: Fake stone plywood paneling or painted on floor.
- LAWN: Outdoor carpeting or Astroturf.
- ORCHARD: Branches and bushes—artificial or real.
- SIDEWALK: Painted on floor.
- GARAGE: Wood siding. Wood, one-piece GARAGE DOOR. Wood SIDE DOOR. Small WINDOW on side. Tile or asphalt shingles. Garage lamp fixture with electric wire stretching to HOUSE optional.

SET FURNITURE:
- PORCH CHAIRS—Metal "Tulip" style. Any color. Cloth cushions.

SET ACCESSORIES:
- MILK BOX: Square wooden box with hinged lid. Dairy company logo painted on front of box.
- MAIL BOX: Black metal box with flip top and curled strips on the bottom to hold the newspaper.
- U.S. FLAG—48 stars.
- BIRDBATH—Cement or plaster.

(GOOD REPRESENTATION)
SET ELEMENTS:
- HOUSE: Minimal facade at stage right.
- AWNING: Small over FRONT DOOR.
- No ORCHARD (just referred to beyond stage right).

Production Notes

Set Design Narrative
- No GARAGE (just referred to beyond stage right).
- LAWN, PATH, and SIDEWALK painted on floor.

(MINIMAL REPRESENTATION)
SET ELEMENTS:
- Open space representing the entire front lawn. Exit stage right for going into the HOUSE, GARAGE, or ORCHARD. Exit stage left when coming or leaving the DUNN home.

Lighting and Sound Requirements

LIGHTING:
- Normal Lighting DAY.
- Dimmed Lighting EVENING/NIGHT.

SOUND:
- Telephone (Live connection would work best).

Prop List (In keeping with the play's title, there are a few **PROPS** that will enhance the "Americana" environment. These items are obtainable, but could be difficult to find or expensive to purchase. Although alternatives are provided, it's recommended that procurement of at least one or two of these "vintage" items be pursued aggressively. A ★ symbol identifies these vintage items.)

- BICYCLE—(**MASON'S** BICYCLE) can be a little banged up. The style of the era is a large seat, big fenders and balloon tires with wide whitewalls. A few vintage bicycles of the style are: 1940-1941 Elgin; 1940 Firestone; 1940 Western Flyer. Pictures of these and other bicycles of the era can be found on the internet. Rental of these retro bikes is also available at some sites. ALTERNATIVES: Because this is not a rich family, a bare-frame bicycle stripped of ornamentation and painted all one color would do. NOTE: Although finding a vintage bicycle is possible, **MASON'S** age and size makes it difficult to find something to fit him. A girl's bike might suffice (**PENNY'S** hand-me-down?). Training wheels? To accomplish the illusion of a 1940's bicycle apply the following: 1. The appearance of the bike being repainted. 2. The bike should have only metal and rubber pieces. A foot propelled scooter could substitute for the bike.
- FLYPAPER STRIPS—Yellow wax paper strips. (Still found at Hay'n Feed Stores).
- FOLDING CARD TABLES and CHAIRS—Wooden with square and flat backs and seats. Or metal chairs with thin, flat, and square backs and seats. Not rounded or molded to body.
- BOX of FABRIC SCRAPS—Cardboard box with no print on it unless it's an era appropriate label. FABRIC SCRAPS.
- RED MATERIAL—Piece of red material long enough to stretch across the PORCH opening.

Production Notes

Prop List

- GARDENING PARAPHERNALIA—Hand trowel, clippers, shears, etc. Metal and wood. No plastic or rubber on them.
- WAGON—Radio Flyer Wagon. Dented and rusty or painted all one color. No plastic on it.
- DUFFEL BAG—Tan or white canvas tubular bag of World War II issue.
- CLOTH LETTERING—White felt letters making up "SWEET 16". Large enough to be seen from the audience.
- DRINKING GLASSES—Large glass tumblers. Clear glass. Not colored or plastic.
- PLATES—Stoneware, not china. Not fancy. Plain or old fashioned floral pattern.
- SILVERWARE—Traditional or classical design. Not fancy.
- NEEDLE and THREAD.
- SCISSORS—Metal with painted black handle.
- PAPER SACKS—Plain, brown (no print on sacks).
- METAL POT and KNIFE.
- PLANTS in TIN PANS.
- STEEL WOOL—Roll.
- STEPLADDER—Tall wooden ladder.
- HAMMER—Iron head with wooden handle.
- NAILS.
- GLASS BOWL—Round, clear or smoked glass for potato salad. Do not wrap with plastic wrap or aluminum foil.
- TABLECLOTHS—Red or blue gingham.
- JEWELRY BOX and ENGAGEMENT RING—Small velvet covered, hinged box. Small ring.
- PLATTER—For fried chicken. Not plastic.
- MEAT CLEAVER—Very large. Metal with wooden handle.
- TELEPHONE—Two piece, black rotary dial, straight cloth cord.
- ROPE—Approximately ¼ inch thick. Not nylon.
- WALLET—Leather and worn for **OWEN**.
- PIECE OF PAPER—With numbers written on it. Also worn.
- STRIPED MATERIAL—Piece of cloth for **OWEN**.
- TELEGRAM—Printing on yellow paper.
- CLOTHESPIN DOLL—Wooden, one-piece decorated to look like a bride.
- SMALL BOWLS—Glassware for ice cream.
- SECOND PIECE OF PAPER—With **ALICE'S** address on it.
- FIRST PRIZE RIBBON—Blue.
- ROSE—Red, long stemmed.

FOOD ITEMS
- SALTINE CRACKERS
- ICE
- WATER
- POTATOES
- POTATO SALAD
- FRUIT PUNCH
- FRIED CHICKEN
- CORN
- LOAFS OF BREAD
- ICE CREAM

Production Notes

Set Design Floor Plan

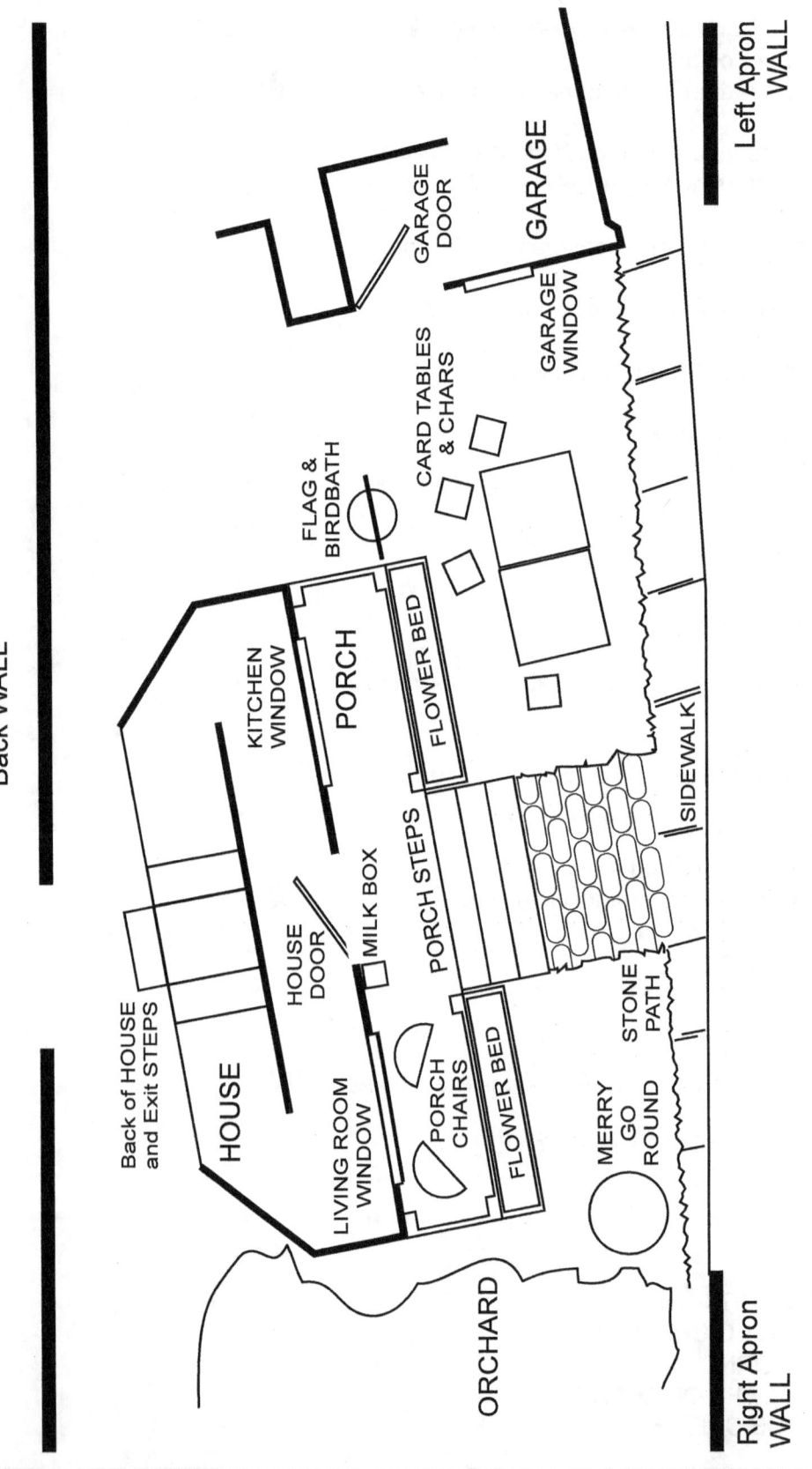

Americana
a Drama
by Joan Garner

CAST OF CHARACTERS *(in order of appearance)*

MASON DUNN—LaVonne's son—Five years old
LAVONNE DUNN—Matriarch of the Dunn family—Late thirties to early forties
GLORIA d'BUSEY—LaVonne's neighbor—Early thirties
JACK COLLINS—War veteran recently returned statewide—Mid to late thirties
ALICE JENNINGS—LaVonne's neighbor—Late thirties to early forties
NOREEN DUNN—LaVonne's sister in-law—Early twenties
OWEN BARTON—LaVonne's neighbor—Sixties
PENNY DUNN—LaVonne's daughter—Sixteen years old
TED EMERY—Penny's boyfriend—Seventeen years old
ELLA BARTON—Owen's wife—Sixties
HANS WELLER—A young German man—Early twenties

ACT I

SET

The FRONT YARD, HOUSE, and GARAGE of the DUNN home. To the right is the beginning of an APRICOT ORCHARD with a winter's overgrowth. To the left is the side of the GARAGE that extends offstage. There is a short DRIVEWAY before reaching the SIDEWALK which runs across downstage, left to right. The FRONT YARD is nearly all grass. The long PORCH extends across the front of the two story HOUSE. The GARAGE is independent of the HOUSE. Nothing is in bloom or planted in the small FLOWER BEDS before the PORCH. The PORCH breaks in the center where three steps come down to meet a STONE PATH. The STONE PATH stretches to the SIDEWALK. Up from the steps—to the back of the PORCH—is the FRONT DOOR with SCREEN DOOR attached. Symmetrically on either side of the FRONT DOOR are two good-sized WINDOWS—the LIVING ROOM WINDOW at right and the KITCHEN WINDOW at left. The WINDOW DRAPES are of a bold, colorful, teetering on gaudy floral pattern. Two metal PATIO CHAIRS rest on the PORCH at right. In the LIVING ROOM WINDOW hangs a red BANNER trimmed around the edge with gold fringe. A smaller white patch sets in the middle of the red field, and a blue star sets in the middle of the white field. The BANNER indicates one member of the family is in the service. The KITCHEN WINDOW has a roll up BLIND pulled halfway down. FLYPAPER STRIPS hang in the corner of the eaves of the PORCH and a MILK BOX stands to the right of the FRONT DOOR with a MAIL BOX above it. The side of the GARAGE has a DOOR across from the PORCH and a small WINDOW insets down from the GARAGE DOOR. A caking of dust and weather is in the corners of the glass panes. The HOUSE is kept in better shape. This is a clean family, but they're not finicky about it. Out from the left side of the PORCH is a BIRDBATH. A U.S. FLAG hangs above the BIRDBATH. To the right, down from the PORCH and next to the ORCHARD is a child's wooden MERRY-GO-ROUND constructed of a round platform attached to a base or rod sticking up in the center. A Card table sits on the FRONT YARD to the left. FOLDING CHAIRS sit around the TABLE.

AT RISE

The front yard of the DUNN HOUSE. All is peaceful and beautiful on this early spring afternoon during the latter part of March, 1944. It's a Friday. The FRONT DOOR is open with the SCREEN DOOR closed.

> *(Enter **MASON DUNN** bicycling in from the left and stopping at the other side of the FRONT YARD near his MERRY-GO-ROUND. [Like most five-year-old boys, **MASON** is excitable, impatient, and embarrassingly honest and blunt, but a good boy.] He drops his BICYCLE, hops up onto the PORCH, and yells into the HOUSE.)*

MASON: Mamma? Mamma, you was gonna help me with my bike! Mamma!

> *(Enter **LAVONNE DUNN** from the SCREEN DOOR toting a tattered BOX OF FABRIC SCRAPES under her arm. [**LAVONNE** is in her late thirties to early forties—living slightly below her station in life; friendly, sincere, and primed for companionship and conversation.])*

LAVONNE: I hear you, son. The whole neighborhood hears you, and should you continue to holler like that, people will think I'm raising a half-wit.

> *(**LAVONNE** places the BOX on the PORCH and she and **MASON** sit on the STEPS on either side of it as they rummage through the SCRAPS OF FABRIC while she corrects the boy.)*

LAVONNE: *(Continued.)* Besides, it's not "you was gonna." Goodness, how easily influenced you are by the other boys. A better way is to say, "Mamma, I thought you were going to help me with my bicycle."

MASON: *(Repeating.)* "Mamma, I thought you were going to help me with my bicycle."

LAVONNE: Yes, my love, I am. But right now I'm fixing Penny's birthday supper. You must learn to be patient.

MASON: But the parade's tomorrow.

LAVONNE: The parade doesn't start until three o'clock in the afternoon. That gives us the entire morning to decorate your bicycle. I promise we'll make it magnificent.

MASON: *(Disappointed, but—)* Okay. *(He pulls out a large piece of RED MATERIAL from the BOX.)* I want to use this.

LAVONNE: We're going to put letters on that for Penny's banner.

(A despondent MASON tosses the RED MATERIAL back into the BOX and turns outward from the PORCH putting his elbows on his knees and face in hands. LAVONNE observes her dispirited son, shoves the BOX behind her, and slides up close to him—placing a motherly arm around his shoulders.)

LAVONNE: Now Mason, this is Penny's big day. A young lady turns sweet sixteen only once in her life, so we should make a special point of it. First thing in the morning we'll take the banner down and cut up the fabric to decorate your bike. You wait and see. It will be the grandest victory bike in the parade. But today we have to be happy for Penny. Can you do that for your sister?

MASON: *(Looking up with excitement once again.)* Uh, huh.

LAVONNE: *(Hugging him tightly.)* That's my man... Do you think you can do another favor for Mamma? Mr. Barton said he would bring over his table and set it up, but it's getting late and I haven't seen Mr. Barton or his table. Would you go over and see what's keeping him?

MASON: *(Jumping down and heading for his BICYCLE.)* Sure. You ain't gonna start the ice cream without me?

LAVONNE: No, I'm not going to start the ice cream without you, but I may if you persist in using the word "ain't." And "gonna" is just as bad.

MASON: Tommy and Steven say "gonna."

(LAVONNE tucks the BOX OF FABRIC SCRAPS under an arm, stands, and crosses to the CARD TABLE while speaking.)

LAVONNE: Tommy and Steven are lazy little boys. Children unwilling to better themselves are resigned to working as clerks and gas station attendants. Now there's nothing wrong being a clerk or attendant if that's what you want to do. But if you're an educated man, Mason, the world is yours. If the time ever comes when you want to leave this town and explore the many wonders beyond Hardin, Utah, you should be literate and that begins with speaking properly. I may not be well educated myself, but I can teach you what I know.

MASON: *(Taking it all in.)* Yes, ma'am. Thank you, Mamma.

LAVONNE: Why, thank *you*, Mason. Hurry along now.

MASON: *(Hopping onto his BICYCLE.)* Okay.

*(**MASON** rides his BICYCLE back out stage left while **LAVONNE** watches after him in reflection.)*

LAVONNE: "Thank you, Mamma." Isn't that something? I'll have to put that in a letter to Guthrie.

*(**GLORIA d'BUSEY** enters from stage left wearing gardening togs and gloves. She's holding a HAND SPADE and pulls a little rusty WAGON behind her. The WAGON carries various GARDENING PARAPHERNALIA. [**GLORIA** is an average if not homely woman in her early thirties—devout and judgmental.])*

GLORIA: How are you making out, Sister Dunn?

LAVONNE: Laws, Gloria, you're not going to work on that garden today? You should be getting ready for the party.

GLORIA: Oh, it won't take me that long to get ready. Those potato sprouts need tending. It turned warm so early this year; I planted a new row under your bedroom window. We'll see if they come up. I have to keep my eye on them or they'll be crawling with bugs.

LAVONNE: *(Spreading the RED MATERIAL out on the CARD TABLE.)* You go get'm, Gloria.

GLORIA: *(Chuckling.)* I will.

*(**GLORIA** exits between the HOUSE and GARAGE. **LAVONNE** steps into the HOUSE. Momentarily, **SERGEANT JACK COLLINS** enters from the ORCHARD. He pauses briefly on the grass to dust off his pant legs and DUFFEL BAG. [**JACK** is an attractive man in his mid to late thirties—generous, and personable.] Rising, he looks over to the HOUSE appreciatively. He then swings the DUFFEL BAG up over a shoulder and steps up to **MASON'S** MERRY-GO-ROUND. He pushes it and smiles watching it turn. **LAVONNE** comes out of the SCREEN DOOR putting a handful of CLOTH LETTERS in order. She glances up and immediately notices **JACK**.)*

LAVONNE: Oh, my word. Hello.

JACK: *(Turning to **LAVONNE** while removing his cap.)* Good afternoon.

LAVONNE: Did you just come out of that orchard, Sergeant?

JACK: Yes, ma'am. I didn't realize it was such a long stretch or I would have gone around.

LAVONNE: That poor orchard's been overgrown since Guthrie left. And it's coming out of winter which doesn't help.

JACK: I shouldn't have trespassed, but when the driver dropped me off, he said Hardin was this way and pointed across the orchard.

LAVONNE: Well, he was right. You're in Hardin now, or the outskirts of Hardin. Our block is the farthest west of town. Hardin proper is down four blocks and up one.

JACK: Thank you.

LAVONNE: Are you visiting family here, Sergeant? Maybe I can steer you their way.

JACK: No ma'am. I'm just passing through.

LAVONNE: I see. Where are you headed?

JACK: *(Looking around, he smiles a bit embarrassed.)* Oh, nowhere in particular. Everywhere. I'm not sure.

LAVONNE: Just mustered out?

JACK: *(Holding the RUPTURED DUCK PIN on his shirt collar.)* Last week in New York.

*(**LAVONNE** steps down to the CARD TABLE with her CLOTH LETTERS.)*

LAVONNE: How did you get clear out here in the desert so fast?

*(**JACK** leaves his DUFFEL BAG by the MERRY-GO-ROUND and crosses to **LAVONNE**.)*

JACK: I traveled day and night on train straight to Elko. I thought I'd make my way back to the east coast a little slower this time.

LAVONNE: have family in Elko?

JACK: I thought I did. I found out I haven't much of anything in Elko anymore.

LAVONNE: Sorry to hear that. This war has changed lives all over the world.

JACK: Yes, ma'am.

LAVONNE: Well, sit yourself down here and rest awhile. Anyone cutting through our apricot orchard can use a little breather.

JACK: *(Backing up a little.)* Thank you, ma'am, but you don't know me and—

LAVONNE: —Well, we can fix that. What's your name?

JACK: Sergeant— *(He catches himself and smiles once again embarrassed.)* Jack Collins.

   *(**LAVONNE** steps over to him with an outstretched hand.)*

LAVONNE: Jack, I'm LaVonne Dunn.

   *(**LAVONNE** and **JACK** shake hands.)*

JACK: Miss Dunn.

LAVONNE: See how simple that was? Now we know each other. And it's *Mrs.* Dunn. Laws, it better be Mrs. Dunn. I have two children. But please call me LaVonne. Say now, we have two cartons of Coca-Cola for my daughter's birthday party. Would you like a Coca-Cola, Jack?

JACK: Oh, no, ma'am. You save that for your daughter's party. I would appreciate a glass of water if it's not too much bother—and....

LAVONNE: And what?

JACK: This is going to sound a little odd, but would you happen to have any ice? I can't get enough ice since I've been back.

LAVONNE: You servicemen miss the little things when you're over in those strange countries, don't you? Were you stationed in a jungle or somewhere where you didn't have any ice?

JACK: North Africa mostly.

LAVONNE: Oh, my word. No wonder you're craving ice. I'll get you a great big glass of ice. We have plenty. We're going to make ice cream tonight.

   *(**LAVONNE** steps back up onto the PORCH.)*

LAVONNE: *(Continued.)* You sit there and be comfortable, and I'll be right back.

*(JACK remains standing until **LAVONNE** exits into the HOUSE. He then sits down putting his hat back on. **MASON** flies in on his BICYCLE and skids out when he see **JACK**.)*

MASON: Hi.

JACK: Hi.

*(**MASON** drops his BICYCLE on the SIDEWALK to the right and rushes over to **JACK**.)*

MASON: Hey, you're a Sergeant.

JACK: Hey, I know.

MASON: *(Inspecting the insignia on **JACK'S** sleeve and speaks in awe.)* Second Corps—and look!

*(**JACK** kneels down to **MASON** who fondles **JACK'S** MEDALS.)*

JACK: Nifty, huh?

*(**MASON** holds out the EUROPEAN, AFRICAN, and MIDDLE EASTERN CAMPAIGN MEDAL.)*

MASON: What's this one?

JACK: That one is for being over in Africa.

*(**MASON** holds out the PURPLE HEART with two Oak-Leaf Clusters. He looks to **JACK** for identification.)*

MASON: This one?

JACK: That's for getting shot. How about that? They give you medals for getting shot up.

MASON: Yeah.

*(**MASON** holds out the last MEDAL—the DISTINGUISHED SERVICE CROSS.)*

MASON: *(Continued.)* What's this one for?

JACK: Oh, that's for just doing what I was supposed to do.

MASON: It's the best one.

(**LAVONNE** *comes back out the SCREEN DOOR with a LARGE GLASS OF ICE WATER and a PLATE OF SALTINE CRACKERS. Excitedly,* **MASON** *rushes to his mother as* **JACK** *stands again.*)

MASON: *(Continued.)* Mamma, look!

LAVONNE: I know, dear.

(**MASON** *pulls* **LAVONNE** *towards* **JACK**.)

LAVONNE: *(Continued.)* Oh, Mason, be careful.

(**LAVONNE** *sits the PLATE OF CRACKERS on the CARD TABLE and hands* **JACK** *the GLASS OF ICE WATER.*)

LAVONNE: Jack, this is my live wire son, Mason... Mason, this is Sergeant Jack Collins.

JACK: *(Shaking* **MASON'S** *hand.)* How do you do, Mason.

MASON: *(So excited he could bust.)* You're a hero, Jack.

LAVONNE: Mason, it's Sergeant Collins to you.

(**JACK** *puts* **MASON** *on his lap as he sits.*)

JACK: He can call me Jack if he likes. And I'm not a sergeant anymore. I guess I should get me some civvies to wear.

LAVONNE: Oh, there's plenty of time for that... Here. I thought you might be hungry. I suspect a strapping man like you is hungry even after eating. Guthrie is the same way.

(**LAVONNE** *holds the PLATE OF CRACKERS out for* **JACK**.)

JACK: *(Taking a couple of CRACKERS.)* Thank you, ma'am.

(*When* **MASON** *reaches for the CRACKERS* **LAVONNE** *pulls the PLATE back.*)

LAVONNE: Mason, they're not for you.

JACK: Growing boys are always hungry, too. Aren't they, Mason?

MASON: Uh, huh.

LAVONNE: *(Holding the PLATE back for* **MASON**.*)* All right, but just one, young man. We have a big supper coming up.

MASON: *(Mimicking JACK as he takes a CRACKER.)* Thank you, ma'am. *(Eating.)* Are you coming to the party, Jack?

JACK: No. I have to be moving on.

LAVONNE: Well now, Jack, Mason has a good idea there. Why don't you stay for supper? My Penny's celebrating her sixteenth birthday. We're only having a few neighbors and Ted.

MASON: Teddy's sweet on Penny.

LAVONNE: Thank you for clearing that up for the Sergeant, son. *(To JACK.)* There will be more than enough for everyone, and I'm sure Penny would love having you with us.

MASON: We're having fried chicken and ice cream.

JACK: Boy, that's really tempting, but I couldn't impose.

LAVONNE: It's not imposing, it's... Well, I think Guthrie would like us including a fellow serviceman since he can't be here himself.

JACK: Thank you. I'd like that as long as I pay.

LAVONNE: I wouldn't hear of it. With what you've been through, you deserve a good home cooked meal. We don't get many GI's passing through a little speck on the map like Hardin, but the church elders see that the ones who venture in don't leave hungry. We'll just catch you before they do.

(MASON slides off JACK'S lap to stand next to LAVONNE.)

MASON: Mamma, Jack's been shot up.

LAVONNE: Mason! *(To JACK.)* I'm sorry, Sergeant. The boy's only five and short on manners when excited. I'm afraid having you around has wound him up more than his usual spirited self.

JACK: It's all right. It's encouraging to see a healthy, happy kid again. The children overseas are the saddest looking urchins.

(LAVONNE will begin to pin the CLOTH LETTERS to the RED MATERIAL during the next sequence.)

LAVONNE: We see how it is over there in the newsreels. Those poor families. It's appalling. Thank the Lord the war isn't here.

JACK: Yes, ma'am.

LAVONNE: Oh, Mason, what did Mr. Barton say about that extra table?

MASON: He wasn't there. He's down at the Post Office. Mrs. Barton said she'd send him scoot'n right over as soon as he got back.

LAVONNE: *(To JACK.)* Owen Barton is our retired Postmaster, except they neglected to tell the Post Office of this fact. They're forever calling him down there for one thing or another.

   (LAVONNE has been moving things on the CARD TABLE, but can't find what she's looking for.)

LAVONNE: *(Continued.)* Laws, I know I gathered the scissors with the rest of this.

JACK: Is there anything I can help with?

LAVONNE: You wouldn't happen to know how to sew, would you?

JACK: Yes, ma'am. Well, I can sew on buttons and darn my socks—that kind of sewing.

LAVONNE: That's right. I forgot about that. In boot camp they teach you how to sew and shoot a gun, don't they? I was flabbergasted when Guthrie wrote to say he sewed on his own stripes after basic training. I never thought I would see the day when Guthrie Dunn would pick up a needle and do a woman's sewing.

   (By this time LAVONNE has pinned the letters on the RED MATERIAL to read "Sweet 16." She threads a NEEDLE.)

LAVONNE: *(Continued.)* We need to tack these letters on to make a banner and then we're going to string it up over the porch. Noreen said she would try to get home early to help, but things are beginning to pile up. Do you think you could tack them on? A couple of stitches at the corner of each letter should do.

   (LAVONNE hands JACK the NEEDLE.)

JACK: I can try.

LAVONNE: Like I said, it doesn't have to be fancy. Mason, you come inside and help Mamma find the scissors.

   (MASON hops up in the PORCH followed by LAVONNE.)

LAVONNE: *(Continued.)* Would you like another glass of water, Jack?

JACK: No, this is fine. Thank you.

LAVONNE: I'll only be a minute.

(LAVONNE helps MASON into the HOUSE. Though a little awkward at it, JACK begins stitching a LETTER onto the BANNER. Briefly, ALICE JENNINGS enters from stage left with two SACKS OF GROCERIES in her arms. [ALICE is around the same age as LAVONNE—reserved, mysterious, and tempered.])

ALICE: Good evening.

JACK: *(Immediately standing.)* Hello. *(He looks at the NEEDLE in his hand.)* Uh, this is for Penny's birthday.

ALICE: It's pretty. I brought over a few things for LaVonne. Is she home?

JACK: Yes, she's... *(He realizes his hat is still on and drops the NEEDLE to remove it.)* I'm Jack Collins.

ALICE: *(Sitting a SACK on the CARD TABLE.)* Alice Jennings.

(LAVONNE comes out the SCREEN DOOR with a PAIR OF SCISSORS.)

LAVONNE: Alice, have you met the handsome Sergeant here?

ALICE: Yes, I have.

LAVONNE: He's staying for Penny's party. Isn't that nice?

(ALICE smiles and moves the SACK OF GROCERIES towards LAVONNE.)

ALICE: Here are the extra potatoes you asked for, Von. And there's a sack of sugar in there, too. I know you're using up this month's ration with the cakes you're making for the potluck tomorrow.

LAVONNE: Oh, hon, I couldn't take your sugar.

ALICE: Please take it. I don't use that much—just for my mush in the morning mostly.

(LAVONNE hugs ALICE.)

LAVONNE: Bless you... Come sit down and we'll have a little chat while we're sewing this.

ALICE: I'd like to, but I have a couple of things to do first. I have to take this sack of groceries over to Mrs. Thurmon, but I'll be back shortly to peel the potatoes.

LAVONNE: Okay, dear. You hurry back and we'll start the party early.

ALICE: Sergeant.

JACK: Mrs. Jennings.

(ALICE exits out stage left. LAVONNE notices JACK watching ALICE leave.)

LAVONNE: Attractive, isn't she?

JACK: Very.

(The two sit and resume sewing on the BANNER while they talk.)

LAVONNE: Mrs. Thurmon is a shut-in. She's very old. She lives three houses down— *(Pointing out stage left.)* —next to Alice. Alice buys Mrs. Thurmon's groceries. We asked Mrs. Thurmon to Penny's party, but she said no. She shakes now and doesn't like to have other people watch her eat. So I told the little lady we would bring over a plate of cake and ice cream later and this pleased her. Mrs. Thurmon said she would sit in her rocker and watch the festivities from her big bay window... Alice will be here.

JACK: Is Alice's husband in the service?

LAVONNE: Oh, no... You're interested in Alice, aren't you, Jack? I can tell by the little sparkle in your eye.

(JACK bows his head with a smile almost blushing.)

LAVONNE: *(Continued.)* Well, I'll tell you what I know about Alice which isn't much. I'll tell you what I know and let you draw your own conclusions. Ordinarily I'm not one to spread gossip or rumor, but it may be best coming from me and not others in this town. People in Hardin look down on Alice. This is a small, clutchy town and Alice is mostly a stranger who keeps to herself. And she's not Mormon. As you're probably well aware, this is Mormon country. Are you a Latter Day Saint, Jack? I know we have a goodly group of followers in Nevada.

JACK: No, ma'am. I was baptized Presbyterian.

LAVONNE: I'm a converted Mormon myself. You see, Guthrie is a Latter Day Saint, so I became a Latter Day Saint. To tell you the truth, there's a lot about the religion I don't understand—me being born a Portland

Protestant. But I guess that can be said about any religion. They do have some unusual ways and traditions, but let me say this—a more organized group of people you'll never find. If you're in crisis, this is the bunch to be with. In no time at all they have assessed the situation, figured out what must be done, and do it. And they're a good hearted people. I'm not a devout Mormon, but I send the children to the church functions, and we go to Sacrament every Sunday, so the more avid and faithful do their best to put up with me.

JACK: About the only thing I know about Mormons is they have more than one wife.

LAVONNE: *(Laughing.)* Yes. Laws, I'm afraid we'll never live that one down... It was a necessary decision at the time, but I don't imagine the rest of the world will ever accept that part of our past. But getting back to Alice... The bishop and a couple of elders invited her to attend church. Even if you're not of the faith, you can come to know the entire town by attending church. It was an innocent enough gesture but from what I'm told, Alice was a little sharp with them. I'm not certain if Alice believes in God—at least it hasn't entered the conversation. And then she's a divorced woman so there are rumors all over the place about what happened there. Alice hasn't confided in me, and what's her business is her business. To me, she's just a pleasant and caring person.

JACK: That's a shame about rumors. They're only made up to hurt people.

LAVONNE: Alice is so quiet and unassuming; I don't understand why anyone would start gossip like that.

*(**LAVONNE** stops and studies **JACK** for a moment.)*

LAVONNE: May I ask you a very personal question? I know we only just met, but it's going to be asked, so I'd like to have the right answer. You don't have to go into any detail....

JACK: What is it?

LAVONNE: Your medals and you being mustered out. I know you boys usually don't like to talk about what you've been through, but can you say something I can tell the others?

JACK: There isn't much to tell. I was in Africa when I broke my leg. It took awhile to recuperate from that. Then I was hurt in Sicily the first day we landed. I've spent the rest of my time restricted to a military hospital in London.

LAVONNE: How dreadful.

JACK: At least I'm able to come home.

LAVONNE: That's the only thing I want—Guthrie back here in one piece.

JACK: Where is your husband?

LAVONNE: Somewhere in the South Pacific. Whenever I get his letters there's this big stamp over the back that says "Somewhere in the South Pacific."

*(**GLORIA** wheels her WAGON in from between the HOUSE and GARAGE.)*

GLORIA: Sister Dunn, I'm going to leave these cherry tomatoes on the porch here and plant them in this flower bed tomorrow.

*(**LAVONNE** stands and crosses to **GLORIA** who is busy placing the PANS OF PLANTS on the edge of the PORCH.)*

LAVONNE: I was going to plant a few pansies there, Gloria. I'm hoping to get a little color back in the yard this spring. Roy Fuller has promised me some starts. Mercy, Gloria, you have my entire backyard for a vegetable garden, can't I have the porch?

GLORIA: Well, I have the plants right here and I don't know where else to put them. They should be in a protected spot and we can't let them root in the pans.

LAVONNE: *(Drolly.)* Heaven forbid that should ever happen... I'll make you a deal. If I can't find a place to put the tomatoes by Monday, I'll plant them here myself—damn the pansies.

GLORIA: I didn't mean for you to get upset over this, Sister Dunn. But this is important.

LAVONNE: Yes, Gloria. Lord knows how lucky we are having you help us like this. The children are especially grateful for the fruit and vegetables you have harvested in the backyard these past years. But I haven't had flowers by the porch since Guthrie left. I thought that if I put a flower garden in this year that maybe—well, it's a ridiculous idea, but....

GLORIA: I understand, Sister Dunn. If I thought it would bring back Bill, I'd plant my whole yard in pansies. I'll be busy until after church Sunday. If I can leave these here until then, we'll find another place to plant them.

LAVONNE: Thank you, Gloria.

GLORIA: I'll be getting myself home now and ready for the party.

LAVONNE: Come over whenever you're ready... Oh, Gloria, this is Jack Collins. He'll be here. Jack, this is my good friend Gloria d'Busey.

GLORIA: Mr. Collins.

JACK: *(Standing.)* Mrs. d'Busey.

GLORIA: Well, if you're staying we can talk at the party, but I must be off now.

JACK: Yes, ma'am. I'll be looking forward to it.

(**GLORIA** *exits back out between the HOUSE and GARAGE pulling her WAGON behind her.*)

JACK: *(Continued.)* Is Gloria your sister or Guthrie's?

LAVONNE: My sister? Oh, she called me Sister Dunn, didn't she? It's a Mormon thing. We call everyone Sister or Brother. It's like declaring we're all in this together or something like that. It's a nice thought, but personally I find it confusing. Noreen and I are both called Sister Dunn. When we're standing together and someone says, "Sister Dunn?" Who do they want?

JACK: *(Amused.)* I see what you mean.

LAVONNE: Gloria is very Mormon. She's one of them that puts up with me and my Coca-Cola. Mormons aren't supposed to drink soda pop... She lost her husband early in the war.

JACK: I'm sorry to hear that.

LAVONNE: At least she can get on with her life; she's not sitting here in limbo wondering and not knowing. Lloyd Fielding is courting her. He's a sensitive man and a nice distraction for her. There was a time when all Gloria had to fix on was these victory gardens. Needless to say, she went at it with a vengeance. Gloria loves to get the potato bugs. She puts a spoonful of gasoline in the bottom of a can, pulls the little buggers off the plant and dumps them into the gas. Then she watches as they squirm around and eventually kick off. It brings her great delight... This makes me think there's a bit of a dark side to Gloria.

(**MASON** *comes out of the SCREEN DOOR and crosses to his BICYCLE.*)

MASON: Momma, do you think I could start making my bike up—just me?

LAVONNE: Well, I tell you, son, we're not going to touch that bicycle until you wash off all the dust and mud.

MASON: Ah, Maaaaa....

LAVONNE: "Ah, Ma" nothing. The best thing you can do is take it out back and put some water on it. You can't expect to win a prize with a dirty bicycle no matter how pretty it's decorated.

MASON: But I can never get the pedals and spokes clean.

JACK: Do you have any steel wool?

LAVONNE: Gosh, I don't know. Guthrie might have a roll in the garage. When he left we closed the doors with the Plymouth inside. It's hard getting gasoline for the car and Noreen is the only one who really needs to get around. But she takes the bus to the Base and has Walker to take her to their social events. Noreen cleans the garage out every summer, but at the moment I couldn't tell you what shape its in.

   (**JACK** stands and crosses to the GARAGE DOOR.)

JACK: I'll take a look. Steel wool is the army's answer for cleaning anything and everything. It should take care of those spokes. That is if you don't mind, LaVonne. I'm not much of one with a needle.

LAVONNE: Go ahead. I suspect you'd rather be puttering with a bike anyway.

JACK: Thanks. Mason, you go hose off your bike and I'll be there in a minute.

MASON: Yes, sir.

   (**MASON** happily moves his BICYCLE around to the back of the HOUSE while **JACK** slips into the GARAGE. Enter **NOREEN DUNN** from stage left. She carries her high heels while wearing slippers. [**NOREEN** is a beautiful young woman in her early twenties—feminine, sincere, mildly possessed of sophistication.])

NOREEN: Sorry I'm late, Von. Ten blueprints came back at the last minute and I wanted to file them away before I left.

LAVONNE: It wasn't a problem, Noreen. I've had some help.

NOREEN: *(Sitting at the CARD TABLE.)* Did Alice drop by?

LAVONNE: No, she's busy doing things for Mrs. Thurmon.

   (**JACK** comes out of the GARAGE and continues to exit behind the HOUSE. He's fiddling with some STEEL WOOL and doesn't notice the women noticing him.)

NOREEN: *(Changing back into her high heels.)* Who's that?

LAVONNE: That's who dropped by. His name is Jack Collins and he's making his way from Elko back to the east coast. He fought in Europe and Africa and has three medals on his chest. He's also hurt. I think it's pretty bad. They discharged him.

*(**NOREEN** begins to help tack the CLOTH LETTERS onto the RED MATERIAL.)*

NOREEN: How long has he been here?

LAVONNE: Just a little while.

NOREEN: You found all that out about him in a little while? You're a wonder, LaVonne—an absolute wonder. I suppose he knows all there is to know about our family, too.

LAVONNE: Nooo, but he's staying for Penny's birthday, so if you want to get your two cents in, you can later... Is Walker coming?

NOREEN: He wanted to start turning the fields today for the spring seeding. If he makes it, it will be late.

LAVONNE: That's too bad. Well, without Walker or Ted's parents, we'll have more than enough for Sergeant Collins.

NOREEN: What's the problem with Ted's parents?

LAVONNE: Oh, they're tied up with the victory parade.

NOREEN: I bet.

LAVONNE: Now, Noreen.

*(**ALICE** enters from stage left.)*

ALICE: Okay, LaVonne, I'm all yours.

LAVONNE: Oh, good. Would you like to help me with the chicken, or stay out here and peel potatoes?

ALICE: I'll stay out here. After being cooped-up in the house all winter, it's nice to be outside.

LAVONNE: I can't blame you there. I'll fetch you a knife and pot....

*(**LAVONNE** exits into the HOUSE.)*

ALICE: That's a beautiful dress you're wearing, Noreen.

NOREEN: Thank you. I wasn't sure I'd have time to change when I got home, so I wore it to work. It may not have been the smartest thing to do.

ALICE: Why?

*(**LAVONNE** is quickly out the SCREEN DOOR taking a POT and KNIFE to **ALICE**. **ALICE** will dig into the SACK OF POTATOES on the CARD TABLE and peel as they talk.)*

LAVONNE: Are you still having problems with those POWs, Noreen?

NOREEN: Uh, huh.

ALICE: What POWs?

NOREEN: *(To **LAVONNE**.)* You mean you haven't told Alice about my POWs? You're slipping, LaVonne.

LAVONNE: *(Playfully tapping **NOREEN** on the shoulder.)* Oh, behave yourself.

NOREEN: They're resurfacing the roads at the Base and trucking in POWs to do the heavy work. Right now they're redoing the parking lot in front of our building. Our office has a big plate glass window and eye level outside is exactly at my leg level inside.

ALICE: Oh, no.

NOREEN: Oh, yes. They whistle and make suggestive gestures when the guards aren't watching. The German boys aren't too bad, but those Italians... Martha and I put boxes under our desks so they can't look up our dresses when we're sitting, but we still have to climb up on the ladders to file the blueprints. This drives them crazy.

LAVONNE: Well, you're a stunning woman, Noreen. You have driven the boys crazy since birth.

NOREEN: I believe that's why Guthrie grew up so big and strong. He was constantly fighting off the boy's advances and protecting his little sister. Whether he developed his muscles because of me or to spite me, I couldn't say.

LAVONNE: If that's how Guthrie got his muscles, I thank you. I fell in love with those muscles the moment I saw him. I thought he was a prizefighter.

NOREEN: It must have been disappointing to discover he was only a milkman.

LAVONNE: Not in the least. It merely made him a muscle-bound milkman.

ALICE: You must like the men in all shapes, LaVonne. That Sergeant isn't as muscular as Guthrie, but he's as good-looking.

LAVONNE: You stop your teasing, Noreen. You know Guthrie is the only man I've ever looked at twice— three times— four times. Laws, I begin to get hot just thinking of Mr. Guthrie Dunn.

(The women laugh.)

ALICE: LaVonne, what has gotten into you tonight?

LAVONNE: What's gotten into *me*? Why don't you ask Noreen about her German boy?

NOREEN: He's not *my* German, LaVonne.

ALICE: What German?

NOREEN: There's one German soldier in the group that acts differently from the others. Sometimes when I look out—well, I have to look out— they're right there. But when I look over and see him, he stands quietly and doffs his cap. His is a chagrin smile, demoralized because he's a prisoner I guess, but pleased I would notice him. The rest of the time he looks so pathetic; like a little lone puppy whimpering in the store window wishing someone would come and take him home. I know he's the enemy, but he must be lonely for his family like anyone else. After all, here he is in the middle of a strange country not knowing what's going to happen to him.

LAVONNE: He's a human being, too, hon. Maybe you remind him of a girl back in Germany. I'm sure that's all it is. I wouldn't let it upset you.

NOREEN: Oh, I'm not upset. I'll just be glad when they're done with the parking lot and move on.

LAVONNE: Well, I best get the chicken on to fry or we won't be having any supper.

*(**LAVONNE** exits into the HOUSE. Shortly, **MASON** rides out from behind the HOUSE on a shiny clean BICYCLE with **JACK** following. **JACK** has his shirtsleeves rolled up and there is a wet rag in his hand.)*

JACK: *(Calling out to MASON.)* Don't go riding into any more mud puddles or your mother will thrash us both!

MASON: *(Offstage.)* I won't!

(JACK steps over to the CARD TABLE.)

JACK: *(To NOREEN.)* I see you got my job.

NOREEN: Would you like it back?

JACK: No thanks. I'm sure you're doing a much better job of it.

ALICE: Noreen, this is Sergeant Jack Collins. Jack, this is LaVonne's sister-in-law, Noreen Dunn.

NOREEN: Sergeant.

JACK: Evening.

NOREEN: LaVonne tells us you were over in Europe fighting.

JACK: Yes. To be honest, I didn't do that much fighting. I spent the better part in hospitals. First in Tripoli and then in London.

NOREEN: War creates many ways of fighting, Sergeant.

JACK: Yes, ma'am.

NOREEN: *(Standing and looking the BANNER over.)* How does this look?

ALICE: It's great. Penny should be pleased.

JACK: Where is the guest of honor? I haven't met the birthday girl yet.

NOREEN: Ted has the assignment of keeping Penny away from the house until six o'clock so we better get this up before she gets home. Sergeant, will you help me?

JACK: Happy to.

NOREEN: I'll go downstairs and get Guthrie's hammer and nails. The ladder is—

JACK: —In the garage. I saw it.

(JACK quickly exits into the GARAGE. NOREEN watches, taken aback at how comfortable JACK moves about the place. She

*(smiles while watching him cross to the GARAGE, and then exits into the HOUSE. When **JACK** comes back out of the GARAGE with the LADDER, he steps to the CARD TABLE and props the LADDER against him while he waits for **NOREEN**.)*

JACK: *(Continued.)* I haven't had the opportunity to tell you how nice you look this evening, Mrs. Jennings.

ALICE: Thank you.

JACK: Would you... This is going to sound like it's coming from a high school sophomore, but it would be an honor to sit next to you during dinner. I promise not to drink or embarrass you in any way.

ALICE: This is Hardin, Utah, Sergeant. You couldn't find a drink in this town to save your soul. As for setting next to me, I'd be surprised if LaVonne hasn't already arranged that.

JACK: This won't be a problem, then?

ALICE: No, Jack, it won't be a problem.

*(**NOREEN** comes back out of the HOUSE with a HAMMER and CAN OF NAILS.)*

NOREEN: We'd like to hook it up over the steps here if you think it's possible.

*(**JACK** crosses to the PORCH STEPS with the LADDER.)*

JACK: Can't see why not.

*(**NOREEN** hands **JACK** the HAMMER and NAILS then crosses to the CARD TABLE to gather the BANNER. She gives **JACK** a corner of the BANNER once he sets the LADDER and climbs a few steps to reach the top of the PORCH. He proceeds to tack up the one end and easily hammers in a second NAIL in the middle of the BANNER. But when it comes to nailing in the other corner, he doesn't move the LADDER. Instead he feels he can reach it by staying where he is. He must stretch to get there, and when he does and begins to pound the NAIL, a tremendous pain catches in his stomach and he doubles over.)*

NOREEN: *(Alarmed.)* Sergeant, are you all right?

JACK: *(Trying to catch his breath.)* Just a minute....

*(**ALICE** crosses to the PORCH concerned.)*

NOREEN: Don't trouble with it anymore. Alice and I can finish putting it up.

(*JACK comes down off the LADDER.*)

JACK: (Trying to play it down.) Well, that's pretty bad when I can't even nail up a little banner.

(*After a BEAT—in anger—he flings the nail he still has in his hand out into the ORCHARD. Embarrassed with this sudden outburst, JACK exits stage left.*)

ALICE: How he must be hurting.

NOREEN: I think more than his injuries are hurting him right now.

ALICE: Maybe I should go after him.

NOREEN: Maybe we should leave him alone.

(*NOREEN moves the LADDER and climbs up to finish hanging the BANNER while ALICE crosses back to the CARD TABLE and continues peeling POTATOES. Enter from stage left OWEN BARTON with a SECOND CARD TABLE under one arm and FOLDING CHAIRS under the other. [OWEN is an elderly gentleman—kind and gentle, living in his own uncomplicated world.]*)

OWEN: Alice, I bet Sister Dunn is ready to tan my hide. I promised to bring these over this morning and here it is almost time for the party.

ALICE: As long as they're here, Mr. Barton.

(*OWEN sets the SECOND CARD TABLE up against the FIRST CARD TABLE.*)

OWEN: I was down at the Post Office today.

(*NOREEN finishes with the BANNER and comes down the LADDER.*)

NOREEN: Sometimes I wonder why you ever retired, Mr. Barton.

OWEN: Oh, it wasn't a big catastrophe—just something they thought I should see. They do it on purpose, you know. I'm called down there all the time. They ask my advice on this and that. I know darn well those people can carry on without me, but I think they do it to make me still feel useful and important. It pleases me that young people would regard me like that.

LAVONNE: *(Looking out the KITCHEN WINDOW.)* Oh, good. I thought I heard you, Owen.

*(**LAVONNE** is quickly out carrying two TABLECLOTHS, DISHES, and EATING UTENSILS. Meanwhile **NOREEN** has moved the LADDER away and leans it up against the side of the GARAGE.)*

NOREEN: How does the banner look, LaVonne?

LAVONNE: *(Looking back.)* It's wonderful, Noreen. Thank you... Where's Sergeant Collins?

NOREEN: Uh, I believe he set out to look for Mason.

OWEN: Who's Sergeant Collins?

LAVONNE: Jack's a veteran passing through town. He must be a war hero if the medals on his chest are any indication. Mason has fallen instantly in love with him.

OWEN: It's nice for a boy to have a young fella to look up to for a spell what with Guthrie not here.

LAVONNE: He looks up to you, too, Owen. You've been like a substitute father to my son and I'm so grateful for that.

OWEN: I've tried, but it's not the same. A boy like Mason will take a man's word as gospel. Advice coming from an old goat like me is nothing.

NOREEN: You're not an old goat, Mr. Barton.

OWEN: Tell that to Ella. I can't keep her as happy as I used to, and that's a definite sign of being old and rundown.

LAVONNE: Why, Owen—you rascal, you.

OWEN: Speaking of keeping Ella happy, I better get back and help her carry over the potato salad. What with the party tonight and the potluck tomorrow, she's made enough for a whole Ward Conference. I've seen nothing but potatoes, pickles, and hard-boiled eggs for two days... We'll be back in a bit.

*(**OWEN** exits stage left.)*

LAVONNE: *(Calling after **OWEN**.)* Thank you, Owen. Be sure to bring your appetite.

NOREEN: How old is Owen now, LaVonne?

LAVONNE: Well, let's see... He must be close to sixty-eight. Imagine him talking about trying to keep Ella happy.

*(The three chuckle at the thought as **JACK** reenters from stage left.)*

LAVONNE: Jack, did you find Mason?

JACK: Find Mason? I saw him up by the creek.

LAVONNE: Is he getting his bike dirty again? I'll have to spank him if he is.

JACK: No, he's riding up along the path.

LAVONNE: Well, that's a miracle... Laws, my chicken.

*(**LAVONNE** hurries back into the HOUSE.)*

JACK: I'd like to apologize for that outburst a moment ago. Sometimes I forget what's happened and try to do things like I could before I got this hole in my stomach. I get mad, but I shouldn't have taken it out on the two of you.

ALICE: Are you feeling better? Would you like to lie down?

JACK: No, I'm fine—really.

NOREEN: We managed to get the banner up. See?

JACK: *(Looking over.)* It's terrific. Thank you.

LAVONNE: *(Calling from the KITCHEN WINDOW.)* Noreen, I could use you in here, hon.

NOREEN: I'm coming, Von.

*(**NOREEN** exits into the HOUSE.)*

JACK: Nice family.

ALICE: Yes, they are.

JACK: Do you have family?

ALICE: Why?

JACK: No reason. I just asked because I didn't know what else to say.

ALICE: Sorry. Sometimes I get a little testy, too. I was married. That was the only family I had.

JACK: What happened?

*(**ALICE** looks coolly at **JACK**.)*

JACK: *(Continued. Embarrassed.)* Sorry. I shouldn't be asking personal questions.

ALICE: We say that a lot, don't we? "I'm sorry." Even if we're not directly responsible or have no control over the situation, we're still sorry. I think half of our nature is to fumble through life making mistakes, and the other half is to be sorry for it. People are a sorry lot.

LAVONNE: *(Calling out from the KITCHEN WINDOW.)* Alice, we need to get those spuds on to boil pretty quick here.

ALICE: *(Gathering her things.)* Yes, LaVonne, I almost have it all done.

LAVONNE: *(Calling out from the KITCHEN WINDOW.)* Jack, will you call Mason for me? He should be home now.

JACK: Yes, ma'am.

*(**ALICE** steps up into the HOUSE while **JACK** exits stage left. You hear the women chattering inside the HOUSE for a moment or two when **PENNY DUNN** and **TED EMERY** enter from stage left. [**PENNY** is a pretty little thing of sixteen—mature in some ways, immature in others.] [**TED** is a good-looking young man of seventeen—zealous at times, and angry with his own insignificance.] **PENNY** stops on noticing the banner.)*

PENNY: Oh, Ted, look at that.

TED: Are you surprised, Penny? Your mother has planned this big party for you.

PENNY: Smell that—fried chicken. My favorite.

TED: And mashed potatoes and corn. Sister Barton is bringing her potato salad, and Sister d'Busey is making her homemade sourdough bread. Later we're having ice cream and cake.

PENNY: You knew about this?

TED: Uh, huh.

(They hug.)

PENNY: Are your parents coming?

TED: No, they said they'd be too busy with the victory parade and potluck preparations. You'd think that just once—it's your sixteenth birthday for crying out loud.

PENNY: It's okay. I understand.

TED: I don't.

PENNY: You parents still dislike the thought of us seeing each other. If they ever accepted any of our invitations, it would be as if they approved. So there will always be a victory parade or a church meeting or some other excuse for them not to come.

TED: It makes me so mad.

PENNY: Well, it shouldn't.

TED: You'd think they'd get used to the idea by now. We've been together since we were ten.

PENNY: Wishful thinking is a hard thing to stop—whether it's us wanting them to accept us as a couple or them wanting us to break-up.

TED: I guess you're right.

    (**TED** pulls a small JEWELRY BOX from his pocket.)

TED: *(Continued.)* Here, I want to give you your present before things get started.

    (**PENNY** happily takes it and kisses **TED** on the cheek.)

PENNY: Thank you.

    (Opening the JEWELRY BOX, **PENNY** is nearly speechless.)

PENNY: *(Continued.)* Oh, Ted.

TED: Do you like it?

PENNY: Is this what I think it is?

TED: I certainly hope so.

*(**TED** takes the RING out of the JEWELRY BOX and places it on **PENNY'S** wedding finger.)*

TED: What do you think?

PENNY: It's gorgeous, but I can't accept it.

TED: Why not?

PENNY: Teddy, I'm only sixteen. I can't marry you now.

TED: Who said anything about getting married now? This will let everyone know what we have in mind—especially my parents.

PENNY: But I can't wear it.

TED: You don't have to wear it on your hand. Maybe you can put it on a gold chain and wear it around your neck for awhile.

PENNY: Ted, I wear your class ring around my neck, not an engagement ring.

TED: You don't like it.

PENNY: I love it. I love *you*. Only, I was expecting this to come in two or three years.

TED: I wanted to make my intentions clear because....

PENNY: Because?

TED: I've been thinking about enlisting.

PENNY: Enlisting! You have another year before—

TED: —I have another whole year before I'm drafted, I know. By that time the war will be over. I want to go now. It's not fair that other guys have to risk their lives while I stay here in a big house living off my father's ball bearing business.

PENNY: The war *will* be over. You don't have to do this.

TED: I know I don't have to—I want to.

PENNY: Your parents will never sign the papers to let you go in before you're eighteen.

TED: There are ways of getting around that. I have to do my part, Penny.

PENNY: Then stay here and make ball bearings. The war effort needs ball bearing, too. Look at Walker. They wouldn't let him enlist because he grows wheat. It's the same for you.

TED: No, it's not. Walker runs the farm, I don't run the factory.

PENNY: This is a fine present. First you give me a ring that says you want to spend the rest of your life with me, and then with your next breath you're talking about going off to Heaven only knows. Were you considering my feeling when you decided this?

TED: Of course I was. But I know what people are thinking. They're thinking I'm a coward. Penny, could you marry me if I'm looked at as a coward?

PENNY: *(Tearing up.)* You're not looked at as a coward. But they'll think you a fool if you go in before you have to.

TED: Do you think I'm a fool?

*(There's a strained pause between **TED** and **PENNY** until **LAVONNE** peeks through the KITCHEN WINDOW to see them. **LAVONNE** hollers on her way out the SCREEN DOOR.)*

LAVONNE: Here she is. Everyone, Penny's here!

*(**NOREEN** and **ALICE** follow **LAVONNE** out. **LAVONNE** crosses down to hug her daughter.)*

LAVONNE: *(Continued.)* Happy birthday, honey.

PENNY: *(Trying to hold back the tears.)* It's wonderful, Mamma.

LAVONNE: Sweetheart, what's wrong? *(**LAVONNE** sees the RING on **PENNY'S** finger.)* What on earth is this?

PENNY: It's pretty much what it looks like, Mamma. Ted just gave it to me.

TED: We're planning a very long engagement, Mrs. Dunn.

LAVONNE: It had better be.

PENNY: It will be the shortest engagement in history if you go off and get yourself killed! Mamma, Ted wants to enlist.

*(In tears, **PENNY** buries her head in her mother's shoulder.)*

LAVONNE: But why, Ted?

TED: Because I'm a patriot.

LAVONNE: No one doubts that, but there are different ways of being patriotic. Listen, if you want to be the patriot, I have a can of lard you can take down to the collection center.

TED: Mrs. D.!

LAVONNE: Settle down, Ted, I was only being silly. But look what you're doing. You're ruining the party.

TED: Well, forgive me for wanting to serve my country.

NOREEN: Ted, LaVonne didn't mean you were ruining the party. What we hope you'll do is not make any definite plans until we've had a chance to talk it over with you.

LAVONNE: That's right, Ted. What do your parents think of this?

TED: I haven't told them yet. But I know what they'll do: Mom will start balling her eyes out and Dad will smack me across the room.

NOREEN: If you decide this is what you really want to do after we've talked about it, we'll come with you when you tell your folks. Would that help?

TED: Yeah, it sure would. Thanks.

NOREEN: We'll let this idea rest for a day or two. Let's give Penny time to adjust to the idea. You've dumped quite a bit on her all at once.

TED: I suppose you're right.

   (TED takes PENNY into his arms.)

TED: *(Continued.)* I'm sorry, Penny.

PENNY: It's all right, Ted. I just don't want to lose you.

TED: Well, I don't want to lose you either, Pen.

LAVONNE: Penny, you come in the house with me and wash up. We can't have our birthday girl with red and puffy eyes, can we?

   (LAVONNE takes PENNY inside the HOUSE. ALICE follows. NOREEN unfolds the TABLECLOTHS onto the CARD TABLES and sets the TABLES.)

TED: I didn't think everyone would get so upset. Noreen, doesn't Walker feel bad about not being in uniform?

NOREEN: At times. You're only seventeen, Ted. Why are you in such a rush to grow up?

TED: I don't know. Sometimes it seems like if I don't hurry something along, I'll miss out on it.

NOREEN: I understand what you're going through, Ted. When you're in your last year of high school you begin to see all of these possibilities right before your eyes you're afraid if you don't grab them right away, you'll lose out. But it's a funny thing... If you take the time to look at what's available like what job to do or when and whom to marry—you realize how important these decisions are. What you do now affects the rest of your life. Don't you want to slow down a little and make sure you make the right choices?

TED: Is that why you and Walker haven't gone through the Temple yet?

NOREEN: The reasons are personal.

TED: Shoot, if you were my girl, I wouldn't lollygag around like Walker. I'd snatch you up and marry you before someone else did.

NOREEN: Maybe Walker isn't the one lollygagging around.

(*JACK enters from stage left with MASON. MASON rides his BICYCLE between the HOUSE and GARAGE and back out.*)

NOREEN: *(Continued.)* Sergeant, this is Ted Emery. Ted, Sergeant Jack Collins.

(*TED and JACK extend greetings by shaking hands.*)

NOREEN: *(Continued.)* Ted is thinking of enlisting early.

JACK: You are? That's great. My entire Platoon volunteered—four of them were underage.

TED: *(To NOREEN.)* See?

NOREEN: Where are these young men now, Jack?

JACK: *(Reluctantly.)* Well, they're all dead.

TED: *(After a BEAT.)* I'm going to see if Mrs. D. needs my help. Nice meeting you, Sergeant.

JACK: Same here.

*(**TED** exits into the **HOUSE**.)*

NOREEN: Thank you.

JACK: Any time.

*(**OWEN** enters from stage left with a huge bowl of **POTATO SALAD**. **ELLA BARTON** follows carrying two **PRESENTS**. **GLORIA** also enters from stage left carrying a loaf of bread on a wooden cutting board. [**ELLA** is a gentle looking elderly woman—of the old school, a typical rural grandmother.])*

OWEN: Here we are. Let's get this show on the road. *(Calling out.)* So where's the birthday girl?

*(**PENNY** dashes out of the **SCREEN DOOR** bubbly and excited about her party. She bounds down the **PORCH STEPS** and crosses to hug **OWEN**.)*

PENNY: Here I am, Mr. Barton.

OWEN: Looky here—the prettiest sweet sixteen I've ever laid my eyes on.

PENNY: Oh, Mr. Barton, Noreen was much prettier than me.

OWEN: Well now, I didn't know Noreen when she was sixteen, so you're the prettiest one I've ever seen.

ELLA: Happy birthday, Penny.

PENNY: *(Hugging **ELLA**.)* Mrs. Barton, I'm so glad you're here.

*(**PENNY** steps over to **GLORIA**.)*

PENNY: *(Continued.)* Mrs. d'Busey, is this your homemade bread?

GLORIA: Wouldn't make anything else for such a special occasion.

*(**PENNY** hugs **GLORIA** as **LAVONNE**, **TED**, and **ALICE** come out of the **SCREEN DOOR** and **MASON** races in from the back.)*

LAVONNE: Has everyone met Sergeant Collins? He's going to have supper with us. Jack, this is Owen and Ella Barton. They live in the red brick down on the corner. Gloria you've met. How about Ted?

JACK: Yes, ma'am. We were introduced a few minutes ago.

(*JACK* crosses and takes *PENNY'S* hand.)

JACK: *(Continued.)* Happy birthday, Miss Penny.

PENNY: Thank you.

LAVONNE: Now that everyone knows everyone else, we can start getting things ready. Ella, you can check on the corn. Noreen, see if the potatoes are boiled enough to mash. Gloria, you can help me with the chicken. Penny, I need you to pull down a few more bowls and plates. Alice, why don't get the punch and start pouring? The chicken will take a few more minutes and then we'll start carrying things out.

OWEN: What do us men do?

LAVONNE: You men do what men do best—sit tight and get ready to eat.

(*The women file into the HOUSE as the men watch.*)

OWEN: I think we men have just been insulted.

(*OWEN grabs MASON and tickles him in a loving manner.*)

OWEN: *(Continued.)* What do you think, Mason?

(*MASON laughs with delight.*)

OWEN: *(Continued.)* So, Sergeant, when did you get back stateside?

MASON: He's been shot up.

OWEN: Say, I'm sorry to hear that. So many of our good young men are coming back hurt—it's a crying shame, but a necessary thing. Where were you?

JACK: North Africa mostly.

OWEN: North Africa. Imagine that. That must be some place.

MASON: Jack's in the Second Corps. *(He points to JACK'S insignia.)* See?

(*ALICE comes out of the SCREEN DOOR with a PITCHER of PUNCH and will start pouring GLASSES of PUNCH while the men talk.*)

OWEN: Now how did you know that, Mason? It simply amazes me how such a little fella knows all those symbols and signs. I get them mixed up all the time.

TED: North Africa? Did they put you up against the tiger tanks?

JACK: Our troop was assigned the "strays" as we called them. They marked me an explosives expert and taught me right where to place the plastics on the tigers. When it blew, it disabled the tank. We had two jeeps with eight men. Whenever the call came in that two or three tigers were spotted by themselves, we'd take out after them.

OWEN: Now that sounds about as dangerous as you can get.

JACK: It wasn't a picnic. We blew up about six before....

TED: Before what?

JACK: Well, before we ran into trouble. Then the troop was disbanded.

TED: What kind of trouble?

(*JACK looks over at ALICE, reluctant to tell the story.*)

ALICE: Don't press him, Ted. Perhaps the Sergeant would rather not talk about it.

(*There is another slight pause as JACK and ALICE continue to watch each other.*)

JACK: There were two tanks down in a gully hiding behind a small sand dune about the size of a building. We thought we could sneak up from behind, plant the explosives, and then back out without anyone seeing us. Lester and I—that was my best friend, Keith Lester—we slipped down and set everything when a kraut came out the hatch and dropped down to the ground. He shouted the alarm and the others scrambled out of their tanks and began shooting. We hightailed it out of there as fast as we could, but they sprayed Lester across the back and I got it in the leg. When the guys in the jeep heard the gunfire, they came busting over the dune shooting back. By this time the krauts were back in their tanks turning the turrets around. They blew up both jeeps and the men in them. Then the explosives went off and leveled the tanks. When the smoke lifted, Lester and I were the only ones left. I carried him back to camp.

TED: You carried him back with a bullet in your leg?

JACK: Yeah, it broke my leg. I didn't even know it. The doctor's said it was impossible for me to walk little alone carry anyone with a break like I had, but somehow I did. All I wanted to do is get Lester to the medical tent. An artillery column picked us up three miles from camp. I had carried Lester about ten miles I figured.

ALICE: What about your friend? Is he all right?

JACK: *(As a matter-of-factly, though one can see the hurt in his eyes.)* No, he died.

(ALICE watches JACK for a moment, then quietly turns and exits into the HOUSE.)

OWEN: *(Reflecting.)* Terrible... Terrible, terrible thing.

JACK: It took several months for the leg to heal—because I walked on it, I think. Then they shipped me out with another unit to Sicily. The first day on the beach I tried to play hero by jumping on a grenade before it went off in the middle of a bunch of guys. I ended up with a big hole in my gut. Thirteen months in a hospital in London and they send me home. Such is the complete war record of Sergeant Jack Collins.

OWEN: Well, bless the Lord you're alive, son. Gloria's husband isn't coming back.

JACK: Yes, sir.

(LAVONNE comes out of the HOUSE with a PLATTER OF CHICKEN. The other women follow with food they place on the CARD TABLES.)

LAVONNE: Mason, are your hands washed?

MASON: They got washed when I cleaned my bike.

LAVONNE: Well, you better wash them again.

MASON: But they're clean, Mamma.

LAVONNE: That's good. Go clean them again. Hurry now, we're going to eat now.

MASON: Mamma, isn't Penny going to open her presents?

LAVONNE: Penny can open her presents when we've finished supper.

MASON: But Mamma, I think Penny wants to open her presents now.

LAVONNE: You do?

MASON: Don't you, Penny?

PENNY: Do you want me to open my presents now, Mason?

MASON: Yeah.

NOREEN: We could cover the food, LaVonne. It will stay warm enough.

LAVONNE: All right. If that's what you want. Mason, go help your sister get the gifts—they're all in the living room.

(MASON take's hold of PENNY'S hand and drags her up the PORCH STEPS and into the HOUSE while ALICE, ELLA, and GLORIA begin to cover the food with TOWELS.)

OWEN: *(Watching after PENNY and MASON.)* Who's going to open these presents, Penny or Mason?

NOREEN: Penny always let's Mason help.

GLORIA: Ted gave Penny an engagement ring for her birthday.

OWEN: A what?

ELLA: I'll fill you in during supper, Papa.

(PENNY and MASON are back out carrying the PRESENTS. They sit the PRESENTS at the top of the STEPS and PENNY sits on the PORCH. MASON unwraps a PRESENT before PENNY can situate herself.)

PENNY: Mason, you're going too fast. I don't know who this one is from.

NOREEN: It's from me, Penny.

PENNY: Oh. Thank you, Noreen. *(PENNY opens the box and is about as surprised to see this gift as she was TED'S.)* Oh, Noreen, where did you ever find these?

NOREEN: J.C. Penney down on Washington in Ogden.

PENNY: *(Pulling a PAIR OF SHOES out of the box.)* They're real leather, aren't they?

NOREEN: Well, it's your sixteenth birthday. I thought you should have something elegant.

LAVONNE: Laws, Noreen. How did you get your hands on a pair of leather shoes?

NOREEN: Maxine special ordered them for me.

*(Thrilled, **PENNY** steps down to hug **NOREEN**.)*

PENNY: Thank you, Noreen.

*(As the two women exchange a hug, and the others comment on the unusual and obviously expensive gift, **MASON** steps up onto the PORCH and crosses to the end where the ORCHARD begins.)*

MASON: Mamma, there's something in the trees.

LAVONNE: What?

MASON: *(Pointing.)* Look.

*(**LAVONNE** steps up to the PORCH and joins **MASON** at the end.)*

LAVONNE: *(Calling out.)* Who are you? Come out of there. Come on.

*(Reluctantly, a tall and skinny young man rises from behind the dead bushes in front. He removes his cap and steps onto the grass with arms raised high. **LAVONNE** quickly places a protective arm around **MASON**.)*

ELLA: Good gracious!

*(**PENNY** quickly flies into **TED'S** arms while **OWEN** places himself between the young man and **ELLA** and **GLORIA**. **JACK** steps out in front of the group. The cause for alarm is the young man is wearing a dowdy gray uniform of sorts with POW letters sewn on the back. This is **HANS WELLER**. [**HANS** is a slight man in his early twenties—personable but leery and on guard because of his circumstance.] Meanwhile, the poor POW shouts in a German accent, trying to ease the fear of the moment.)*

HANS: Friend! I am friend! No harm. No hurt.

JACK: Everyone stay back. He may be armed.

HANS: No. No arms. I surrender.

*(**TED** has slipped out around the back of the HOUSE.)*

GLORIA: Penny, go get your father's hunting rifle.

LAVONNE: That won't do any good, Gloria. It's not loaded because of Mason.

GLORIA: He didn't have to know that, LaVonne!

LAVONNE: Wait. I know.

(LAVONNE shuffles MASON in as she exits into the HOUSE. HANS jumps a little, frightened by the movement. The others jump a little, frightened by HANS.)

JACK: No one move, dammit!

HANS: No harm. Friend.

(LAVONNE is quickly out the SCREEN DOOR and at the top of the STEPS with the biggest MEAT CLEAVER ever made. HANS sees the MEAT CLEAVER and turns white.)

HANS: *(Continued.)* NO!

(HANS drops to his knees and covers his head the best he can with his arms when TED comes charging in from between the HOUSE and ORCHARD and pounces on HANS. The two go rolling on the ground which gives JACK the opportunity to join in the scuffle. TED and JACK stand HANS up, holding him on either side.)

JACK: Search him.

(TED bends down and begins to frisk HANS.)

LAVONNE: Jack, what do we do?

JACK: Call the police.

OWEN: I have a better idea. My nephew works out of 2nd Street. I bet this fella is one of theirs. *(Taking a PIECE OF PAPER out of his wallet.)* I'll call down there and see if I can get Mickey.

(OWEN hurries into the HOUSE.)

(TED finishes frisking HANS and stands on the other side of HANS to hold him.)

TED: Nothing on him.

HANS: No, I have nothing. I come in peace. No harm. I come to see the beautiful rose.

JACK: The what?

HANS: *(Pointing to NOREEN.)* The beautiful Fräulein.

LAVONNE: Oh, my word. This is Noreen's German POW—the one she can see outside her window at the Base.

JACK: Ted, there's a piece of rope hanging in the garage. Go get it.

(*TED* *heads for the* *GARAGE* *while* *OWEN* *steps out of the SCREEN DOOR and onto the PORCH with TELEPHONE in hand.*)

OWEN: Thelma's patching me through. *(Into the TELEPHONE.)* Hello...? Hello, Corporal Eddie Hampton. You're not the Eddie Hampton whose folks live up from the Randell's canning factory in North Ogden, are you...? Well, I'll be. Eddie, this is Owen Barton, the Postmaster in Hardin... I saw your grandpa the other day, he's looking much better—

ELLA: —Papa, for Heaven sakes!

OWEN: Oh, yeah... Say, Eddie, I have a nephew stationed there, a Lieutenant Michael Barton. We have a problem here and... Oh, you know him...? He is...? Yes, that would be good. Thank you, Corporal. *(OWEN holds the TELEPHONE RECEIVER to his chest while informing the others:)* Mickey's still there.

(*Meanwhile,* *TED* *has crossed back to* *JACK* *and* *HANS* *with a ROPE.* *TED* *ties* *HANS'* *hands in front of him.*)

OWEN: *(Continued. Listening into the TELEPHONE RECEIVER.)* Mickey? Hi, Mickey, this is your Uncle Owen. How are you doing, son...? Good to hear it. And Beverly and the kids...? Let me tell your Aunt Ella. *(OWEN presses the TELEPHONE RECEIVER to his chest and speaks to ELLA:)* He says they're all fine.

ELLA: Good gravy, Papa, we can find out about the family later.

OWEN: Oh, right. *(Talking into the TELEPHONE RECEIVER.)* Say, Mickey, I think we have one of your POWs in Sister Dunn's front yard... No, no cause for alarm. We have an Army Sergeant here who has everything under control. He's kind of a scrawny little fella—I think I could have taken him myself... No, only a few of us here for Penny's birthday party... Well, me and your Aunt Ella, Gloria d'Busey, Alice Jennings, and of course Ted Emery.

LAVONNE: Laws, Mrs. Thurmon. She's probably having a heart attack!

ALICE: I'll let her know what's going on.

(*ALICE* *exits stage left.*)

OWEN: *(Still on the TELEPHONE.)* No, we called you first. Do you want us to get the police...? Oh, okay... Well, sure, I guess we could lock him in a closet or something. To tell you the truth, he looks like he's ready to fall down. Don't you feed these boys...? Okay, Mickey, whatever you say... Oh, two houses down from my place. It's at the end of our block next to the apricot orchard... Okay, we'll do that. Bye-bye, Mickey. *(OWEN hangs up the TELEPHONE RECEIVER.)* It sounds like things have been mighty hectic down there when the truck got back without this fella. Mickey said they'll send a car out to pick him up.

LAVONNE: What about the police?

OWEN: Mickey told me not to involve the police if we can help it. We're not to tell anyone what's happened. They don't want to start a panic.

LAVONNE: I imagine they're a little embarrassed about it, too—letting one get away like this.

OWEN: I told Mickey we would hold him 'til they got here.

ELLA: We could put him in the basement.

TED: Basements have windows.

LAVONNE: We're not locking him up anywhere. Look at that poor boy.

GLORIA: He's the enemy, LaVonne.

LAVONNE: I know that, Gloria. But you can see what kind of shape he's in. If this is what they're throwing at our soldiers, we should have this war wrapped up before the end of summer. No wonder you felt sorry for him, Noreen.

ELLA: Is this the boy you told us about, Noreen? The one in the parking lot?

OWEN: What parking lot? What boy?

LAVONNE: They're using a bunch of prisoners to resurface the parking lot outside Noreen's office at the Base. She can see them through the window.

NOREEN: I only slightly smiled at him a couple of times....

HANS: *(Ready to fall down.)* Excuse, please. I must sit down.

*(**TED** and **JACK** lead **HANS** over to the MERRY-GO-ROUND to let him sit while they remain vigilant on either side.)*

PENNY: Is he sick?

*(**LAVONNE** steps down, takes a GLASS OF PUNCH off a CARD TABLE, and crosses to **HANS**.)*

LAVONNE: *(Handing the GLASS OF PUNCH to **HANS**.)* What's your name, son?

HANS: Hans. Hans Weller. *(He gladly takes the GLASS of PUNCH.)* Danke. *(He drinks.)*

*(**OWEN** sits the TELEPHONE on the PORCH and steps down to join the group around **HANS**.)*

OWEN: Where were you captured?

HANS: England—three years ago.

OWEN: In England? Was your plane shot down?

ELLA: Mercy, Papa, don't start up a chitchat with the boy like he was a neighbor come in to the Post Office to mail a letter.

OWEN: This isn't chitchat, Mamma. This is interrogation.

ELLA: What's he going to tell you they don't already know?

OWEN: Well—like how he escaped and how he got here.

HANS: *(Willingly.)* I can tell that. How I got here. *(He gives the GLASS OF PUNCH back to **LAVONNE**.)* Danka. This way very good.

OWEN: He speaks English pretty well for a German.

HANS: Learn English in camp. Have been in camps a long time. Not much to do there—I learn English. Lately I find words I can use to speak about the beautiful Fräulein. I learn many pretty words to use about the lovely rose.

JACK: How did you escape?

HANS: Have been sick most of day. Could not keep morning meal down. Did not eat at noon. When we get in truck to go back to camp, I rest on floor. The guards—they do not watch because they think I will be sick again. When I look up to get air, I see.... *(**HANS** points to **NOREEN**.)*

LAVONNE: Noreen.

HANS: *(Appreciating knowing her name.)* Noreen. Her name is Noreen... She gets on bus. I was there—no one watching—no one paying no mind because I am sick. I slip out of irons. *(**HANS** demonstrates how he slipped out of the irons by casually slipping the rope off his hands.)* I can get out of things. I have thin hands.

(HANS casually lips the rope back on as ALICE reenters from stage left.)

ALICE: Mrs. Thurmon is fine. Once I told her what happened and that we were all right, she began to laugh.

ELLA: Thank Heavens.

GLORIA: This is no laughing matter. He's a Nazi!

LAVONNE: Calm down, Gloria. Jack and Ted have him. He's not going to do anything.

OWEN: *(To HANS.)* Son, if you got out of your irons today, you could have escaped any time you wanted.

HANS: Not always. But past month, I lose much weight. And where am I to go? They bring us here, but where is here? Then I see beautiful Noreen and I think this is where I can go. I can see beautiful Noreen and hear her speak. I dream of what music there must be when the precious rose speaks... No one watching. I crawl out of truck and under bus.

LAVONNE: You rode all the way from Hill Air Force Base under a bus?

HANS: I get up behind the wheels. This is why I am so dirty. I mean not to come so dirty. I watch as bus stops and Noreen gets off. I roll into ditch. This, too, why I am so dirty. Fräulein Noreen walks here, I come here. No one watching for prisoner of war. No one sees me.

LAVONNE: Did you do all this just to hear Noreen's voice?

(HANS stands formally and takes a few humble steps towards NOREEN.)

HANS: The darkness of the world sits heavy in my eyes. For long-time, I see nothing but black doom and red blood. I hear nothing but cries, sorrow, innocence dying. I feel pressing in heart, and alone in this nothing. Then one day in this darkness comes the bloom of a beautiful rose; the light of tender eyes; the glow of pale pink petal cheeks. And I think the world cannot be so dark to have such a lovely rose as Fräulein Noreen. I think of you when I work and the world is no longer black with gloom. I dream of you and sleep when I cannot. I laugh when I think I never laugh again. I want to tell you this—what your kind smile has given me. I want to thank you for this.

(A stunned NOREEN pulls out a CHAIR and sits down.)

HANS: *(Continued.)* I go back now.

*(Silence. **HANS** stands for a moment smiling sweetly at **NOREEN**, and then sits back on the MERRY-GO-ROUND.)*

LAVONNE: Hans, would you like something to eat?

GLORIA: LaVonne, I can't believe you. He's a Nazi—one of Hitler's inhuman monsters who would just as soon cut your head off as pass the time of day.

LAVONNE: Gloria, I understand how you feel—I do what with you losing Bill and all. And I'm really sorry about that. We all are. I hate the Axis Powers and what they're doing just like you. The greed and lust for power of a handful has set this whole world upside-down. So many families are dying and being left homeless—thousands more losing their husbands, fathers, sons and brothers—it's simply unforgivable. I know I should hate this young man because he's a part of this terrible thing we're fighting, but I can't. This boy isn't defending or bragging about his part in the war. He just wants to tell Noreen how lovely he thinks she is. I can think of nothing more human than that. Besides, I promised to give Penny a special birthday party, and we're going to do it to spite Mr. Weller's untimely appearance. It's going to take awhile for the army to get here anyway, so we might as well include Hans in our celebration and act like the decent people we were brought up to be. If it makes you uncomfortable, you can go home.

OWEN: But don't tell anyone. Mickey said not to tell anyone—security reasons.

HANS: Please, I sit here and wait for the soldiers. I want no hard feelings.

LAVONNE: Come over here, Hans—everyone. The food is getting cold. We can all sit down and—oh laws, I left Mason hiding in the pantry!

*(**LAVONNE** hurries up into the HOUSE while the others just stand for a moment not knowing what to do until **PENNY** steps up to the CARD TABLES and begins uncovering the food.)*

PENNY: Ted, do you want a chicken leg?

TED: *(Still not sure what to do.)* Uh, sure.

*(**TED** steps up to the place setting that **PENNY** is fixing for him. **ALICE** steps up to **HANS** and helps **JACK** lead **HANS** to a CARD TABLE.)*

ALICE: I'll pour you another glass of punch.

HANS: *(Willingly led.)* This kindness. I know not what to say.

NOREEN: *(Coming out of her daze and sliding over one seat.)* He can sit here, if he likes.

*(Almost in tears, **HANS** smiles and quietly and shyly sits next to **NOREEN** as the others slowly begin to step up to their places. **LAVONNE** comes out of the HOUSE carrying **MASON** who has his head buried in her shoulder.)*

LAVONNE: See, honey? Everything is just fine. Mamma's so sorry, baby.

OWEN: Poor little fella. We scared the willies out of you, didn't we, Mason?

*(**MASON** looks up tentatively. He's been crying. **JACK** steps to **LAVONNE** and holds out his arms.)*

JACK: Here, Mason, you come with me.

*(**MASON** let's **JACK** take him. After holding **MASON** tightly for a moment, **JACK** carries him over to **HANS** who stands.)*

JACK: This is a soldier just like me.

HANS: I mean not to scare you.

LAVONNE: He came to visit Noreen—that's all. Are you okay, dear?

*(**MASON** sniffles and nods his head "yes," although he's still not too sure about it. **LAVONNE** takes **MASON** back and carries him to their place settings.)*

LAVONNE: Here, honey. You come sit next to Mamma and she'll fix you a nice plate of food. Everyone please sit down.

*(All gather around the CARD TABLES and sit. Still not happy, **GLORIA** sits as far from **HANS** as she can. **LAVONNE** begins passing around food and conversations begin with **LAVONNE** telling **MASON** how brave he was waiting in the pantry. **OWEN** tells **TED** how courageous he was to sneak up behind **HANS**. A concerned **ALICE** places a hand on **JACK'S** shoulder asking if he's all right after the scuffle. His cheerful self again, **MASON** kneels on his chair asking for a chicken wing. **ELLA** asks **GLORIA** to please cut her a piece of that wonderful homemade bread—using it as a distraction. **NOREEN** turns to **HANS** and hands him a plate of food. He takes it and just holds it a moment, staring at her with the most grateful of smiles.)*

End of ACT I of Americana

ACT II, Scene 1

AT RISE

Later that evening. The FOOD is cleared from the CARD TABLES. Lights are on in the HOUSE and GARAGE. **LAVONNE**, **ALICE**, **GLORIA**, and **ELLA** are in the kitchen washing dishes. You can hear their chatter at times. **MASON** and **OWEN** are in the GARAGE decorating **MASON'S** BICYCLE. The DOOR of the GARAGE is open and a light shines out from it. The BANNER across the PORCH has been taken down. **JACK**, **PENNY**, and **TED** are out front talking.

TED: I still don't see why we can't tell anyone—not even my parents.

JACK: Lieutenant Barton said for security purposes and that it might start a panic around here.

TED: But no one, ever?

JACK: That's what he said. It's a classified matter. Maybe after the war, but not until then.

PENNY: Who would believe us, anyhow? It happened right before my eyes and I still don't believe it.

TED: But we didn't make it up. You had a Nazi in your front yard!

PENNY: Shh. Quiet, Ted. You'll get Mrs. d'Busey riled up again.

TED: *(Whispering loudly.)* She has every right to be riled up. The fact is we had the enemy staring us in the face. I think everyone but Mrs. d'Busey is taking this too lightly.

PENNY: Well, Ted, what would you have us do? We called the army and they came and got him. You knocked him to the ground and tied him up so no one would be in danger—not that there was any threat to begin with. Would you rather we have shot him?

TED: Cut it out. You're making me sound like an idiot.

PENNY: You're not an idiot, Ted. You took command of the situation and protected us. I'm very proud of you.

(PENNY takes TED'S hand and moves him towards the left.)

PENNY: *(Continued.)* Come walk with me.

TED: You're proud of me?

PENNY: I'm always proud of you. I love you... Would you like to walk with us, Sergeant?

JACK: No thanks. You go on.

PENNY: We'll be back soon.

(TED and PENNY exit. JACK sits at a CARD TABLE for a moment sipping on a drink until ALICE enters from the HOUSE to gather the TABLECLOTHS.)

ALICE: Where is everyone?

JACK: Mason and Owen are in the garage decorating the bike. Ted and Penny went for a walk.

ALICE: Young love... Why aren't you in the garage helping decorate?

JACK: Didn't feel like it.

ALICE: Are you sure you're all right? It worried me when you went down with that POW.

JACK: It didn't hurt. Ted did most of the wrestling.

ALICE: Poor Ted. He wants to be a hero so badly.

JACK: He's a nice young man.

ALICE: Yes, he is. *(She gathers the TABLECLOTHS and prepares to reenter the HOUSE.)* But you shouldn't be out here by yourself. Why don't you come in and join us?

JACK: I'm comfortable sitting right here, thanks. I was just thinking.

ALICE: About what?

JACK: Hans Weller.

ALICE: Imagine that man risking his life to spend but a moment with a beautiful woman.

JACK: He must have been pretty desperate.

ALICE: We're all a desperate people, Sergeant... To have your every thought and wish concentrated on a girl you only saw through a window. Such devotion is mind-boggling.

JACK: When you're in love, you do the unexpected and the impossible.

ALICE: I suppose.

JACK: Alice, may I ask you a question?

ALICE: I suppose.

JACK: I was wondering what you're doing here in Hardin.

ALICE: I'm hiding. Hardin, Utah is a good town to hide in, don't you think?

JACK: What are you hiding from?

ALICE: The world. Life.

JACK: Life's a difficult thing to hide from.

ALICE: So true. But I think I've been pretty successful at it as of late.

JACK: Is life that bad?

ALICE: I find it remarkable you still have this positive attitude after all you've been through.

JACK: What's the alternative? If I wasn't hopeful, I'd go crazy.

ALICE: To keep from going crazy, I hide... But hiding isn't the only reason I'm here. In my own inconspicuous way, I'm contributing to the war effort. I processed a Japanese family through the Interment Camp in Topaz after Pearl Harbor. There name is Lito. Kee and Amata Lito with two of the most adorable children you ever saw.

JACK: What were you doing in Topaz?

ALICE: *(Ignoring **JACK'S** question.)* They're second generation Americans. Kee's great-grandfather or great-great grandfather helped build the Transcontinental Railroad. When they finished it northwest of here at Promontory Point, the older Lito sent for his family and settled along the Wasatch—doing mostly migrant work at first. There are hundreds of orchards along this mountain range, so that kind of work is plentiful... Kee owns the house I'm living in. He also has a little restaurant next to the bank. He's famous for his meat loaf and mashed potatoes.

   *(**JACK** and **ALICE** chuckle at the thought of a Japanese man cooking American foods.)*

JACK: Meat loaf?

ALICE: He swears this to me... The restaurant's boarded up. I know nothing of running a business like that, but I said I'd come here and hold it for them—pay the taxes and such until they're released. If I didn't, they'd lose everything.

JACK: That's awfully generous of you.

ALICE: It's not generous. It's an obligation. I couldn't do much else to help out. I'm not a very good nurse, and can't wield a screwdriver, so I thought the least I could do is keep things together for this family. They write me every week and there's talk of letting them come home soon. The government moved them to the Heart Mountain Relocation Center in Wyoming. When this is over, they'll be able to come back and pick up where they left off—for the most part. So many won't have anything to go back to. I can only hope this little community accepts them back.

JACK: Where did you get the money to pay the taxes? If you don't mind me asking.

ALICE: I have a comfortable inheritance.

JACK: Lucky you.

ALICE: In many respects, yes... What about you, Sergeant? What are you doing here in Hardin?

JACK: I had a small automotive parts store in Elko. Before they shipped me overseas, I turned the business over to my Dad. But he had health problems and sold the business. That was okay because the guy who bought it was a good friend of mine, Lowell Underwood. When I got home last week I found out Lowell had married Betty. Betty and I hadn't talked about marriage or anything, but I thought we had something that could grow in time. Anyway, there wasn't much point in sticking around.

ALICE: It never stops, does it? As if you haven't been through enough. That's why I hide, Jack. Because it never stops.

(**ALICE** starts for the HOUSE when **JACK** grabs onto her arm.)

JACK: Wait.

(**ALICE** yanks her arm away and backs up a little frightened.)

JACK: (Continued.) I'm sorry. I didn't mean... I never manhandled a woman in my life. I don't know what's wrong with me anymore. I get so frustrated. I'm sorry.

ALICE: I'm sorry I overreacted. I don't know why I jumped like that. *(Smiling slightly.)* Here we go again being sorry.

JACK: You're not angry?

ALICE: No, Jack. I'm not angry.

JACK: Then stay and talk with me.

ALICE: I have been talking with you. I've told you more than I have LaVonne and she's my best friend.

JACK: You may have told more than you're used to, but you really haven't said anything.

ALICE: I told you quite a lot. You weren't listening.

*(**LAVONNE** comes out of the SCREEN DOOR.)*

LAVONNE: Well, that's all cleaned up. How about getting the ice cream made?

ALICE: Ice cream so soon after dinner?

LAVONNE: So soon? We've had the army drive up and cart off that POW, Penny finished opening her birthday presents, Owen and Mason have been holed up in the garage for nearly an hour decorating that bicycle, and we've washed the dishes. It's not so soon at all.

ALICE: All right—I've been corrected.

*(**LAVONNE** steps to the left side of the PORCH and calls over to the GARAGE.)*

LAVONNE: Mason! Mason, do you want to start making the ice cream?

*(**MASON** is out of the GARAGE. He heads for the PORCH.)*

LAVONNE: *(Continued.)* Do you want to make it out here or inside?

MASON: Don't care.

LAVONNE: Well, all right. You come in and we'll start breaking up the ice.

*(**MASON** exits into the HOUSE.)*

LAVONNE: *(Continued.)* Owen, we need you to break the ice!

JACK: I can do that, LaVonne.

LAVONNE: You don't have to bother, Jack, you're company. You shouldn't have to work for your supper. Besides, Mason and Owen have this system worked out.

*(**OWEN** comes out of the garage with a STRIP OF MATERIAL over his shoulder. He's holding another PIECE OF CLOTH.)*

OWEN: Do you have some rackety string, LaVonne?

LAVONNE: Rackety string?

OWEN: You know, the fancy stuff you ladies put on your clothes?

LAVONNE: Rickrack?

OWEN: That's what I said. We could use some blue colored rackety string if you have it.

LAVONNE: I think I might. Come in and we'll check.

OWEN: That would be swell.

*(**OWEN** heads into the HOUSE.)*

OWEN: *(Continued.)* Okay, where's this ice cream making commencing?

*(**OWEN** exits into the HOUSE with **LAVONNE**. **JACK** and **ALICE** watch them exit.)*

JACK: It's like nothing happened here tonight. They're so gentle. You have to love them.

ALICE: I do. They restore your faith in people, don't they?

*(There is a tender moment between **JACK** and **ALICE**.)*

JACK: You have a wonderful smile. Can I tell you a funny story? I'd love to hear you laugh.

ALICE: *(Amused.)* All right. Tell me a funny story.

JACK: The seas were really choppy on our trip over to England. We had a good number of boys hung over the side of the ship at any one time. If you passed by, the sounds and smells would make you sick and there you'd be joining right in. But there was this one poor slob who was sick every minute of the trip.

ALICE: I get the picture. Are you sure this is a funny story?

JACK: Well, that's not the funny part. You have to let me finish the story.

ALICE: Sorry. Go ahead.

JACK: Like I said, this one poor devil hung over the side the whole time—day and night with no relief. When we were ready to disembark, a group of sailors got together and planned this ceremony. When the sick GI got off the boat, the band there began to play "Blow the Man Down." Then they presented him with a sailor's cap and made him an honorary seaman in charge of the intensive watch over the starboard side of the ship. The entire dockside irrupted in laughter.

ALICE: Except for the poor GI.

JACK: Oh, no. He got a big kick out of it.

> (**JACK** reaches into his back pants pocket and pulls out a SAILOR'S CAP. **ALICE** takes the cap while the two laugh. They share a special moment until **LAVONNE** calls out from the KITCHEN WINDOW.)

LAVONNE: Why don't you two come inside? It's getting chilly and you'll freeze to death eating ice cream out there now the sun's down.

> (**ALICE** gives **JACK** his SAILOR'S CAP back and he escorts her into the HOUSE. After a BEAT, **PENNY** and **TED** enter from stage left. **PENNY** wears **TED'S** jacket over her shoulders.)

TED: Are you okay now?

PENNY: I was never not okay, Ted.

TED: I get so mad when this happens. I didn't know they would be in the park setting lights. I thought they would be at church.

PENNY: I know, Ted. It's not your fault.

TED: They could have at least said hello. Even if they didn't want to, they should have acknowledged your presence. You were standing right in front of them for crying out loud. I didn't know they were going to be there or we wouldn't have gone.

PENNY: It was an enjoyable walk, Ted. Let's drop it.

TED: They're outright snobs. I hate them.

PENNY: Oh, Ted, you don't mean that. They're your parents.

TED: They may have had me, but they're not my parents. If they were they would welcome you into our house and make you feel like one of the family like your folks have done with me—not try to ignore you or deny you even exist. Just because we have some money, they think they're so high-and-mighty. To hear them talk, there's this halo over their heads and they have a direct line of contact with Heaven.

(**PENNY** *chuckles.*)

TED: What's so funny?

PENNY: Your eyes flare so when you're upset. It reminds me of the mad scientist in that bad movie we saw.

TED: You're trying to settle me down by changing the subject, aren't you?

PENNY: Is it working?

TED: Yeah. I don't know if you're more like your Mother or Dad, but you have this way of always making me feel better.

PENNY: Noreen says I'm like Daddy.

TED: You have a great dad. I wish my father was more like yours.

PENNY: I wish he were home. I miss him so much.

TED: *(Taking **PENNY** into his arms.)* I know, Pen. I know.

(**LAVONNE** and **NOREEN** *come to the* **SCREEN DOOR**.)

LAVONNE: There you are. You two best come and get in line for some ice cream.

PENNY: We're coming, Mamma.

(**NOREEN** *holds the* **SCREEN DOOR** *open for* **PENNY** *and* **TED** *to pass through. She then comes out and leans against a* **PORCH POST**. **LAVONNE** *notices* **NOREEN'S** *forlorn manner and joins her.*)

LAVONNE: You look a little tired, hon.

NOREEN: I'm fine.

LAVONNE: Hans is going to be okay, Noreen. I asked Lieutenant Barton to go easy on him. When Owen explained why Hans escaped, Mickey seemed genuinely sympathetic.

NOREEN: They're going to lock him up in a little room all by himself, I know it.

LAVONNE: Well, he did escape, Noreen.

NOREEN: When he took the plate of food from me, his hands were shaking so badly. He's very sick, LaVonne.

   (*LAVONNE puts a comforting arm around NOREEN.*)

LAVONNE: Hon, you can't let it get to you. He was just a boy who wanted to see you.

NOREEN: That's the whole point, Von. He was just a boy who wanted to see *me*. He was just a boy who risked his life and future to see *me*. What if he dies?

LAVONNE: My darling, you're getting worked up for no reason. You're not responsible for what happens to that young man. In a way, you've already helped him a great deal.

NOREEN: How's that?

LAVONNE: Weren't you listening to his testimony? Hans dreams about you. He sees your face and the world is no longer black with gloom for him. Meeting you has given him something good to think about. In his days in prison he thinks of you. If and when he gets to go home, he doesn't know if he'll have a home to go to or a family or country. These are going to be bad times for him, but I think he'll get through it because he'll remember meeting a lovely young woman who reminded him of a rose.

   (*NOREEN ponders for a moment and then hugs LAVONNE.*)

NOREEN: Thank you, LaVonne. You have a knack of putting things in their proper perspective.

LAVONNE: Why don't you go in and call Walker. He'll help you feel better.

NOREEN: I'll do that.

   (*NOREEN exits into the HOUSE as OWEN, ELLA, and GLORIA come out. They notice NOREEN'S despondent nature.*)

ELLA: Is there something wrong with Noreen? She looked a little pale.

LAVONNE: No, there's nothing wrong. She's going to call Walker.

ELLA: Have those two set a date yet?

LAVONNE: Not yet.

OWEN: Well, LaVonne, it's been a real interesting night, but we're going to say good night.

LAVONNE: You're not going already? The ice cream isn't done.

OWEN: We'll pass on the ice cream. It was a delicious supper, but we have to get up early and haul two tons of potato salad over to the park.

ELLA: Oh, Papa, it's not that much.

OWEN: *(Teasing.)* Not that much? I may have to call Walker and borrow his tractor to get it all over there.

ELLA: Now stop your teasing.

(*JACK* and *ALICE* step out onto the PORCH joining the others.)

OWEN: If it's okay, I'll pick up our table and chairs in the morning.

LAVONNE: Sure. I'm so glad you could come.

(*OWEN* hugs *LAVONNE*.)

OWEN: Wouldn't miss it. You give that pretty girl of yours an extra kiss tonight for me.

LAVONNE: I'll do that.

(*ELLA* hugs *LAVONNE*.)

ELLA: It was very nice, LaVonne. Thank you.

GLORIA: *(Hesitantly.)* I'm sorry I ruined your party, LaVonne.

(*LAVONNE* hugs *GLORIA*.)

LAVONNE: You didn't ruin the party, Gloria. I'm just sorry there wasn't a better way to handle the matter. It's hard to know what to do sometimes.

GLORIA: *(Smiles.)* I know. Good night.

(*OWEN*, *ELLA*, and *GLORIA* exit stage left.)

ALICE: I should leave, too.

LAVONNE: Please stay, Alice.

JACK: I need to be heading out as well.

LAVONNE: You're not going back out on the road this time of night. Stay with us tonight.

JACK: I couldn't do that.

LAVONNE: Why not? You can sleep downstairs in Aunt Fannie's bed. Mason is currently using it as a battleship, but I'm sure he'd be happy to move his things for you to sleep there.

JACK: Thank you, but it wouldn't look right.

LAVONNE: Well, who's looking? You have to stay over for the victory parade and potluck. Look what you'd be missing if you left tonight.

JACK: Maybe I can get a room in town.

LAVONNE: Alice, will you tell him how silly he's being?

ALICE: Leave me out of this.

JACK: All right, I'll stay—but only if I sleep in the garage.

LAVONNE: But....

JACK: I insist.

LAVONNE: Very well, I give up. I'll have Ted lug up the mattress for you.

JACK: You don't have to—

LAVONNE: —I won't hear any more argument. This time *I* insist.

JACK: *(BEAT.)* I've been had.

ALICE: *(Chuckling.)* You can't get around LaVonne. That's the first thing I learned when I got here.

(OWEN reenters from stage left. He's more reserved than before.)

LAVONNE: Owen, did you forget something?

OWEN: Well, I thought I better do this now... I....

LAVONNE: What is it, Owen?

OWEN: *(Taking a yellow PIECE OF PAPER out of his pocket.)* I didn't want to say anything before Penny's birthday, but you should know.

LAVONNE: *(Becoming concerned.)* Know what?

OWEN: Remember how they called me down to the Post Office today? That's why I was late bringing over the table and chairs.

LAVONNE: Yes, I know, Owen. What's wrong?

OWEN: They called me down there. They thought I should be the one to give you the news.

LAVONNE: *(Horror.)* Guthrie.

OWEN: I'm afraid so.

LAVONNE: He's gone.

(OWEN gives LAVONNE the TELEGRAM.)

OWEN: They don't know. He's missing in action. It says his ship was hit hard and went down. The Navy was able to fish a bunch out of the water, but Guthrie is still unaccounted for.

ALICE: Oh, no.

OWEN: I wasn't going to tell you until the morning what with all that's been going on, but I showed it to Ella and she said I better get my behind over here and give it to you.

(LAVONNE sits in one of the CHAIRS as she stares at the TELEGRAM.)

LAVONNE: It says the ship went down last week. Don't they know more after a whole week?

OWEN: I bet things are real confusing when something like this happens. It takes times to sort out exactly who's okay and who's not.

JACK: It could be that Guthrie is on one of the ships that picked the guys up and the news just hasn't gotten to the officials yet.

ALICE: He's alive, LaVonne. I know he's alive.

LAVONNE: Well, of course he's alive. I was thinking of him out there somewhere swimming his little heart out. He never liked to swim in the first place. It has always puzzled me why he joined the Navy if he didn't like the water... I'll have to tell the kids—in the morning. Oh, no, it's the parade tomorrow... I'll have to change the star in the window. It's a different color star for someone missing, isn't it? Or maybe it's just if they're dead... Oh, Jack, I forgot your mattress....

(*LAVONNE heads for the PORCH.*)

OWEN: LaVonne....

LAVONNE: Owen, will you ask Ella to keep this between the two of you until I have a chance to tell the children? Sunday after church will be the best time. If it took a week to get me the news, it won't hurt putting off telling the kids for a day or two. Please, I would appreciate it if everyone acted like nothing happened.

ALICE: Of course.

OWEN: You can count on Ella and me, LaVonne.

LAVONNE: Thank you, Owen.

(*LAVONNE heads into the HOUSE while calling:*)

LAVONNE: *(Continued.)* Ted, I have a favor to ask you.

(*LAVONNE exits into the house. OWEN stands for a moment not knowing what to say, then quietly turns and exits stage left.*)

JACK: Poor LaVonne. This shouldn't happen to someone like her—she's too good a person.

ALICE: She's so crazy about her husband. She'll put on a good act for the children and Noreen, but I know she's really aching inside. I wish there was something I could do.

JACK: We do what we can. The rest is up to God.

ALICE: I would expect to hear that from LaVonne.

JACK: Her goodwill must be contagious.

ALICE: I better go home.

JACK: Alice....

(*JACK stops ALICE by taking her hand, then bends over and gently kisses her on the cheek.*)

JACK: *(Continued.)* Good night.

*(**ALICE** stares at him for a moment surprised at his tenderness.)*

ALICE: Good night, Jack. I'll see you tomorrow.

JACK: I'll be here.

*(**ALICE** exits stage left. As **JACK** watches her leave, **LAVONNE** comes back out of the SCREEN DOOR. **JACK** turns to her.)*

JACK: I'm sorry, LaVonne. Is there anything I can do?

LAVONNE: That's the worst part of something like this, isn't it? There's nothing anyone can do. I feel so helpless.

JACK: If there is anyone in this world that isn't helpless, it's you, LaVonne.

LAVONNE: I'm so glad you came traipsing through that orchard this evening.

JACK: Me too.

LAVONNE: Come inside and help me pretend everything is all right.

*(**JACK** climbs the PORCH STEPS and opens the SCREEN DOOR for **LAVONNE** to pass through. When he closes the SCREEN DOOR behind him, he also closes the HOUSE DOOR.)*

End of ACT II, Scene 1 of Americana

ACT II, Scene 2

AT RISE: Late, the day of the victory parade and potluck. Saturday. The HOUSE is closed. A light can be been through the LIVING ROOM WINDOW. The LIGHT over the GARAGE is also on. Hand in hand, **TED** and **PENNY** come strolling from stage left. PENNY holds a small CLOTHESPIN DOLL done up like a bride.

PENNY: I think I'll put this on my nightstand next to your picture.

TED: I'll need to get a photograph of you to have when I ship out.

PENNY: Ted, you promised not to bring that up until after my birthday.

TED: It is after your birthday.

PENNY: You know what I mean.

TED: Well, when will your birthday be over?

PENNY: Sixteen is a big birthday. It may take weeks.

TED: You're going to have to get used to the idea eventually.

PENNY: I'll never get used to the idea.

TED: Resigned to the idea, then.

PENNY: Please, Ted, I don't want to fight—not tonight. Everything was so nice; the parade and potluck. We didn't even run into your parents. So let's not talk about enlisting or we'll end the day on a sour note.

TED: Don't expect it to go away. I am going to enlist.

PENNY: Well, maybe I'll just find someone else if you do.

TED: It's not like you to be mean, Penny.

PENNY: It's not like you to be mean either. But you are when you keep harping on leaving me.

TED: This is something I have to do. I was hoping you'd understand. If you really loved me, you would understand.

PENNY: And if you really loved me, the idea of going away would have never entered you mind.

   (TED pulls PENNY to him.)

TED: I do love you.

   (PENNY pulls away.)

PENNY: Don't.

TED: *(BEAT.)* What if I'm shipped over to Europe? What if I'm killed? You'll never know how much I love you because we haven't shared our love for each other in that special way. Maybe we should think about that before it's too late.

PENNY: What are you talking... Oh, Ted, how could you? Is that what this is about? Just to—

TED: —No, of course not. What kind of man do you think I am? I love you, that's all. I want you. Dammit to Hell!

PENNY: Don't swear at me, Ted Emery. I've never been so ashamed in my life. You can get yourself another girl if what you want is someone to "share that special way" with.

TED: I didn't say that.

PENNY: You keep telling me I'm the only one and that you love me and respect me, and then you pull a trick like this.

> (**PENNY** runs into the HOUSE and slams the HOUSE DOOR behind her. **TED** follows and knocks.)

TED: Penny! Do you really think I could be such a louse?

PENNY: *(From behind the HOUSE DOOR.)* Go away, Ted.

TED: *(Trying to open the HOUSE DOOR.)* Penny, let me in.

PENNY: No. Go home, Ted. I don't want to see you anymore tonight.

TED: Penny! *(Angrily, he pounds on the HOUSE DOOR.)* Penny!

> (**TED** turns and kicks the PORCH POST in rage. He then stomps offstage left. **LAVONNE**, **NOREEN**, **OWEN**, **ELLA**, **JACK** and **ALICE** enter stage left, looking back after **TED**.)

LAVONNE: *(Calling back.)* Ted, what happened?

OWEN: That young fella is sure in a huff.

LAVONNE: He and Penny must have had a fight.

OWEN: Golly, it must have been a wallop-a-loser. I can't remember those young people ever having a fight.

> (**LAVONNE** has crossed up to the HOUSE DOOR. She tries to open it, but it's locked so she knocks.)

LAVONNE: Penny, it's Mamma. Open the door, please.

PENNY: *(From inside the HOUSE.)* Is Ted gone?

LAVONNE: Yes, Ted's gone.

> (The HOUSE DOOR opens, but **PENNY** elects to stay inside. **LAVONNE** turns to the others with a sigh.)

LAVONNE: *(Continued.)* I'll be back.

*(**LAVONNE** exits leaving the HOUSE DOOR open, but closing the SCREEN DOOR.)*

OWEN: Maybe we should pass on the ice cream.

NOREEN: No, please stay. I'm sure it's nothing tragic.

*(**MASON** rides in from stage left on his BICYCLE that's decorated with red, white, and blue streamers. He parks it carefully alongside the GARAGE and unpins the DISTINGUISHED SERVICE CROSS **JACK** had given him to pin on a piece of cardboard on the front of his BICYCLE. **MASON** wears a large BLUE RIBBON that says "1st Prize." All puffed up, he struts up to **JACK** and returns the MEDAL—not saying a word.)*

JACK: Thank you, Mason.

OWEN: You sure had some snazzy bike in that parade, Mason.

*(**LAVONNE** steps out of the SCREEN DOOR.)*

LAVONNE: Come on in. She's all right.

ELLA: Are you sure? We wouldn't want to barge in on a family crisis.

LAVONNE: They had a little quarrel. It will be fine in the morning. Come in, you'll see.

*(**MASON** hops inside the HOUSE as **ELLA** and **OWEN** head for the DOOR along with **ALICE**. **JACK** takes **ALICE'S** arm and holds her back. **LAVONNE** closes the DOOR behind **ELLA** and **OWEN**.)*

JACK: Please stay a moment.

ALICE: What is it?

JACK: I want to thank for allowing me to hang around.

ALICE: We should thank LaVonne to allowing the both of us to hang around.

JACK: Yes, but I wanted to thank you personally for being my companion today.

*(**ALICE** heads to the PORCH STEPS.)*

ALICE: Forget it.

JACK: Alice...

(ALICE stops and looks back.)

JACK: *(Continued.)* Am I doing something wrong here?

ALICE: I don't know what you're expecting of me, Jack, but I can't give it to you.

JACK: I'm not expecting anything. I had a great time today with the sack races and bicycle parade. I know it was hokey, but these things are priceless. I stood in the middle of America again. For the first time in four years I wasn't afraid and it felt good. I felt safe... Then I realized how extra nice it was with you standing beside me and I wanted to thank you for it. I'm probably using the wrong words, but I just wanted you to know.

ALICE: Your words are fine, Jack.

*(There is a pause until **ALICE** moves down and into **JACK'S** arms. They kiss, but **ALICE** breaks away before the kiss turns passionate.)*

ALICE: I'm sorry. I shouldn't have done that.

JACK: Why not?

ALICE: I'm sorry.

*(**ALICE** exits stage left as **NOREEN** comes out of the SCREEN DOOR with two BOWLS of ICE CREAM.)*

NOREEN: Am I interrupting?

JACK: No, I guess not.

NOREEN: I came out to offer you and Alice some ice cream.

*(**JACK** crosses to **NOREEN** making the most of things)*

JACK: Well, I'll have a little.

*(**NOREEN** gives a BOWL to **JACK** and they sit on the STEPS to eat their ICE CREAM.)*

NOREEN: Tempers must be a little on the sharp side tonight.

JACK: I'm trying to be careful with Alice so I don't scare her away. I know she likes me, but she's so... I don't know. Sometimes I think I'll go through the rest of my life doing things wrong.

NOREEN: Alice is skeptical.

JACK: To put it mildly.

NOREEN: Sometimes it's easier to just accept whatever people are willing to offer. It's when you press for more you run into trouble.

JACK: *(Thinking.)* Yeah... You're are as wise as you are beautiful, Noreen. You belong on the faculty of a college or on a magazine cover.

NOREEN: Not everyone can be on a magazine cover, Sergeant.

(LAVONNE, OWEN, and ELLA come out onto the PORCH with their BOWLS of ICE CREAM.)

OWEN: Well, we figured if you weren't going to join us, we'd come out and join you. Can't get enough of that pretty clear sky with the stars shining like everything was right with the world. *(Looking out.)* Isn't it pretty, Mamma?

ELLA: It's the prettiest thing I've ever seen, Papa.

NOREEN: LaVonne, you've been quiet today. Are you all right?

(LAVONNE looks at everyone as they look back knowingly.)

LAVONNE: Well, hon, I suppose you should know... It's bad news and I wasn't sure you could handle it along with the German boy thing.

NOREEN: What is it, LaVonne? Is it Guthrie?

LAVONNE: His ship went down last week. He's missing.

NOREEN: *(Tearing.)* Oh, no.

(The TELEPHONE rings. PENNY is seen in the LIVING ROOM WINDOW answering it.)

OWEN: I came over and told LaVonne after the party last night. I didn't want to spoil Penny's birthday. But there's a good chance they'll find him, Noreen. I read all the time where these fella's have floated on the water for days before they scoop'm up.

(PENNY comes out of the HOUSE with the TELEPHONE. She holds it out to OWEN.)

SCRIPT **Americana**

PENNY: Mr. Barton, your nephew's on the phone. He'd like to speak to you.

OWEN: How'd he know I was here?

PENNY: Well, he asked to talk to Noreen first, but when I said you were here....

OWEN: *(Taking the TELEPHONE.)* Thank you, Pen... Hello, Mickey. What's up? Lose another POW...? Well, we've been at the victory parade all day... Oh, yes, she's here... Okay... Say, that's a shame... You don't say...? Well, that's a crying shame. Sure, sure, I'll tell her... Yes, I'll let them know, too. How do you like that? It's so sad... Thanks for calling, Mickey. Give Beverly and the kids our love... Okay, bye now.

(OWEN hangs up and gives the TELEPHONE back to PENNY.)

ELLA: What did Mickey have to say, Papa?

OWEN: Well, it's mighty heavy news, I'm afraid. Might heavy. That German POW that was here last night? The poor fella died this morning.

LAVONNE: What?

OWEN: The doctors told Mickey that Hans had a blood disorder for a long time now and that there was nothing they could do for him... They didn't know how long he was going to live, and the young man seemed set on going out to the Base to work, so they let him. Had they known how close it was to his passing, they wouldn't have made him work like that.

LAVONNE: How strange. Noreen knew that last night, didn't you, hon? You thought that young man was awfully sick... I don't know what to say.

(There is silence in the group. Everyone is in shock.)

JACK: *(More-or-less to himself.)* It never stops.

OWEN: Mickey said Hans told him he got to see the rose and there is peace. Mickey thought Noreen would like to know that.

(NOREEN breaks out sobbing and hurries into the HOUSE. LAVONNE and PENNY quickly follow.)

OWEN: *(Continued.)* Sad, sad. Mamma, let's go home and give these people time to themselves.

ELLA: Good night, Sergeant.

JACK: Mrs. Barton.

OWEN: Say, it just dawned on me. I'm going to call Mickey back. He may have a few friends in the service who could find out more about Guthrie.

ELLA: Papa, why don't you call Mickey back and invite the family to supper next Saturday?

OWEN: We'll do that, Mamma.

(OWEN and ELLA exit stage left. JACK gathers the ICE-CREAM BOWLS and stands on the PORCH a moment not knowing whether to go inside or not. ALICE reenters from stage left.)

ALICE: Jack, may I speak with you, please?

(JACK turns to recognize her.)

JACK: Maybe we shouldn't. I'll probably do or say something wrong again.

ALICE: I deserve that. I know I've been behaving erratically, especially towards you and I apologize. There are reasons and it has nothing to do with you. I just received permission... Please allow me to explain.

(JACK hesitates, but sits the BOWLS OF ICE CREAM on the MILK BOX and steps down the PORCH STEPS. ALICE sits on the STEPS and motions for JACK to set next to her.)

ALICE: *(Continued.)* First of all, I have to apologize for the kiss.

JACK: I didn't think it was that bad.

ALICE: *(Amused.)* No, it wasn't... Jack, I have to ask you to keep what I'm about to tell you confidential. You can't tell anyone.

JACK: What is it, another classified issue?

ALICE: Actually, it is.

(JACK laughs some, but stops when he sees ALICE is serious.)

JACK: Criminy, now what?

ALICE: My name isn't Alice Jennings and I'm not a divorced woman. I'm a married woman which is why the kiss was very inappropriate. I can't say what got into me. I think I wanted you to know what a nice man you are. I know you're hurting and I wanted to stop it—just for a second or two.

JACK: Well, thank you, I guess.

ALICE: My husband is an Army Colonel working in the division that oversees POW containment in this country and the Japanese internment camps. He's stationed in Washington D.C.

JACK: Sounds like a really important man.

ALICE: He has an important job, that's certain.

JACK: If he's there, what are you doing here?

ALICE: They needed a plant—an operative here. It seems a few of the local girls working at the Air Force Base have taken up with the Italian POWs out at Second Street. They work with Noreen.

JACK: Wait. Noreen couldn't be—

ALICE: —No, no. Noreen is fine. But it was her innocent nature and LaVonne's gift of the gab that led the Army to set-up monitoring here. When they began working this possible problem and realized an interned Japanese family lived a few doors up from the Dunn's, everything conveniently fell into place. They just needed someone to come out and discreetly nose around a little. I was back east with a lot of time on my hands so when my husband suggested I'd be their perfect operative, I happily volunteered.

JACK: With you being a neighbor, Noreen would tell LaVonne what happened during her day at the Base and then LaVonne would tell you.

ALICE: Exactly. The Dunn's are such decent people; we figured they would simply relay the events of their day and think nothing of it. So instead of placing someone on the Base who might raise suspicion, my being here is a less intrusive, gentler watch.

JACK: Did anything happen with the other girls?

ALICE: Thank Heavens, no. The Italian POWs are scheduled to be relocated next week, so I think that will be the end of it.

JACK: And then you'll get to go home?

ALICE: Yes.

JACK: It's ironic Noreen would have this situation with the German POW.

ALICE: Isn't it? Last night when I went to see if Mrs. Thurmon was all right, I called out to Second Street and let them know everything was under control.

JACK: That's why Owen's nephew specifically asked who was here?

ALICE: I report in every day, so they know all my activities here on this block. They thought I might be at the party, so when Owen told them I was *in attendance*, the emergency wasn't such an emergency.

JACK: Huh. And you got the all clear to tell me this?

ALICE: Just now... Talk about someone who has their own secrets... You're quite the talk of Washington, Sergeant Jack Collins. It seems everyone knows about you there.

JACK: Ah, they wanted to make me into this big hero and send me around the country promoting war bond sales. I'm no hero and I'm no salesman.

ALICE: At least your notoriety sped along the investigation process. In case you're interested, you now hold a highly classified clearance status.

JACK: And what do I do with that?

ALICE: Well, if you ever at the Pentagon....

   (They share a chuckle.)

ALICE: *(Continued.)* You did help me in another way.

JACK: How so?

ALICE: Last night I called my husband to see if he could find out more about Guthrie Dunn. Apparently he dropped your name around and the lines of communication opened.

JACK: That would be great if we could find out something for LaVonne.

ALICE: So you see, you're still helping, Jack. I wanted you to know that. And I wanted you to know about me. I hope you feel better about everything.

JACK: A lot better. Thanks.

ALICE: *(Standing and slipping a PIECE of PAPER out of her pocket.)* If you're ever in Washington, please come see us. I mean that.

   *(**JACK** stands as **ALICE** gives him the PAPER.)*

JACK: Maybe I will.

   *(**ALICE** extends her hand.)*

ALICE: It's been an honor, Sergeant. Good-bye.

JACK: *(Shaking her hand.)* Good-bye.

*(**ALICE** exits stage left. **JACK** watches a moment and then opens the PIECE OF PAPER and reads.)*

JACK: *(Continued.)* Good-bye—Emily Singleton.

*(He smiles, carefully refolds the PIECE of PAPER, and pockets it in his breast pocket. **JACK** then steps up to the PORCH to gather the ICE-CREAM BOWLS again and goes into the HOUSE.)*

End of ACT II, Scene 2 of Americana

ACT II, Scene 3

AT RISE: Sunday morning. **MASON** bursts out of the HOUSE and into the FRONT YARD to his MERRY-GO-ROUND. [In this scene, all but **JACK** wear their Sunday go to meeting clothes.] **MASON** is proudly wearing his FIRST PRIZE RIBBON that he won the day before. He begins pushing his MERRY-GO-ROUND. Momentarily, **PENNY** comes to the SCREEN DOOR.

PENNY: Mason, come back in. If you stay out there, you'll get dirty.

MASON: Will not.

PENNY: Will too. Mamma's going to blame me for not keeping you inside.

MASON: Will not.

PENNY: Will too.

MASON: Will not.

*(**PENNY** comes out onto the PORCH.)*

PENNY: Mason, you get back in here before I spank you.

MASON: No, you won't.

PENNY: Yes, I will.

MASON: No, you won't.

*(**PENNY** steps down to the MERRY-GO-ROUND.)*

PENNY: If you don't do what you're told, I'll take your ribbon away and burn it in the compost heap.

MASON: *(Defensively holding onto his ribbon.)* NO!

PENNY: Then come inside!

(LAVONNE pokes her head out of the SCREEN DOOR.)

LAVONNE: Quiet you two. You think I was raising village simpletons.

PENNY: Mamma, I just dressed Mason for church when he bolts out here to get dirty again.

LAVONNE: Mason, do you want some breakfast?

MASON: Yeah.

LAVONNE: Well, breakfast is inside.

(MASON happily bounds back into the HOUSE as LAVONNE continues to hold the HOUSE DOOR open for PENNY.)

LAVONNE: Finesse, my sweet.

PENNY: Next time I'll dangle a Popsicle from the door.

LAVONNE: That's the idea.

(PENNY exits back into the HOUSE while LAVONNE crosses and knocks on the GARAGE DOOR.)

LAVONNE: *(Continued.)* Jack? Jack, are you awake?

(JACK comes out of the GARAGE with his DUFFEL BAG flung over his shoulder.)

JACK: Morning, LaVonne. How are you this morning?

LAVONNE: You're not leaving?

JACK: It's time. I've taken advantage of your hospitality long enough.

LAVONNE: But I was expecting you to stay for awhile. I thought you and Alice—

JACK: —No, not really.

LAVONNE: Oh, what a shame. You made such a handsome couple. I thought you were perfect for each other.

JACK: It's all right. We had a nice talk last night. We're fine.

LAVONNE: That's good. I'm glad everything is okay. I just saw a couple of good people and... You know me, I'm forever the matchmaker.

JACK: You're forever the optimist, LaVonne.

LAVONNE: So where do you figure on going now?

JACK: Back out the orchard if that's all right. I have a half sister in Cheyenne who has invited me to come for a visit, so I'll be going through the canyon.

LAVONNE: That sounds like a good idea. Your family is the most precious gift on earth, Jack. You have to hold onto it tight and treat it with great care.

JACK: Yes, ma'am.

LAVONNE: Well, at least come in and have a good breakfast to get you on your way.

JACK: Oh, no. You're ready for church and I—

LAVONNE: —Church isn't for another hour, and it's only two blocks down. There's plenty of time. Come in and we'll fix you up.

(JACK concedes and exits into the HOUSE. LAVONNE stays at the SCREEN DOOR when she notices TED coming from stage left. He has a single ROSE in his hand.)

LAVONNE: Morning, Ted. Want some pancakes?

(TED steps up to the PORCH.)

TED: No, thank you, Mrs. Dunn.

LAVONNE: My lands, what happened to your face?

TED: It's nothing. I was... Mrs. Dunn, may I speak to Penny, please?

LAVONNE: Sure, hon. *(LAVONNE calls out as she goes into the HOUSE.)* Penny, Ted's here.

(PENNY reluctantly comes out of the SCREEN DOOR. TED offers her the ROSE, but she doesn't take it at first.)

Americana SCRIPT

TED: Please take it. I picked it out of Mom's greenhouse. If I'm going to catch hellfire for it, I'd prefer it be worth it.

(**PENNY** smiles slightly and takes the **ROSE**.)

TED: *(Continued.)* I thought a rose—like Hans thought of Noreen as a rose—that's how I think of you.

PENNY: It didn't sound that way last night.

TED: I was an idiot last night. *(He touches the side of his reddened face.)* The whole world told me I was an idiot last night.

(**PENNY** finally notices **TED'S** face and her anger immediately vanishes. She gently touches his cheek.)

PENNY: Ted, what happened?

TED: This is the result of reality smacking me across the face.

PENNY: Did your father hit you again?

TED: Well, he had cause this time.

PENNY: No one has the right to hit someone else no matter the reason.

TED: We got into a fight. I yelled at him. Dad is the only one allowed to raise his voice in our house. I keep forgetting that little rule and he flattens me.

PENNY: It looks painful. Do you want a cold pack to put on it?

TED: No, it's okay. Really it feels pretty good.

PENNY: Ted, how can you say that?

TED: Because it may be the last time he ever clobbers me. Penny, let me tell you what happened. It's about you, too.

PENNY: You weren't arguing over me?

TED: We were arguing over everything... It started when I told my parents I wanted to enlist in the army. Mom immediately pulled out her nicely starched handkerchief and started crying asking the walls where she went wrong. Dad closed the door so no one could hear us then simply told me he was sending me on a church mission to Detroit. Obviously he's had this in mind for some time. Dad feels that I can learn where ball bearings come into play in the automotive industry by sending me to Detroit. Naturally I would be doing this between bringing souls into the church. When they start sending missionaries out again, I'm going there.

PENNY: But you have never wanted to go on a mission, Ted.

TED: I know, and I've told him this time and time again. But Dad has other ideas. And when he has his mind made up, other choices don't count.

PENNY: Are you going?

TED: Most certainly not. I put my foot down and said I'd rather cross the ocean and kill Japs.

PENNY: Ted, you didn't say that?

TED: You bet I did. And I meant every word. At that point, Dad hauled off and smacked me clear across the room. He meant every bit of that, too... I went sailing through the air and banged my head on the windowsill. They said I was out cold for five minutes. He's never knocked me out cold before. It must have scared him half to death because when I came to, he was as white as a ghost. Then he began calling me Ted. Not Teddy or Ted'm, but Ted. I must have really scared the pants off him—probably thought he killed me—finally.

PENNY: Ted, don't joke like that. He could have really hurt you.

TED: But he didn't. And he sat me down in his chair—*his* chair, Penny. Then he sat across from me on the footstool and we talked like adults. He asked me why I was so set against the factory and running it for him. I told him I didn't have anything against the factory. I like the factory and the people there. I wouldn't mind being the boss and running the place when the time comes. Shoot, I'm not that stupid. So he asked why he hasn't heard anything but my wanting to get out of this town for the past three years... He was right about that. I have a one-track mind. I guess I get it from him, though I'd never admit it and he would deny it. I suppose we have more in common than we'd care to admit.

PENNY: Except you don't hit people. I couldn't love you if you hit people.

TED: Oh, who knows, Pen? I might have ended up exactly like my father. But I met you and your folks and I found out how real families behave lovingly towards one another. That's what changed me. I've grown up with you family, not mine.

PENNY: Could it be that you love my family and not me?

TED: Now see there? If I was really my father's son I'd slap you good for even thinking such a thing. But I'm Ted Emery—my own man. And if it takes the rest of my life to prove to you how much I love you, I'm ready to do that.

PENNY: But you're not going to be around for the rest of you life. You're going off to war or on a mission or Lord only knows.

TED: I'm not going anywhere, Pen... I told Dad I can't live in a town where my family doesn't approve of my wife. I told him that, too—that I asked you to marry me.

PENNY: You did tell him we're planning a very long engagement?

TED: Yes. He appreciated that. He was actually listening for the first time since I can't remember when. So I gathered my courage and went on. I said, "Dad, I love you and Mom, and I want you to be proud of me, but I can't act against my own feelings and principles."

PENNY: He didn't hit you again when you said that, did he?

TED: Believe it or not, he didn't. He told me he didn't like the enlistment thing. He didn't want me enlisting just to get away from him. He said if the war goes on, I'll be drafted soon enough and he'll be proud to see me off and pray for my safe return, but please don't go just to get away from him.

PENNY: Your father said please?

TED: Wait, it gets better. He said I didn't have to go on a mission if I didn't want, but that he wanted me to go to BYU and get a degree in business. He said he would send me down to the university and pay my expenses.

PENNY: Oh, Ted, that's wonderful.

TED: But you won't believe what he said next. He said, "If after four years of college—if you and pretty little Penny still want to marry..." He called you pretty little Penny. It was always that Dunn girl before, but last night it was pretty little Penny.

PENNY: Well, what did he say, Ted? Gees, talk about leaving me in suspenders.

TED: He said, "If you and pretty little Penny still want to marry after you graduate from college, you'll have my and your mother's blessing."

PENNY: Your father said that?

TED: Can you believe it? I can go down to BYU and be back on weekends and holidays. It will be perfect. And this morning as I was leaving the house, Dad asked if I would be walking you to church. Of course I said "yes" like I always do. But this time, Pen—this time he said, "We'll see you in church."

(PENNY tearfully hugs TED with joy.)

PENNY: Oh, Ted! Mamma! Mamma come here!

(LAVONNE rushes out of the SCREEN DOOR.)

LAVONNE: What? What's wrong now?

PENNY: Mamma, Brother Emery said, "See you in church."

LAVONNE: He didn't.

PENNY: And Ted's going to BYU and his father isn't calling him Ted'm anymore.

LAVONNE: Will miracles never cease?

(NOREEN and JACK come out of the HOUSE.)

NOREEN: What's going on?

LAVONNE: Harold is softening up. He said he would see us in church.

NOREEN: He always sees us in church.

LAVONNE: Yes, but before he wasn't looking.

TED: Let's go early, Penny. I want to tell Kenny I'm going to BYU with him.

PENNY: But I have to wait for Mamma and Mason.

LAVONNE: Go ahead. We'll be along shortly... Oh, Penny, say good-bye to Sergeant Collins. He's leaving this morning.

PENNY: You are?

JACK: I'm going to visit my sister in Cheyenne.

PENNY: That will be nice.

(PENNY crosses to JACK and kisses him on the cheek.)

PENNY: *(Continued.)* Good-bye, Sergeant. I'm glad you were here for my birthday.

JACK: So am I.

TED: *(Shaking JACK'S hand.)* Sergeant. Thank you.

JACK: For what?

TED: For helping me see what's important. You too, Noreen... Come on, Pen.

(TED and PENNY almost skip out stage left.)

LAVONNE: They look so happy. Lord bless them.

NOREEN: I wonder what Mr. Emery has up his sleeve.

LAVONNE: I know exactly what he has up his sleeve. He's thinking the minute Ted gets down to BYU, he'll forget all about Penny.

NOREEN: Hardly.

LAVONNE: It eases the problem for the moment. I'm thankful for that. Well, I better get back in the kitchen. You can't leave Mason in the middle of a stack of pancakes for very long and expect him to stay clean.

(LAVONNE exits into the HOUSE.)

NOREEN: *(Watching LAVONNE exit.)* She's taking the news of Guthrie so well—better than I am.

JACK: You had a double shock last night. You need to give things time to sink in.

NOREEN: I'm going to be sorry to see you go.

JACK: It's for the best. I saw many a scrutinizing glance my way yesterday during the parade. People are already talking about LaVonne taking in a perfect stranger and I don't want to add to it. She's a great lady and doesn't deserve that kind of trouble on top of everything else.

NOREEN: She would just ignore it.

JACK: Yeah, LaVonne would do that.

(LAVONNE comes out of the HOUSE with MASON.)

LAVONNE: What would LaVonne do?

NOREEN: We were talking about you, LaVonne. Were you ears burning?

LAVONNE: Laws, what were you saying?

NOREEN: We were commenting on how extraordinary you are.

LAVONNE: Oh, sweetheart, I'm not extraordinary. I'm just—LaVonne.

NOREEN: I'll walk Mason down to the corner for you, Von. It will give you a few minutes to say good-bye to Jack.

LAVONNE: How thoughtful, Noreen. Thank you, hon.

MASON: *(Sad and tearing up some.)* Bye, Jack.

(JACK bends down to hug MASON.)

JACK: Bye, bye, Mason. You be a good boy for your Mamma.

(JACK removes the DISTINGUISHED SERVICE CROSS from his shirt and pins it on MASON.)

JACK: *(Continued.)* Here, you take this.

LAVONNE: Oh, no, Jack. You keep that to give to your little boy someday.

JACK: *(Standing.)* I'd rather Mason have it—really.

LAVONNE: Well, if you're sure. What a wonderful treasure. What do you say, Mason?

MASON: Thank you, Jack.

JACK: You're welcome, Mason. *(JACK turns to NOREEN.)* Good-bye, Noreen. I'm glad I got to know you.

NOREEN: Bye, Jack. You're an extraordinary person yourself... Come along, Mason.

(NOREEN takes MASON by the hand and they exit stage left while MASON turns and waves good-bye to JACK. There is a slight pause.)

LAVONNE: Well, suddenly I feel very sad. Jack, you were a nice interlude. You broke into my little life and added a special time for me to remember when I get a little down.

JACK: Same here. I'll never forget your kindness. I lost sight of the things I value most in those sands of Africa. I forgot how precious and wonderful sharing love can be. You gave that back to me, LaVonne—you and your family. I can't thank you enough.

(There is another awkward pause and then they hug.)

LAVONNE: You're a good friend, Jack.

JACK: So long, Von.

(JACK picks up his DUFFEL BAG and heads for the ORCHARD. He turns and looks at the HOUSE and LAVONNE one more time and exits. LAVONNE watches him leave and then crosses up to close the HOUSE DOOR. Afterwards, she leans against a PORCH POST trying not to break down.)

LAVONNE: Lord, I know it's not a practice of mine to pray in the light of day, but I think I need to stress the importance of our talks today... This thing with Guthrie—he just has to be all right. I'm not a special case and I know too many have lost their loved ones in this war, so to be asking for special consideration seems selfish. But for once in my life I'm going to be selfish. Now everyone in town says LaVonne Dunn is invincible. Why, she simply picked up Guthrie's milk route and went on as if nothing had changed and she'll keep going on if he doesn't come back. But Lord, you know me—I'm an old softy. I'm not invincible, especially where Guthrie's concerned. I don't want the others to see me worry, so I put up this front. But if Guthrie dies, I die with him. As long as I knew Guthrie was okay... Now... So if you could find it in your heart to spare my Guthrie Dunn, I'd—I'd plant these silly cherry tomatoes right out here in the front yard for all to see. I'd... Well, please see what you can do....

(We hear OWEN hollering for LAVONNE as he enters from stage left.)

OWEN: LaVonne. LaVonne, I just got off the phone with Mickey! He called me just now.

LAVONNE: What did he say? Did he find out anything?

OWEN: He said the Navy had a hospital boat going to Hawaii with wounded sailors and GI's onboard. He said they were keeping its whereabouts a secret so the Japanese couldn't intercept it. But an officer called him to say Guthrie's name was on the list. LaVonne, Guthrie's on the hospital boat!

LAVONNE: Oh, Owen.

OWEN: Mickey said you should be receiving official word once the boat is safely at Pearl Harbor.

LAVONNE: But he's on a hospital boat. That mean he's hurt.

OWEN: Not bad. He's not hurt real bad. He's going to be fine.

LAVONNE: Fine?

OWEN: Second degree burns on his arms. Second degree, LaVonne. That's nothing. And his right ear—the top was torn off.

LAVONNE: Mercy.

OWEN: Now there's no need to fret. Guthrie has more than enough ear to lose some of it. He can grow his hair a little longer so it goes over his ears and no one will know the difference... He's coming home, LaVonne.

LAVONNE: Coming home?

OWEN: Well, he lost his hearing in that ear, so they're sending him home. But he can still hear with the other ear. That's not bad.

LAVONNE: What else, Owen? What aren't you telling me?

OWEN: That's it, LaVonne. I swear it. Just an ear and some burns.

LAVONNE: And Guthrie's coming home!

OWEN: Come on; let's go tell the kids their Dad's coming home.

LAVONNE: Yes, let's... Oh, wait a minute.

(*LAVONNE crosses over to the PORCH.*)

OWEN: LaVonne, what's wrong?

LAVONNE: Nothing is wrong, Owen. Nothing in the whole world is wrong.

(*LAVONNE has picked up a SPADE **GLORIA** left with the TIN OF PLANTS and busies herself digging a hole in the FLOWER BED next to the PORCH.*)

LAVONNE: *(Continued.)* I'm just keeping my part of a bargain I made.

(*LAVONNE plants a little CHERRY TOMATO PLANT in the hole, covers the roots with dirt, and stands brushing off her hands. **LAVONNE** then steps back to the side and looks up skyward.*)

LAVONNE: *(Continued.)* I'll plant the others when I get back. Thank you, Lord... Amen.

(*LAVONNE crosses to **OWEN** and takes his arm as they joyfully exit with **LAVONNE** commenting on how they're going to have to have another fried chicken supper to celebrate Guthrie's return.*)

End of AMERICANA

About the Author

An artist by trade and playwright by love of the genre, Joan Garner's first highly successful play compilation *Stagings* (Teacher Ideas Press, 1995) has prompted her to continue with this latest offering. Her lengthy work in community theatre and extensive background in production design lends just the right balance for creating entertaining yet "practical-to-produce" plays.

Living in Colorado, Joan applies her graphics skills as a freelance artist while writing and creating fine art pieces in her spare time.

In recent years the award winning playwright has participated in the Onassis International Cultural Competition, submitted a design for the World Trade Center Memorial, and has assisted other authors with their books.

www.ingramcontent.com/pod-product-compliance
Lightning Source LLC
Chambersburg PA
CBHW080936300426
44115CB00017B/2840